RADICAL DEMOCRACY

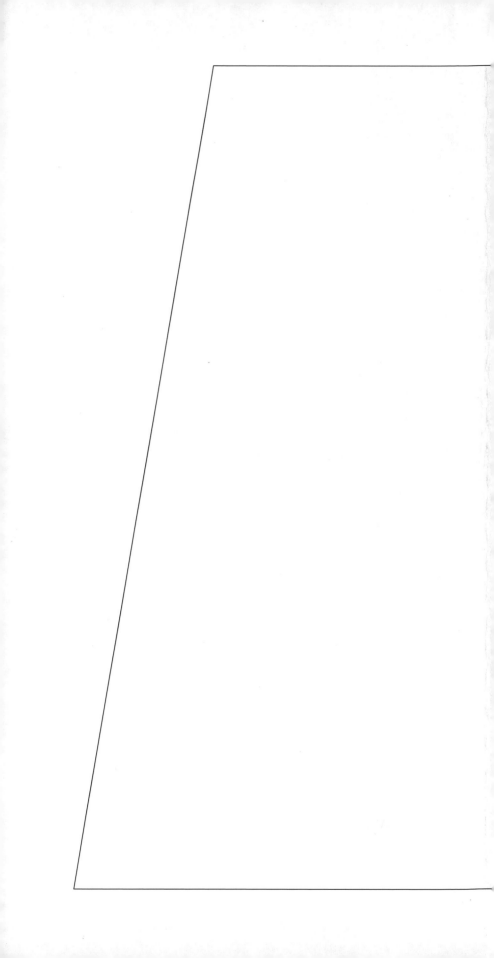

IDENTITY, CITIZENSHIP, AND THE STATE

EMOCRACY

EDITED BY

David Trend

Published in 1996 by

Routledge
29 West 35th Street
New York, NY 10001

Published in Great Britain in 1995 by

Routledge
11 New Fetter Lane
London EC4P 4EE

Library of Congress Cataloging-in-Publication Data

   Radical Democracy: Identity, Citizenship, and the State /
   edited by David Trend.
     p. cm.
   Includes bibliographical references.
   ISBN 0-415-91246-6 (alk. paper). ISBN 0-415-91247-4 (pbk.)
   1. Radicalism—United States 1. Democracy—United States
   I. Trend, David.
   HN90.R3R35 1995   95-8488
   320.5'3'0973—dc20   CIP

Designed by Leslie Sharpe
with Hermann Feldhaus at Cave.

CONTENTS

3 RADICAL DEMOCRACY AND POLITICAL POSSIBILITY 195

ACKNOWLEDGMENTS

A number of individuals and institutions deserve thanks for their help with *Radical Democracy: Identity, Citizenship, and the State.* The anthology originated from a proposal by Stanley Aronowitz to the Center for Social Research and Education to initiate a series of public debates on the future of activism on the left. The project began in 1994 with a special issue of *Socialist Review*, introduced by Aronowitz's essay "The Situation of the Left in the United States." This article questioned both the assertion of "the left" as a unified category and the presumption of socialism as its governing logic, advocating the replacement of the term "socialism" with "radical democracy." Responding to that essay were Amarpal Dhaliwal, Barbara Ehrenreich, Barbara Epstein, Dick Flacks, Michael Omi, Howard Winant, and Eli Zaretsky—each of whom tested and expanded the scope of Aronowitz's proposal.

As anticipated by its original design, the ensuing discussion of left-ist politics in the United States expanded considerably. The issue of *Socialist Review* was followed by a plenary session at the 1994 Socialist Scholars Conference where Bogdan Denitch and Cornel West joined the debate over radical democracy. Soon other contributors expressed interest in writing on the topic. And as the conversation expanded, most of the original participants felt compelled to rewrite their essays. For these reasons, *Radical Democracy: Identity, Citizenship, and The State* constitutes more than a simple expansion of a journal issue—and would not have been possible without the subsequent assistance of numerous people.

Editorial advice on the initial *Socialist Review* issue was provided by that publication's west coast collective, whose members at the time included Marcy Darnovsky, Amarpal K. Dhaliwal, Cynthia Kaufman, Karl Knapper, Arlene Keizer, Jacki Orr, René Francisco Poitevin, and Francine Winddance Twine. As the project began to unfold, I received increasingly important intellectual and practical help from Jason Frank, a doctoral student in political science at Johns Hopkins University. In addition to providing research assistance, Frank helped clarify the direction of this book. Other conceptual guidance came from my friend Henry A. Giroux, whose long-time commitment to radical democracy as a political ideal informed the expansion of this project along interdisciplinary lines. David Milton and Homay King also pro-vided crucial editorial assistance. Finally, great credit is due to Jane Fargnoli at Routledge, who supported this effort from its earliest phases and whose encouragement made it possible.

Earlier versions of the chapters by Barbara Ehrenreich and Eli Zaretsky originally appeared in *Socialist Review* 23, no. 3 (1994). Chantal Mouffe's "Radical Democracy or Liberal Democracy?" was originally published in *Socialist Review* 20, no. 2 (1990). Manning Marable's "A New American Socialism" was first published in *The Progressive* (February 1993). Bogdan Denitch's "A Foreign Policy for Radical Democrats" was first published in *Social Policy* (Fall/Winter

1992/93). Ellen Willis's "Let's Get Radical: Why Should the Right Have All the Fun?" was first published in *The Village Voice* (December 14, 1994). We are thankful to the various authors and publishers for permission to reprint these materials.

David Trend
1995

RADICAL DEMOCRACY

INTRODUCTION

PICK UP ANY NEWSPAPER AND IT'S CLEAR THAT DEMOCRACY
in the United States is facing a crisis. Conventional definitions of citizenship and national identity have been thrown
into question by ruptures in the global political landscape,
changing post-industrial economic relations, shifting racial
demographics, and new attitudes toward sexuality and religion. In a post-cold war era lacking in superpower conflicts,
old fears of foreign insurgency have been supplanted by anxieties about trade deficits, declining educational standards, and a
loss of common purpose. As social inequities continue to
increase, citizens are losing faith in the government and the
master narratives supporting it.

Few could have predicted the speed with which Europe
would be reconfigured by the collapse of the Eastern Bloc. Yet rather
than easing international tensions, these events have triggered new forms
of national chauvinism and regional antagonism. Complicating

DAVID TREND

matters further is the so-called post-Fordist restructuring of global capitalism. As the world evolves into a transnational marketplace and the production of goods and services becomes more fluid and decentralized, the distance between rich and poor nations continues to widen.

Meanwhile, within the United States a dominant white majority is quickly being diminished by communities of color. Factor in the growing influence of feminism, challenges to the traditional nuclear family, and more recent activism supporting the rights of lesbians and gay men, and it becomes clear that a massive movement—indeed, a *majority movement*—is rising to confront the reigning order.

Not surprisingly, these shifts have produced considerable public tension along with a disturbing tendency to reach for quick and easy ways to settle disputes. Witness recent social unrest in cities from Los Angeles to Atlanta, the broad-based hostility toward legislative and judicial figures, and the remarkable popularity of such reactionary personas as the self-proclaimed "doctor of democracy," Rush Limbaugh. Claiming to appeal to populist sentiments, a new breed of would-be demagogues has emerged to promote a xenophobic politics of fear and hatred propped up by an ever more puritanical set of cultural standards.

In foreign policy, this translates into an increasingly predatory role for the United States in the expansion of capitalism in the name of democracy. More and more reluctant to commit further resources to the protection of human rights, the United States portrays itself as the militaristic force of reason in a world overrun by savage tribes and mad dictators. Even as the efficacy of old legal conventions and bureaucratic structures is thrown further into doubt, new justifications are advanced for consolidated power and political control on a global scale. For a growing number of conservative ideologues, these new international dynamics call for a familiar and anti-democratic foreign policy: the return of colonialism.

At home, the process of national identity formation is less obvious, particularly as the Clinton administration continues to be undermined by an oppositional Congress. Lacking the threat of the Red Menace, neo-liberals and conservatives find common ground in assaulting the very underclass that dominant culture exploits most. In a post-civil rights era this bigotry is executed in new and sometimes subtle ways. Rather than identifying the poor as victims of discrimination and inequality, the disadvantaged are cast as the source of a decaying national infrastructure. Too sophisticated to directly name specific groups, this new rhetoric frames its objects by allusion and exclusion. Within this discourse, policy makers even appropriate the vocabulary of "empowerment" and "free choice" once thought to be the province of radical activists.

In the face of this political turmoil, the amalgam of interests identified as the "left" is strangely silent and ineffective. With the apparent triumph of liberal democracy worldwide, the unifying capacities once provided by socialism are now undeniably compromised. To many groups, the economic emphasis of socialism has become an insufficient explanation for problems like ethnic cleansing, gay-bashing, or sexual harassment. A more encompassing paradigm is needed.

For many on the left, the concept of radical democracy provides just such an alternative framework. Radical democrats argue that traditional democracy has failed to deliver on its promises of equality and civic participation. They accuse liberal democracy in particular of being too willing to sacrifice the interests of diverse groups in the name of a broad consensus. Most importantly, radical democrats claim that democratic principles underlie critiques of capitalism and that the creation of an egalitarian society will entail extending these democratic principles into ever expanding areas of daily life: work, education, leisure, the home.

Despite its commonsense appeal, radical democracy has yet to be implemented on any large scale. The theoretical character of radical democracy has drawn fire from those who fault the program for a lack of specificity. These critics accuse radical democracy of offering little more than a set of philosophical ideals, lacking any concrete explanation about its implementation in practical circumstance. Socialists in particular have asserted that in deemphasizing a critique of capitalism, radical democracy is reduced to an academic exercise that is ultimately more cultural that political.

Such criticisms notwithstanding, one of radical democracy's primary contributions to political theory has been its ability to rekindle debates within the left over issues of representation, equality, and freedom. *Radical Democracy: Identity, Citizenship, and the State* seeks to document these discussions while extending the conversation into a practical context. Assembling an interdisciplinary range of commentators from the social sciences, humanities, and the arts, *Radical Democracy* also intends to complicate these discussions in terms of both theory and practice—in part by frustrating easy distinctions between the two terms. Beyond this, the anthology explores particular implications of radical democratic principles in a variety of applications from the local to the global.

Part One, "Genealogies of Radical Democracy," provides a philosophical grounding for the more specific and speculative discussion to follow. The selection opens with "Democracy's Crisis of Meaning," which discusses the myriad applications and names democracy has taken, while asking whether the current ubiquity of democracy has exhausted the significance of the term. Chantal Mouffe's comparison of radical democracy and liberal democracy further demarcates the philosophical terrain of the anthology by explaining the reasoning behind the radical program. This is followed by essays by Seyla Benhabib and Amarpal Dhaliwal, which discuss the need for new democratic models while also criticizing alternatives that have been offered thus far. Both essays acknowledge the need for a new political agenda but question the way discussions are often foreclosed in the process. The final chapter by J. Peter Euben explores the role of theoretical reflection in the process of democracy itself.

Part Two, "Debating Radical Politics in the United States," opens with four essays assessing the current condition of the "left." In "Toward Radicalism: The Death and Rebirth of the American Left," Stanley Aronowitz argues that in its emphasis on equality and statism, the left has permitted assertions of freedom and individualism to be coopted by the right. He suggests that a language of radical democracy offers a means to reclaim these underemphasized values. Richard Flacks takes a similarly broad view of recent political events in arguing for a multivalent approach to democratic activism. In the following essay, Ellen Willis discusses recent congressional advances by conservatives, while warning leftists to resist the impulse to move toward the political center. Bogdan Denitch makes a related point in sketching a foreign policy for radical democrats.

The three essays which follow challenge the claims radical democracy makes against socialism. Barbara Epstein, Eli Zaretsky, and Manning Marable each argue that a democratic society emerges from a critique of capitalism, rather than the other way around. Epstein says that in emphasizing new social movements, identity politics, and cultural issues, radical democrats have minimized the importance of class. More seriously, Epstein warns that by emphasizing the dispersion of democracy into ever more local contexts, radical democrats cede the contest over the state to the right. Making a complimentary argument, Zaretsky states that socialism should not be abandoned because it has historically nurtured and encouraged the interests of new social movements. This position is extended by Manning Marable, who puts forth a model for "A New American Socialism" that accommodates diversity under its umbrella of anti-capitalism.

The last articles in this section reengage the issue of radical democracy in specific areas. Michael Omi and Howard Winant focus on race, noting that radical democrats should be careful not to overemphasize cultural concerns at the expense of social structure. Jeffrey Escoffier discusses ways of mobilizing lesbian, gay, and bisexual communities around issues of civil rights, especially in light of the growing efforts of the religious right to foreclose such democratic principles. Finally, Henry A. Giroux looks at recent debates around education and political correctness. Giroux cautions that the tendencies of both left and right to enforce orthodoxies argues against a democratic ethos.

Part Three, "Radical Democracy and Political Possibility," presents four articles of a more speculative character that suggest future directions in the radical democracy debate. Nancy Fraser anchors her discussion in conflicts within feminism between deconstructive anti-essentialists and pluralist multiculturalists. Fraser argues for a new, yet unnamed, means of cooperation among seemingly disparate groups. Gayatri Chakravorty Spivak and David Plotke explore these issues of coalition and strategy on a global scale, discussing the increasing political and economic permeability of national borders. They conclude that radical democracy can only have significance if it considers these newly emergent transnational relationships. Barbara Ehrenreich takes a similarly broad view in arguing that although "socialism" is experiencing a crisis of meaning, the greater problem facing leftists is a generalized loss of hope. Finally, bell hooks suggests that the means exist to forge political alliances across differences—if we are able to broaden our conception of alliances in ethical terms.

As an ensemble, *Radical Democracy: Identity, Citizenship, and the State* offers a wide-ranging overview of differing perspectives on radical political thinking. At a time when the "left" is in crisis, this volume seeks to provide a catalogue of suggestions for possible strategies to alleviate this crisis from both activists and academics. The message that emerges from this anthology is that single, uncomplicated answers are no longer sufficient for the complex issues of the current political environment. Clearly, radical democracy offers an important framework for addressing these concerns, if not as an immediately achievable goal, then as a meaningful horizon.

1

GENEALOGIES OF RADICAL DEMOCRACY

1

DEMOCRACY'S CRISIS OF MEANING

"**D**EMOCRACY" IS A RELATIVE TERM. LIKE ANY OTHER
expression, its meaning is a matter of interpretation, debate,
and contest; and in recent years it is a word we have heard
a great deal: from the "democratic" protests in Tiannamen
Square, to the "democratic" reforms throughout Eastern
Europe, to "Operation Restore Democracy" in Haiti. While
rival ideologies seem ever more flawed and uncertain,
evidence abounds of the so-called "triumph" of liberal
democracy. As a term nearly synonymous with the foreign policy objectives of the United States government, democracy has
witnessed the fall of many who once vowed to stand in its way.
Perhaps not so coincidentally, it is also nearly always equated
with the global economic order of market capitalism.

Despite these historic advances on the international front, the
domestic state of democracy could not be more in question. If

DAVID TREND

democracy implies the enfranchisement of all voters, how is it that the majority of citizens do not participate in electoral politics? If democracy means equal rights for all citizens, how can one explain the chronic disrepair of the social service network and the continued tolerance of predatory business interests? If democracy suggests unmediated communication and access to information, what is one to make of the consolidation of media in a handful of corporations? If democracy entails a role for citizens in their common governance, what explains the wide scale resentment toward government officials and the rise of fringe personas like Ross Perot and Oliver North? While totalitarian regimes and oppressive bureaucracies tumble around the globe, within the United States the tenents of justice and equality continue to weaken.

These apparent contradictions in American democracy suggest more than a simple gap between theory and practice. They signify the profoundly fictional character that the democratic ideal assumes in the public mind. The very slipperiness of the term permits its exploitation by a range of politicians, bureaucrats, and philosophers for purposes ranging from electoral sloganeering to military intervention. For this reason, an initial step in the salvaging of participatory politics may well entail an analysis of democracy's crisis of meaning. This entails asking such questions as whether democracy functions primarily as a form of decision making or as an instrument of popular empowerment, whether democracy constitutes an abstract ideal or an achievable goal, or whether democracy emerges from within a group or can be externally imposed.

Such questions begin to suggest that the very idea of a single democracy is a fallacy. Instead democracy serves as a marker for a wide variety of interests, philosophies, and political programs expressed in the continual flux of labels like direct democracy, liberal democracy, juridical democracy, associative democracy, socialist democracy, and radical democracy, among numerous others. At the same time, these questions throw into relief the way democracy has become essentialized as an undefined norm—joining such ambiguous expressions as "mainstream opinion" and "family values," which lack a clear definition, yet are highly effective in discrediting selected groups. It is therefore in the interest of "democratic" ideals to attempt to unpack the various discourses of democracy.

This inquiry into the crisis of democratic meaning motivates the discussions anthologized in *Radical Democracy: Identity, Citizenship, and the State*. Whether or not one agrees that democratic principles prefigure other forms of economic and social change, the ubiquity of democratic rhetoric demands clarification at a time when its meaning is so profoundly debased in the global environment. This is not to promise an analysis distinguishing between "true" or "false" democracies. Put in its most optimistic terms, this conversation will delineate the shifting meanings and applications of the concept within various power relations and consequently enhance democracy's productive uses.

DIRECT DEMOCRACY

One way of envisioning democracy is at the end of a participatory continuum, the other end of which marks the complete exclusion of people from common decision making. Yet contrary to much contemporary rhetoric, even this simple view of democracy also implies a set of limits on human behavior—a series of restraints on freedom itself. Any subscription to democracy presupposes a degree of faith in the possibility of politics—a belief that human need can be addressed within communities, as opposed to the anarchy of absolute privacy, liberty, and individualism. Put this way, debates over different forms of democracy all boil down to arguments over what kind of common compacts are desirable or possible in a given society.

Like other social formations, democracy is enabled by the agents of the populous who call it into being. Classical theory located this agency in the category of the citizen, bound in a contractual relationship with the state to cede certain freedoms in order to gain corresponding rights. The exact terms of this contract vary with the form of democracy used. In direct or "pure" democracies, citizens engage in common decision making without the mediation of a legislature or other representative body. Such democratic structures originated on nearly every continent, although the first written records of such practices are commonly attributed to the ancient Greeks.

The privileging of Athenian democracy over other "preliterate" models has become a matter of no small consequence in its historic deployment to assert the primacy of European culture and to justify its "natural" posture of dominance. This issue receives detailed examination in Martin Bernal's *Black Athena*, an ongoing study of the colonization of ancient Greece by Egyptian and Phoenician peoples.[1] Bernal asserts that European historians systematically suppressed the Afroasiatic roots of classical Greece to promote ethnocentric narratives of superiority and progress. Specifically, he locates pre-Athenian elements of democratic practice in late-Egyptian religious beliefs of spiritual equality.

The irony of this European historiographic self-interestedness is nowhere more apparent than in the suppression of democratic legacies in colonized nations. For example, various participatory governments were thriving among the indigenous peoples of North America at precisely the time when anti-democratic monarchies were driving populations from the so-called "civilized" world. The egalitarian character of certain tribes and nations so impressed colonial leaders that they appropriated aspects of native organizational structure into their own governments. Benjamin Franklin freely acknowledged his emulation of the Iroquois League in formulating the Articles of Confederation during the 1780s—a series of documents which would later form the basis for the US Constitution.

One aspect of indigenous democracy the early American colonists did not adopt was the tribal model of consensus decision making. The choice instead of Athenian principles of majority rule has raised questions ever since about the ultimate representational fairness of this European model. Classical participatory theory holds that although decisions are made in "winner take all" voting, the regularity of polling assures that no majority is permanent. If any agreement proves inadequate it will be overturned in a subsequent ballot. For this reason, any majority has reason to remain sensitive to the needs of the minority—or so the theory goes. In practice, however, majorities have often used their political leverage to maintain dominance. Commentators from Alexis de Tocqueville to Lani Guinier have criticized this fundamental precept of democracy for its inability to fairly represent all citizens.[2] The frequently evoked concept of the "tyranny of the majority" results not only from winner-take-all electoral systems, but from the persistent failure of democracies to enfranchise potential voters without discrimination.

Critics of this particular shortcoming often begin by pointing to the internal contradictions of Athenian society. Although credited with the "invention" of democracy, ancient Greece permitted only one social group access to this sanctified realm. All "citizens" may have had equal and unmediated participation in civic life, but women, slaves, and non-Greeks were excluded from the fraternity of citizenship. Far from a mere historical "problem" in classical democracy, this very issue of who counts as a voting citizen has plagued Western democracies ever since. It is important to point out that even within the United States— the purported "model" of world democracy—such a fundamental issue as women's suffrage was contested well into the twentieth century. Even these advances remained in question for subsequent decades in such purportedly enlightened nations as Germany, Italy, and Spain, where the right to vote was systematically withheld from certain groups. The denial of voting rights within the United States to African-Americans and other immigrant groups remained a point of severe acrimony through the 1950s and 1960s.

Despite these problems, Athenian direct democracy retains relevance for many as a philosophical ideal. The notion of active citizenship as a defining principle of public life informs many contemporary debates over issues ranging from radical pluralism to communitarianism. Indeed Bill Clinton's exhortations about "public service" in the name of the "national family" emanate from a nostalgic yearning for a pre-liberal sense of civic responsibility. At issue is the degree to which direct democracy or active citizenship can be realized in massive post-industrial societies. Such idealized political models flourished in the relatively immobile atmospheres of small, oral cultures in which face-to-face meetings constituted an organic part of daily life. But as European society became more complex, so did its forms of democracy. With the rise of the Roman empire, the era of classical Italian republicanism marked a transition to elected leadership, and along with it the beginning of a gradual distancing of civic governance from the citizenry. Rome's mixed government, with its interlocking system of consuls and people's tribunals, became a model for an intermediate form of democracy—in which the people remained the ultimate source of accountability, but in which forms of elected representation became a necessity.

The ethical dimensions of this transition from direct democracy cannot be overstated, for the shift to representative forms of government signaled a weakening of the sense of personal responsibility in community governance. The profound influence of the Christian church in the middle ages helped displace secular morality as a motivation for involved citizenship. This inducement to defer civic responsibility was later enhanced by the growth of market capitalism and the resultant competition for material goods. In such an environment the state evolved into an abstract arbiter of the public interest, and as a consequence grew ever more suspect as an impediment to personal autonomy. This called for new forms of political organization that could accommodate and contain both general and individualism impulses.

LIBERAL MODELS AND ALTERNATIVES

Liberal democracy evolved in direct response to the perceived encroachment of the state on personal liberty. At the center of the liberal democratic ethos lies the western notion of the autonomous individual, capable of free choice and motivated by self-interest. Individualistic "private" concerns are viewed as clearly separable from "public" issues of the community at large. Hence, the private sphere encompasses the realm of personal gain and subjective interest, as mediated by the competition of the market, while the public comprises the arena of laws, legislatures, and other civic structures, whose ultimate logic is reducible to an apolitical ideal of the common good.[3] The formation of a disinterested and distinct public sphere reveals the uniquely western belief in Cartesian epistemology—a belief in the possibility of a knowable independent ground apart from humanity's base instincts.

Another key principle for liberal democrats is a belief that individual interest is actually enhanced by mutual cooperation. As John Locke put it, "the great and chief end therefore of men uniting into commonwealths and putting themselves under government . . . is the mutual preservation of their lives, liberties, and estates, which shall call by the general name property."[4] This impulse for accumulation is both enabled and limited by the state. Hence, liberal democracy assumes a two-stroke function as a justification and limit for the exercise of state authority. Regular elections serve the philosophical goal of obliging the public to clarify public issues while assuring that no government or set of public officials will remain in office forever.

Opinions differ among liberal democrats over how much the general consensus should apply to all citizens. This is both the rationale for local government and the reasoning behind various pluralist versions of liberal democracy. Pluralists agree that different groups deserve different degrees of influence over various matters according to the proportion of their interest in them. Within the liberal logic of self-interest, people are more likely to exercise their agency as citizens over matters that affect them most directly.

This belief has led some liberals to advocate a strengthening of the civil society as a means of decentralizing democracy and lessening the role of the state. The civil society argument, occasionally termed the "associationalist" view, asserts that the goals of social justice and human welfare are best served by voluntary and self-governing private bodies, such as unions political parties, and religious organizations.[5] This position gained popularity in the western world during the nineteenth century but was squeezed out of existence as the tension between collectivist and individualist politics foreclosed such compromises. The civil society argument departs from conventional liberal democracy by according voluntary bodies a primary role in organizing social life, rather than an ancillary function to government. These smaller private entities, which may or may not be governed by democratic principles, are viewed as more flexible and responsive to community needs. Representative government assumes a regulatory function as guarantor of services, rather than acting as their provider. Limited to this overseeing role, government bureaucracy purportedly is lessened and its efficiency enhanced as a consequence.

A related trend has been the growing popularity of communitarianism, in which the ethical dimensions of voluntarism are emphasized over the mandates of self-interest. As espoused by Amitai Etzioni and William Galston, the trouble with conventional liberalism is that it focuses too much on individual rights and not enough on shared values.[6] To overcome these problems, communitarians suggest that people should become more involved in developing the "social glue" that holds society together through such entities as schools, neighborhoods, and the family. The communitarian emphasis on the traditional nuclear family, in particular, has drawn the fire of those who claim that communitarianism masks a traditionalist agenda. Others have faulted the doctrine's cultural and micro-institutional approach, arguing that social problems like structural unemployment and entrenched racism cannot be addressed strictly on an interpersonal level.

SOCIALISM AND DEMOCRACY

More extreme opponents of liberal democracy locate its problems in the economic mandates of capitalism. Critical of the liberal emphasis on competition, Karl Marx and Friedrich Engels viewed material inequities not merely as by-products of such a model but as necessary components of it. To create winners in the game of acquisition, a system must also generate losers. The much ballyhooed "opportunities" for liberty offered by liberal capitalism mean little if they are not universally accessible. The resultant inequities in turn spoil the very functioning of democracy. As the state becomes little more than the tool of the privileged, the very idea of a separation between private and public is thrown into question. Rather than serving as an idealized and apolitical mediator of the common good, government is perverted by the ability of some citizens to exert undue control over it.

Beyond this analysis of social structure, Marxism holds significance in democratic discussions for its contributions to the understanding of ideology. Rather than being an objective set of relations among people, politics devolves into a struggle of class interests. Critical strategies are thus required to reveal the machinations of exploitive capitalists and to restore government to the interest of all citizens. Just how to accomplish this became a matter of no small debate, dividing Marxists into either Leninist camps favoring top-down strategies of vanguardist theorizing or Gramscian groups promoting populist programs derived from practical experience.

For similar reasons, the actual applications of socialist democracy vary greatly. One common formula is the merger of the government with private institutions to eliminate any advantages held. Within this logic, preoccupations with individual liberty become irrelevant, as do assertions of groups claiming rights on the basis of identity. Social inequities are perceived primarily as economic matters, resolvable by the dissolution of capitalism. With the elimination of the non-productive aspects of market exchange, efficiency becomes maximized and scarcity is eliminated. Citizens find themselves no longer driven by artificially induced needs and thus lose their egotistical impulses for acquisition. As the social hierarchies of class distinction are eradicated, the need for personal autonomy is diminished. Indeed, individual freedom becomes a redundancy in a society where all needs of the citizenry are addressed. As a consequence, the very need for a state diminishes. So does the necessity for politics itself, as "government" gives way to "administration."

But history has demonstrated the elusiveness of such utopian goals. Like liberal democracy, the principles of socialist democracies have suffered somewhat in practical application. The so-called "transitional" phase between capitalism and communism proved impossible for most regimes to transcend. One explanation for this shortcoming lies in the problem of transforming a mechanism for seizing power into an instrument for the exercise of power. Another factor in the anti-democratic drive to single-party conformity was the incremental development of a managerial class of party bureaucrats and government officials. As demonstrated by the Soviet Union and other nations of the Eastern European bloc, difficulties emerged in the capacities of huge, single-party bureaucracies to remain responsive to local constituencies. Moreover, the structure of state ownership of property has the effect of denying resources to oppositional groups. The ability to mount political alternatives to the state, while not completely foreclosed by a socialist system, is significantly hampered. Not unlike the elite-driven governments of the West, many socialist democracies evolved structures distanced from popular rule.

PLURALISM AND RADICALISM

The post-World War II atmosphere of growing Cold War tension produced a range of efforts to ameliorate antagonisms between liberal and socialist democrats.[7] Groups in Europe and the United States began to argue that neither approach sufficiently represented the complexity of civic subjectivity. Needed was a way of more fairly accounting for the complex differentiation of individuals into groups and identities. The emphasis on locating a "middle ground" between state authority and individual autonomy was further tempered by an antagonism toward the elitist tendencies of both liberal and socialist states.

Not surprisingly, pluralist democracies differ considerably. One of the most significant distinctions lies in the degree to which these hybrids emphasize material or cultural matters. The materialist camp is exemplified by the work of John Dunn, Samuel Bowles, and Herbert Gintis, who focus on the systemic inequities of capitalism in their calls for economic democracy (what Bowles and Gintis term "postliberal" democracy).[8] These authors argue that democracy emerges from the participatory management of property and production. Yet unlike traditional socialists who advocate the centralized organization of this authority, economic democrats typically favor more heterogeneous sites of power, where decisions can be made by constituencies identified by rights claims.

In contrast to economic democracy, the culturalist line argues that capitalism will be undone by enhanced civic participation itself. In this respect, the culturalist camp can be seen as an important precursor to the radical democracy movement. Once people understand the potentials of equality in one sphere, they will attempt to extend it into every other area of life. This approach to politics was codified by Norberto Bobbio, who was strongly influenced by the populist critiques of pure economism posed by Antonio Gramsci. Although critical of the inequities inherent in liberal capitalism, Bobbio saw the modernist assertion of individual agency as a social force too powerful to be undone. To accommodate the values of freedom and equality, Bobbio proposed a strongly constitutional democracy, in which competitive parties would represent constituent interests. The importance of the party stemmed from his perception that society is too diverse to achieve a single "common sense." Setting this form of politics apart from typical representative democracies would be a series of compacts designed to block what Bobbio termed the "invisible powers" of industry and finance from exerting undue influence. To achieve this, citizens would not simply be given equal "political rights," but also equal "social rights" to assure that their political interests would not suffer interference.

Central to this thinking was a reorientation of conventional distinctions between "public" and "private" realms. Loosely speaking, these terms separate human activity into categories of general and particular concern—with the latter typically considered "off limits" to political discussion. As numerous post-liberal democrats came to believe, this separation creates a dangerous trade-off as so-called public decision making increasingly takes on a life of its own and becomes distanced from the daily lives of the citizenry. To remedy the situation, the means of political representation needs to be spread further into the basic fabric of daily life: work, education, leisure, and the home. The problem of democracy becomes no longer simply "who votes" but "where one votes."[9]

In the contemporary United States this distancing of the general from the particular is manifest in a broad-based suspicion among voters of public officials. These anti-incumbency sentiments led to the massive congressional overhaul in the 1994 elections, when opportunistic conservatives successfully exacerbated public anxieties about a federal government grown too large and intrusive. As in other instances, the conventional solution to the public/private dilemma has been to place increased emphasis on local ballots, in which communities need not acquiesce to general social mandates. Regrettably, this has proven ineffective in serving the needs of diverse groups—such as those defined by age, gender, occupation, race, ethnicity, or sexual orientation—within and across geographical communities. During the last 20 years, this representational failure has led to calls for an enhanced emphasis on pluralism, with approaches ranging from a reassertion of the civil society to more radical prescriptions. The search for an invigorated approach to pluralism found sustenance in poststructuralist theory.

Poststructuralists argued that democratic pluralism marked a significant advance over unreconstructed liberalism in carving out a larger role and a more complex arena for citizens to act politically, but it only did so within existing understandings of citizen roles. The problem lay in the way conventional post-war pluralism was incapable of recognizing the subjects of politics as anything other than members of discrete groups. Theorists such as Ernesto Laclau and Chantal Mouffe proposed what they termed a "radical democratic" reconceptualization of the citizen unencumbered by such compartmentalized categories of subjectivity. Far from an independent member of a particular constituency, within this formulation each person belongs to numerous overlapping groups and multiple intersecting identities. As Mouffe explains, "it is not a matter of establishing a mere alliance between given interests but of actually modifying their identity to bring about a new political identity."[10] As this group-identification model ties its subjects irrevocably to the social, individuality is also maintained because of the relatively unique mix of association within each person.

This radical democratic model of the subject has profound implications for political organization, for it shatters convenient distinctions between public and private. As suggested by Kirstie McClure, this formulation provides a reinscription of the "subject of rights" that implies not so much an escape from the state, nor an "abdication from political participation more conventionally understood, but rather a potential refusal of a unitary construct of citizenship as exhaustive of the political tasks of the present."[11] Such a reformulation of the subject need not be understood as a simple collapse of former private concerns into the public arena, or vice versa. According to Laclau and Mouffe, this should be seen instead as an opportunity for the creation of "new political spaces."[12] In the expanded view of the multiple subject, the very definition of the political becomes broadened to a new range of sites beyond the conventional jurisdiction of state institutions and into the far more dynamic domain of cultural representations and social practices.

In such a context, the poststructuralist approach to pluralism does not negate subjective agency as it is often accused of doing. Instead, by opening new territory for scrutiny, the model gives vitality to the impetus for democratic principles. The politicization of social spaces formerly considered neutral makes apparent the often unacknowledged power relations in everyday activities. In this way, such off-limits territories as culture, education, and the family become sites of critical investigation and emancipatory contestation. Rather than diminishing a sense of political agency by negating essential notions of the subject, the principles of radical democracy have the potential of reinvigorating the subject within new spheres of activity. Just as importantly, in arguing against the notion of a fixed or universal subject, the project of a radical democracy is by definition never complete.

TRANSNATIONAL ISSUES AND BEYOND

Despite their utopian aspirations (and perhaps because of them), prescriptions for radical democratic pluralism have been subject to strenuous critique. Many on the left assert that a focus on identity and on generalized definitions of the subject minimizes the importance of economic issues and the particulars of social structure.[13] Radical democracy may promise an egalitarian program but does little to spell out the details of how it will address issues of redistribution. This lack of specificity is similarly critiqued from postcolonial quarters as one indication that this purportedly "postmodern" approach to politics simply may constitute another brand of modernism in disguise.[14] This critique of radical pluralism's failure to articulate where and how its program will be implemented is interpreted as a universalizing theory incapable of engaging the practical aspects of social change. The general "right" of citizens to vote is undermined by the absence of other privileges that such universalizing rhetoric obscures. Without acknowledging the ethnocentric character of these absences, radical democracy becomes "the latest" chapter in an enlightenment program of western progress. Evidence of this evolutionary view comes, for example, from radical democracy's preservation and adaptation of certain liberal principles. Due to this allegiance to the liberal legacy, still other critics claim that radical democracy represents little more than a new name devised by disaffected socialists, who are drifting toward liberal democracy but can't bring themselves to embrace it.

Regardless of definition, the proliferation of democratic societies around the globe is abundantly evident—even though the precise meaning of this proliferation is difficult to gauge. Clearly in certain contexts this democratic globalization is far from an innocent or "natural" occurrence, as democracy is deployed to mask foreign intervention and neocolonial expansionism. In other situations these changes are more benign. Either way, the ubiquity of democracy can become a way of envisioning global political relations—not merely *within* nations, but *among* them as well. This concept of a global democracy becomes especially important in light of the growing concentration of economic relations across sovereign borders. The post-Fordist restructuring of global capitalism makes the issue of national borders increasingly irrelevant. To many analysts, a *de facto* world government is emerging, led by transnational corporations in cooperation with the International Monetary Fund (IMF), the World Bank, the newly established World Trade Organization, and other structures, to promote a new imperial age.

This new world community is replacing the Westphalian model of national sovereignty, in which each country was regarded as internally homogeneous, self-interested, and minimally cooperative with other states. Former isolationist understandings of statehood have given way to a view of nations as interdependent entities. Like the postmodern conception of identity, nations are seen as heterogeneous bodies with multiple points of intersection among each other.

Consequently, nations are not only connected on a state-to-state basis through such issues as non-aggression pacts. They are imbricated with much more complexity through the micropolitics of such matters as health, population, and ecological concerns. Within this heterogeneous model, anything less than an internal democracy becomes extremely difficult for individual states to maintain, for it works against the grain of the emerging global structure. Yet this inherently democratic trend for affinities and allegiances to emerge across national borders does not necessarily imply fairness or equality of development. Quite the opposite.

Since many of these transnational relationships are shaped by the mandates of multinational capital, inequities seem axiomatic in what the World Bank has termed the "international civil society." In a recent address to the group of 77, an organization representing 100 of the world's less-developed nations, chair-person Luis Vernon Jaramillo of Colombia remarked that the states comprising the transnational regime dominated by the IMF and the World Bank are characterized by "their undemocratic character, their lack of transparency, their lack of pluralism in the debate of ideas and their impotence to influence the policies of industrialized countries."[15] In this light, the need for transnational regulatory body along the lines of the United Nations becomes even more pronounced. This transnational view can be interpreted as a call to extend democracy into yet another area of contemporary life, a gesture compatible with the current growth of democracy in general.

Increasingly, the question raised by this proliferation of democracy returns to the issue of meaning. At what point in the expansion of democracy into every corner of human existence does the concept begin to lose significance. Has that moment already arrived? *Radical Democracy: Identity, Citizenship, and the State* seeks to address these issues by engaging democracy's identity crisis from a range of disciplinary perspectives in the humanities and social sciences. Even if the pervasiveness of democracy is emptying the term of its significance, such democratic ideals as participatory government and egalitarian politics retain merit nevertheless. Rather than mourning the loss of a means to achieve these ideals, one can argue that the very fragmentation of democratic strategies opens a field of application by unsettling any dominant version. In this sense democracy becomes radicalized as its very definition becomes a matter of contest and debate. In this radicalized vision of pluralism there is a source of political possibility even in democracy's crisis of meaning.

NOTES

1. Martin Bernal, *Black Athena: The Afroasiatic Roots of Classical Civilization Volume 1: The Fabrication of Ancient Greece 1785–1985* (New Brunswick: Rutgers University Press, 1987).

2. Alexis de Tocqueville, *Democracy in America* (New York: A.A. Knopf, 1945); Lani Guinier, *The Tyranny of the Majority: Fundamental Fairness in Representative Democracy* (New York: Free Press, 1994).

3. John Dewey, *Democracy and Education: An Introduction to the Philosophy of Education* (New York: Macmillan, 1944); John Rawls, *A Theory of Justice* (Cambridge: Harvard University Press, 1971).

4. John Locke, *The Second Treatise of Civil Government* (Buffalo: Prometheus Books, 1986), 413.

5. Paul Hirst, "Associational Democracy," in *Prospects for Democracy: North/South/East/West*, ed. David Held (Stanford: Stanford University Press, 1993), 112–135.

6. Amitai Etzioni, *Capital Corruption: The New Attack on American Democracy* (New Brunswick: Transaction Books, 1988); Amitai Etzioni, *The Spirit of*

Community: Rights, Responsibilities, and the Communitarian Agenda (New York: Crown Books, 1993); William Galston, *Liberal Property: Goods, Virtues, and Diversity in the Liberal State.*

7. See, for example, Robert Dahl, *A Preface to Economic Democracy* (Berkeley: University of California, 1984); David Held, *Models of Democracy* (Stanford: Stanford University, 1987); C. B. Macpherson, *The Life and Times of Liberal Democracy* (Oxford and New York: Oxford, 1977); Joshua Cohen and Joel Rogers, *On Democracy* (New York: Penguin Books, 1983).

8. John Dunn, ed., *The Economic Limits of Modern Politics* (Cambridge: Cambridge University Press, 1990); Samuel Bowles and Herbert Gintis, *Democracy and Capitalism: Property, Community, and the Contradictions of Modern Social Thought* (New York: Basic Books, 1986).

9. Norberto Bobbio, *Which Socialism? Marxism, Socialism, and Democracy*, trans. Roger Griffin (London: Polity Press, 1987), 24; See also, Norberto Bobbio, *The Future of Democracy: A Defense of the Rules of the Game*, trans. Roger Griffin (London: Polity Press, 1987).

10. Chantal Mouffe, "Democratic Politics Today," in *Dimensions of Radical Democracy*, ed. Chantal Mouffe (London and New York: Verso, 1991).

11. Kirstie McClure, "On the Subject of Rights: Pluralism, Plurality and Political Identity," in *Dimensions of Radical Democracy*, p. 109.

12. Laclau and Mouffe, *Hegemony and Socialist Strategy*. Jaramillo as cited by Chomsky.

13. The recurrent accusation that radical democracy constitutes a linguistic argument with little material consequences emerged in a well-known exchange of articles in *New Left Review*. See Norman Geras, "Post-Marxism?" *New Left Review* 163 (May/June 1987): 10–72; Ernesto Laclau and Chantal Mouffe, "Post-Marxism without Apologies," *New Left Review* 166 (November/December 1987): 79–107; Norman Geras, "Ex-Marxism without Substance: Being a Real Reply to Laclau and Mouffe," *New Left Review* 169 (May/June 1988): 34–61.

14. See Amarpal Dhaliwal, "Can the Subaltern Vote? Radical Democracy, Discourses of Representation and Rights, and Questions of Race," in this volume.

15. Noam Chomsky, "Democracy's Slow Death," *In These Times* 19, no. 1 (November 28–December 11, 1994): 25.

2

RADICAL DEMOCRACY
OR LIBERAL DEMOCRACY?

THE RECENT EVENTS IN EASTERN EUROPE HAVE BEEN
heralded as the victory of liberal democracy. But what does
that concept mean? What is liberal democracy? Just another
name for capitalist democracy, or can one imagine a non-
capitalist liberal democracy? This is the most pressing question
for the left today, and it cannot be answered without a new
understanding of the nature of the political. It is only if we
conceive of "liberal democracy" as a specific political form of
society that we will be able to elucidate its main characteristics
and its relations both with capitalism and with socialism as specific forms of ownership of the means of production.

For those who refuse to accept "really existing" liberal
democratic capitalism as the end of history and who consider
Western liberal democratic societies to still have an enormous
potential for democratization, the crucial issue should be how to
radicalize and further democratize our present institutions.

CHANTAL MOUFFE

Norberto Bobbio is right to assert that liberal political institutions should be a necessary component of any process of democratization and that socialist goals can only be acceptably achieved within the liberal democratic framework.[1] In *Hegemony and Socialist Strategy*, Ernesto Laclau and I attempt a reformulation of the socialist project in terms of "radical and plural democracy," arguing that it should be conceived as the radicalization and deepening of the democratic revolution—as the extension of the democratic ideals of liberty and equality to more and more areas of social life.[2] The aim is not to create a completely different kind of society, but to use the symbolic resources of the liberal democratic tradition to struggle against relations of subordination not only in the economy but also those linked to gender, race, or sexual orientation, for example. We emphasized that such a perspective requires abandoning the reductionism and essentialism dominant in traditional interpretations of socialism, and acknowledging the contingency and ambiguity of every essence and the constitutive character of social division and antagonism. Our understanding of radical and plural democracy is to be distinguished from many other forms of radical or participatory democracy. What we advocate is a type of "radical liberal democracy"—we do not present it as a rejection of the liberal democratic regime or as the institution of a new political form of society. Such a political project is more pertinent today than ever, and it can provide the only alternative to the debacle of communism.

There is, to be sure, serious resistance from the left to admitting the positive value of an articulation between liberalism and democracy, resulting from an essentialist view of liberalism and a lack of clarity about the specificity of modern democracy. The first problem resides in the conflation, within the term "liberalism," of different discourses that have no necessary relation to one another, but which are articulated together in certain circumstances. Political liberalism, economic liberalism, and the many discourses that constitute the "philosophy of liberalism," among which the dominant discourse is individualism, do not form a single doctrine. Many different articulations can exist among the different forms of liberalism. When we speak of a liberal democratic "regime" we are concerned with a political form of society and with political liberalism. To value the institutions which embody political liberalism's principles does not require us to endorse either economic liberalism or individualism.

At stake is the nature of modern democracy as a pluralist democracy. Pluralism, understood as the principle that individuals should have the possibility to organize their lives as they wish, to choose their own ends, and to realize them as they think best, is the greatest contribution of liberalism to modern society. This contribution is the individual freedom that liberal political institutions help to secure through the separation of Church and State, the division of powers, and the limitation of state power. Any modern democratic project must come to terms with such a pluralism. This means discarding the dangerous dream of a perfect consensus, of a harmonious collective will, and accepting the permanence of conflicts and antagonisms. As soon as the possibility of a substantial homogeneity is abandoned, the role of liberal political institutions appears in a different light. Far from merely covering up the class divisions of capitalist society, as many participatory democrats seem to believe, they guarantee the protection of individuals' rights against the tyranny of the majority or the domination of the totalitarian party or state. This is why political liberalism must be a central component of a project of radical and plural democracy. Under modern democratic conditions, characterized by the absence of a single substantive idea of the good life, the articulation between pluralism and democracy is the very condition for the extension of the principles of equality and liberty.

SCHMITT'S DEMOCRATIC ANTI-LIBERALISM

That modern democracy must be a pluralistic democracy is paradoxically something understood better by reading Carl Schmitt, perhaps the most brilliant critic of liberal democracy. Indeed, Schmitt can help us grasp the crucial importance of the articulation between liberalism and democracy and the dangers involved in any attempt to renounce liberal pluralism.

In his book *The Crisis of Parliamentary Democracy*, Schmitt's main target is liberal pluralism. The intellectual core of liberalism resides for him "in its specific relationship to truth, which becomes a mere function of the eternal competition of opinions."[3] It is to such liberal belief in the openness of opinions that Schmitt objects, not to democracy per se, which he defines as the identities of rulers and ruled, and which for him is perfectly compatible with an authoritarian regime. He declares, for instance, that "Bolshevism and Fascism by contrast, like all dictatorships, are certainly anti-liberal but not necessarily anti-democratic."[4] He considers that it is the representative liberal element in a parliamentary democracy that constitutes the nondemocratic aspect of such a democracy. He declares, "as democracy, modern mass democracy attempts to realize an identity of governed and governing, and thus it confronts parliament as an inconceivable and outmoded institution. If democratic identity is taken seriously, then in an emergency, no other constitutional institution can withstand the sole criterion of the people's will, however it is expressed."[5]

Such an understanding of democracy might be unacceptable to us, but it is not illegitimate. It is clearly incompatible with our understanding of pluralistic democracy, but it reveals that the logic of democracy alone does not guarantee the defense of individual freedom and a respect for individual rights. It is only through its articulation with political liberalism that the logic of popular sovereignty can avoid becoming tyrannical; then one cannot speak of *the* people as if it was one homogenous and unified entity with a single general will.

Schmitt does not and cannot acknowledge that with modern democracy we are in the presence of a new regime because he is hostile to the effects of the democratic revolution. He refuses to accept that a new form of society has emerged in which individual freedom requires the presence of liberal political institutions. Therefore he is blind to the specificity of modern pluralistic democracy as the regime whose principles of legitimacy are the constitutional guarantees of human rights in order to secure freedom and equality for all.

Such a rejection of liberal pluralism can have very dangerous consequences; it was Schmitt's anti-liberalism that made it possible for him to join the Nazis in 1933. This connection provides a topic of reflection for those on the left who aim at the creation of a perfect democratic homogeneity and who see liberalism only as an obstacle to such an ideal.

There is, however, another way in which we can benefit from reading Schmitt, this time by accepting his critique of liberal individualism. In "The Concept of the Political," Schmitt argues that the pure and rigorous principle of liberalism cannot give birth to a specifically political conception. For him, every consistent individualism must negate the political since it requires that the individual remain as both starting point and destination. Liberal individualism is unable to understand the formation of collective identities, and it cannot grasp that the collective aspect of social life is constitutive. This failure is why, according to Schmitt, liberal concepts move between ethics and economics and attempt "to annihilate the political as a domain of conquering power and repression."[6] The liberal idea that the general interest results from the free play of private interests and that a universal rational consensus can result from free discussion prevents liberalism from comprehending the nature of the political. This concept of the political, Schmitt argues, "can be understood only in the context of the ever present possibilities of the friend and enemy grouping, regardless of the aspects which the possibility implies for morality, aesthetics, and economics."[7]

Liberalism implies that by confining diverse issues to the sphere of the private, agreement on procedural rules should be enough to regulate the plurality of interests in society. But this liberal attempt to negate the political is bound to fail. The political can never be eradicated since it can derive its energy from the most varied human endeavors, "every religious, moral, economic, ethical, or other antithesis transforms itself into a political one if it is sufficiently strong to group human beings effectively according to the friend and enemy."[8]

I think Schmitt is right to point out the deficiencies of liberal individualism with respect to the political. Many of the problems facing liberal democracies today—the so-called "crisis of liberal democracy"—stem from the fact that politics has been reduced to an instrumental activity, to the selfish pursuit of private interests. The limitation of democracy to a mere set of neutral procedures, the transformation of citizens into political consumers, and the liberal insistence on a supposed "neutrality" of the state have emptied politics of all its subsistence. It is reduced to economics and stripped of all its ethical components. There is an increasing awareness today of the need to reestablish the link between ethics and politics and to revive political philosophy as a normative approach to politics. The present conjuncture makes such a task more urgent than ever. If liberal democracy is the only alternative we have, it cannot be accepted on the grounds of being the lesser evil. To promote a project of radical and plural democracy we need to create a strong allegiance to the ethical-political principles of modern democracy. Only on that condition will the extension of the ideals of liberty and equality become the driving force of democratic politics. The current dominance of an instrumentalist model of politics is an obstacle to a real understanding of the radical potential of the liberal democratic regime. It leads to apathy and cynicism, both of which very conveniently maintain the hegemony of the neoconservative elites, with their self-complacent and limited definition of the scope of modern democracy.

KANT AND THE COMMON GOOD

In the last two decades, several attempts have been made to recover the normative aspects of politics and renew the tradition of political philosophy. But the different approaches are, to my view, unsatisfactory and fail to provide us with the type of modern democratic political philosophy we need.

Liberals like John Rawls and Ronald Dworkin want to infuse politics with morality. Following the model set by Kant in "On Perpetual Peace," they propose a view of politics bounded by norms and guided by morally defined goals. Their communitarian critics attack liberalism for its individualism. They denounce the ahistorical, asocial, and disembodied conception of the subject, which is implied by the idea of an individual endowed with natural rights prior to society, and reject the thesis of the priority of the right over the good, which is at the core of the new liberal paradigm established by Rawls. They want to revive a conception of politics as the realm where we recognize ourselves as participants in a community. Against the Kantian inspiration of "rights-based" liberals, the communitarians call upon Aristotle and Hegel; against liberalism, they appeal to the tradition of civic republicanism. The problem is that some of them, like Michael Sandel and Alasdair MacIntyre, believe that a critique of liberal individualism entails the rejection of pluralism and political liberalism. So in the end they propose to come back to a politics of the common good based on shared moral values.[9] Such a position is clearly incompatible with modern democracy because it presupposes a premodern view of the political community as organized around a single substantive idea of the common good.

It is important to rediscover notions of civic virtue, public spirit, and political community which have been set aside by liberalism, but they must be reformulated in a way that makes them compatible with pluralism and the defense of individual liberty. At the same time, we cannot accept the solution proposed by Kantian liberals. What they present as political philosophy is nothing more than a public morality to regulate the basic structure of society. The problem with Rawls, for instance, is that by failing to distinguish properly between moral discourse and political discourse and by using a mode of reasoning specific to moral discourse, he is unable to grasp the nature of the political. Conflicts, antagonisms, and relations of power disappear, and the field of politics is reduced to a rational process of negotiation among private interests under the constraints of morality. He believes that it is possible to find a rational solution to the question of justice and establish an undisputed and "publicly recognized point of view from which all citizens can examine before one another whether or not their political and social institutions are just."[10]

Against such a rationalist denial of the political, it is useful to remember with Carl Schmitt that the defining feature of politics is struggle and that "there are always concrete human groupings which fight other concrete human groupings in the name of justice, humanity, order or peace."[11] There will always be a debate about the nature of justice in a modern democracy, and no final agreement can ever be reached. Democratic politics must accept division and conflict as unavoidable, and the reconciliation of rival claims and conflicting interests can only be partial and provisional. It is the very characteristic of modern democracy to preclude the possibility of any discourse establishing a definite closure. There will always be competing interpretations of the principles of liberty and equality, the type of social relations where they should apply, and their mode of institutionalization. This is why the common good can never be actualized; it must remain as a kind of vanishing point to which we constantly refer, but which cannot have a real existence. Consequently, a fully inclusive political community can never be achieved since, as Schmitt tells us, in order to construct an "us," it must be distinguished from a "them," and in politics that means establishing a frontier, defining an "enemy."

A radical pluralist approach, informed as it is by a nonessentialist view of politics, acknowledges the impossibility of a fully realized democracy and of the total elimination of antagonisms. It views all forms of agreement as partial and provisional and as products of a given hegemony. Its objective is the creation of a chain of equivalence among the democratic demands found in a variety of groups— women, blacks, workers, gays, lesbians, environmentalists—around a radical democratic interpretation of the political principles of the liberal democratic regime. Such an interpretation emphasizes the numerous social relations where subordination exists and must be challenged if the principles of equality and liberty are to apply. This challenging should lead different groups struggling for a radicalization of democracy to recognize that they have a common concern; that is, the establishment of a common political identity as "radical democratic citizens." For it is not a matter of establishing a mere alliance between given interests but rather of actually modifying their identity so as to bring about a new political identity.

This distinction is something that many pluralist liberals do not understand because they are blind to relations of power. They agree on the need to extend the sphere of rights to include groups hitherto excluded, but they see that process as a smooth one of progressive inclusion into a (supposedly) neutral conception of citizenship. The problem with such a view is that it ignores the fact that some existing rights are based on the very exclusion or subordination of the rights of other categories, which imposes limits on the extension of pluralism. It is precisely for this reason that a radical democratic politics agrees with Schmitt that the friend/enemy distinction is central to politics. No struggle is possible against relations of subordination without the establishment of a frontier and the definition of the modes of domination to be destroyed. There is no radical politics without a challenge to the existing forms of power. This does not mean a complete transformation of society, but should be understood in terms of the Gramscian model of an unending "war of position." What it is necessary to stress, however, is that the use of the friend/enemy criterion for a project of radical and plural democracy requires conceiving democratic politics as taking place in a multiplicity of political spaces always linked to specific "subject positions" which can never be conflated with social agents. The struggle against racism or sexism, for instance, consists in destroying racist or sexist subject positions and the institutions in which these are embodied, not concrete human beings. The elimination of the "enemy" should not be understood as physical elimination.

This last point illustrates the important link that exists between our understanding of radical democracy and the philosophical critique of essentialism. Indeed, without abandoning the idea of the unitary subject, and its source and the origin of its meanings, such a project cannot be formulated, for it requires conceiving the social agent as constituted by a multiplicity of subject positions whose articulation is always precarious and temporary. Only such a decentered view of the subject can enable us to theorize the multiplicity of relations of subordination in which a single individual can be inscribed and understand that one can be dominant in some groups while subordinated in others. The construction of a political frontier is therefore something that can cut across each individual.

In recent years, a growing convergence between left-liberals and post-Marxists has occurred regarding the radical potential of the liberal democratic tradition. It consists in the recognition that the modern democratic ideals of liberty and equality that constitute the political principles of the liberal democratic regime have provided the political language with which many struggles against subordination have been articulated and won and with which many others can still be fought. Therefore to assert the victory of liberal democracy does not mean to resign oneself to the status quo. But a positive and militant approach to the radicalization of liberal democracy requires a different view of the political. A society in which all antagonisms have been eradicated, far from being a truly democratic one, would be its exact opposite. Pluralism is constitutive of modern democracy, and it precludes any dream of final reconciliation.

Perhaps the real challenge for the left today is how to formulate its project in a properly secular way, without messianic hopes but with a real "enthusiasm," in the Kantian sense of the awareness of limits. This enthusiasm should first of all be directed towards liberal democracy. It is indeed a particularly problematic regime, but therein resides its value. To be sure, its two logics are ultimately incompatible since—as Schmitt was one of the first to indicate—the logic of democracy is a logic of identity, a logic of equivalence, while the liberal logic is a logic of pluralism that impedes the realization of a complete equivalence and the establishment of a total system of identifications. Through the articulation between liberalism and democracy, the democratic logic of equivalence has been intertwined with the liberal logic of difference. The latter tends to construct each social identity as a positivity and therefore imposes a pluralism that subverts the attempt at totalization that would result from a total equivalence. This difference is why Schmitt argues that liberalism negates democracy and that democracy negates liberalism.[12]

NOTES

1. Norberto Bobbio, *The Future of Democracy* (Oxford: Oxford University Press, 1987), 59.

2. Ernesto Laclau and Chantal Mouffe, *Hegemony and Socialist Strategy: Towards a Radical Democratic Politics* (London: Verso, 1985).

3. Carl Schmitt, *The Crisis of Parliamentary Democracy* (Cambridge, MA: Harvard University Press, 1985), 35.

4. Schmitt, *The Crisis of Parliamentary Democracy*, 16.

5. Schmitt, *The Crisis of Parliamentary Democracy*, 15.

6. Carl Schmitt, *The Concept of the Political* (New Brunswick, NJ: Rutgers University Press, 1976), 71.

7. Schmitt, *The Concept of the Political*, 35.

8. Schmitt, *The Concept of the Political*, 37.

9. For a more detailed critique, see my article, "American Liberalism and Its Critics: Rawls, Taylor, Sandel, and Walzer," *Praxis International*, vol. 8, no. 2 (July 1988).

10. John Rawls, "Justice as Fairness: Political not Metaphysical," *Philosophy and Public Affairs*, vol. 14, no. 3 (Summer 1985): 229. This critique of Rawls is developed in my article "Rawls: Political Philosophy Without Politics," *Philosophy and Social Criticism*, vol. 13, no. 2 (1987).

11. Schmitt, *The Crisis of Parliamentary Democracy*, 67.

12. Schmitt, *The Crisis of Parliamentary Democracy*, 17.

CHANTAL MOUFFE

FROM IDENTITY POLITICS TO SOCIAL FEMINISM

A PLEA FOR THE NINETIES

THE PARADIGM WARS OF FEMINIST THEORY

A DECADE AGO A SYMPOSIUM TOOK PLACE AT THE LAW School of the State University of New York at Buffalo as part of the James McCormick Mitchell Lecture Series. The participants were Carol J. Gilligan, Catharine A. MacKinnon, Ellen C. Dubois, Carrie J. Menkel-Meadow and others.[1] This symposium signaled the great clash of paradigms within contemporary feminist theory, which would unfold in the following years. I will use the term "paradigm" in a non-technical fashion to refer to a coherent set of assumptions, some articulated and some not, which guide, influence, structure, or help "format" a vision of theory and politics. In an exchange with Carol Gilligan, Catharine MacKinnon says in reference to Gilligan's work *In a Different Voice*[2]:

SEYLA BENHABIB

I am—it will shock you to hear—ambivalent about it. On the one hand, I feel excited by the strong and elegant sensitivity in the work. There is something deeply feminist here: the impulse to listen to women. . . . On the other hand, what is infuriating about it (which is a very heavy thing to say about a book that is so cool and graceful and gentle in its emotional touch), and this is a political infuriation, is that it neglects the explanatory level. *Why* do women become these people, more than men, who represent *these* values? . . . For me, the answer is clear: the answer is the subordination of women. . . . She has also found the voice of the victim—yes, women are a victimized group. . . . What bothers me is identifying women with it. I'm not saying that Carol does this expressly in her book. But I am troubled by the possibility of women identifying with what is a positively valued feminist stereotype. It is the "feminine."[3]

MacKinnon does not altogether reduce Gilligan's version of an "ethics of care and responsibility," which is claimed to characterize women's moral voices, to an ethic of the victim, although subsequent commentators have done so.[4] Yet she states clearly that given existing patterns of male domination and female subordination, the values of care, the responsiveness to the needs of others, the ability for empathy and for taking the standpoint of the concrete other, all of which Gilligan claimed women were more likely to display than men, would rather hurt than help women. MacKinnon's rejection of Gilligan's ethic of care is an instrumentalist one; like many power theorists before her, she argues that the end, such as ending the subordination of women, justifies the means, i.e. using an ethic of power instead of an ethic of care and responsibility. Gilligan comments:

Your definition of power is his definition.

MacKinnon: This is because the society *is* that way, it operates on his definition, and I am trying to change it.

Gilligan: To have her definition come in?

Mackinnon: That would be a part of it, but more to have a definition that she would articulate that she cannot now, because his foot is on her throat.

Gilligan: She's saying it.

Mackinnon: I know, but she is articulating the feminine. And you are calling it hers. That's what I find infuriating.

Gilligan: No, I am saying she is articulating a set of values which are very positive.

MacKinnon: Right, and I am saying they are feminine. And calling them hers is infuriating to me because we have never had the power to develop what ours really would be.[5]

This dramatic exchange articulated one type of *paradigm* clash within contemporary feminist theory,[6] namely, whether women as social and political agents are the carriers of a different and distinctive set of values (leaving aside the question of how these are acquired, formed, developed, etc.), which they should promote and fight for in the public sphere, or whether women should seek power and equality by mobilizing existing resources and institutions available in the society at large. Name this a paradigm clash between "difference" and "equality" feminism; or name it a clash between "moralism" and "realism," or between "utopianism" and "Realpolitik."

The exchange, which took place more than a decade ago, is a harbinger of developments to come. In the years to follow, not only would utopian feminism(s) clash with a militant radical feminism of power, but varieties of "power/gender" theories (built around Michel Foucault's model of "knowledge/power") would enter into shifting alliances as well as confrontations with psychoanalytic feminism. As a participant in the Gilligan-MacKinnon exchange, Ellen C. DuBois observed, "there are by this time many feminisms. Women are no longer ignored in the political scene. . . . The issues that the women's movement has raised are at the very center of this historical moment."[7] Speaking these words in 1984, DuBois identified the crucial issues for American women as abortion and the election of a female vice president. Today there are still many feminisms; women are no longer ignored in the political scene as much as they were at the beginning of the eighties, but it is not at all clear how, where, when, or why the "issues that the women's movement has raised are at the very center of this historical moment." After a decade of paradigm struggles, we are no longer sure that there is one movement; in fact, we know that there is not a single organization with the agenda of which a majority of women in this country would agree. More importantly, we no longer know what this historical moment is. As a consequence of postmodernist warnings against grand narratives, we have become skeptical about any tale of this or that historical moment, this or that historical sequence, or logic of development. In fact, we no longer know who "we" are. Postmodernist theorists tell us that this "we," even if only invoked as a rhetorical gesture of public speech and writing, is politically suspect, in that it tries to create a seeming community of opinion and views where there is usually none. Relishing in diversity, basking in fragmentation, enjoying the play of differences, and celebrating opacity, fracturing, and heteronomy is a dominant mood of contemporary feminist theory and practice.

I do not celebrate this mood of revelling in difference and basking in fragmentation; nor am I nostalgic for a sense of lost unity in the women's movement, which itself rarely existed. A healthy plurality of visions and strategies about the meaning of women's emancipation has always been an aspect of the various women's movements.[8] From their inception in the eighteenth century and particularly in the period of their articulation in mid-nineteenth and early twentieth centuries, feminism and women's movements have always struggled with dilemmas of equality and difference: equality with males versus being different from them, preserving women's separate sphere versus becoming full members of existing society by giving up women's traditional spaces. These tensions constitute what the women's struggle is all about; what will change from period to period is the construction and contestation around these oppositions, but not the fact that women will always be aware of such oppositions, dichotomies, and conflicts.[9]

Nonetheless, all is not well in the contemporary scene of plurality, heterogeneity, and diversity. In particular, there are two major problems. The first is the rapid shift of research paradigms in contemporary feminist theory from what is usually referred to as "standpoint feminism" to various "postmodernist" feminisms; but neither the presuppositions nor the consequences of this shift have been adequately analyzed. Micro-narratives of class, race, and gender have replaced macro-narratives of women's subordination across cultures, societies, and historical periods. While much is gained in this shift of research paradigms, much is also lost: as the research paradigms in feminist theory have become more complex and concerned with the varieties of oppression which intersect with one another, the concept of the subject and the vision of agency underlying such research have become increasingly simplistic and empty from a normative standpoint. Feminist theory is in danger of losing the forest for the trees and not being able to develop a voice reflecting the difficult issues of conflicting identity claims.

The second problem confronting the contemporary scene concerns the politics of identity and difference, which dominated the eighties and have begun to show ugly developments in the nineties. The clash of multiple identities as well as of the allegiances that surround them have emerged in the public realm; the continuous and inevitable fragmentation of identities has made it almost impossible to develop a common vision of radical transformation. These developments in theory and in politics are linked. The theoretical paradigm shift from standpoint feminism to postmodernism is related to political trends in identity and difference politics insofar as the articulation of a certain form of the politics of identity and difference was aided by and in turn influenced postmodernist critiques of standpoint feminism.

FROM STANDPOINT FEMINISM TO POSTMODERNIST FEMINISMS

The term "standpoint feminism" designates a type of feminist theory and research paradigm exhibiting the following characteristics.[10] First is the claim that philosophical as well social-scientific theories of the past have been cognitively inadequate because they have been "gender blind," i.e., because they have failed to take into account the standpoint, the activities, and the experiences of women. Gender blindness, it is claimed, is not an accidental omission or oversight, but affects the cognitive plausibility of theories. Second, to correct gender blindness, it is necessary to identify a set of experiences, activities, as well as patterns of thinking, feeling, and acting which can be characterized as "female." Third, such experiences, activities, and the like are a consequence of women's social position or of their position within the sexual division of labor. Whereas the male of the species has been active in the public sphere of production, politics, war, and science, women's activities by and large and throughout history have been confined to the "domestic/reproductive" and "private" spheres. Fourth, the task of feminist theory is to make this sphere of activity and its consequences for human life visible, audible, and present at the level of theory. Feminist theory articulates the implicit, tacit, everyday, and non-theorized experiences and activities of women and allows these to come to the level of consciousness. Fifth, by aiding the articulation of female experience, feminist theory not only engages in a critique of science and theory, but it also contributes to the process of transforming women's consciousness by giving female activities and experiences public presence and legitimacy. Hence, a number of seminal works, mostly from the late seventies, had the characteristic titles of *Becoming Visible: Women in European History*; *In a Different Voice*; *Public Man. Private Woman.*[11]

To be sure, the paradigm shift to postmodernist feminisms occurring by the middle of the eighties was influenced by French thinkers, including Michel Foucault, Jacques Derrida, Jean-Francois Lyotard, Luce Irigaray, and Hélène Cixous. As the impact of their theories, no matter how diverse and at times contradictory, was felt upon the core of study of the humanities in the United States, feminist theorists also discovered an attractive ally in these positions for their concerns. What is unique about the American feminist reception of French postmodernist thought is that, rightly or wrongly, the interest in French theory coincided with a set of intense political and cultural struggles within the American women's movement. Linda Nicholson and Nancy Fraser captured this well in their article, "Social Criticism Without Philosophy: An Encounter Between Feminism and Postmodernism":

> The practice of feminist politics in the 1980s generated a new set of pressures which have worked against metanarratives. In recent years, poor and working-class women, women of color, and lesbians have finally won a wider hearing for their objections to feminist theories which fail to illuminate their lives and address their problems. They have exposed the earlier quasi-metanarratives, with their assumptions of universal female dependence and confinement to the domestic sphere, as false extrapolations from the experience of the white, middle-class, heterosexual women who dominated the beginnings of the second wave. . . . Thus, as the class, sexual, racial and ethnic awareness of the movement has altered, so has the preferred conception of theory. It has become clear that quasi-metanarratives hamper rather then promote sisterhood, since they elide differences among women and among the forms of sexism to which different women are differentially subject.[12]

Fraser and Nicholson have put their finger on some fundamental changes in the theoretical landscape of North American feminism, namely the coincidence of postmodernist sensibilities with the politics of identity and difference. But this coincidence is neither obvious, nor self-explanatory, nor always salutary.

Throughout the eighties the theoretical message of the French "masters of suspicion" was at the center of a *political critique* by lesbian women, women of color, and Third World women of the hegemony of white, western European, or North American heterosexual women in the movement.[13] This *political critique* was accompanied by a *philosophical shift* from Marxist and psychoanalytic paradigms to Foucauldian types of discourse analysis and Derridean practices of textual deconstruction. In terms of *social research* models, there was a shift from analyzing women's position in the sexual division of labor and the world of work in general to the analyses of identity: its constitution and construction, the problems of collective self- and other-representation, and issues of cultural contestation and hegemony.

No concept reveals the nature of this paradigm shift more explicitly than the one that is central to feminist theory, namely "gender." Competing theoretical attempts to define "gender" also indicate what has been gained and what has been lost in this theoretical shift. The historian Joan Kelly Gadol provides a clear statement of the assumptions of early standpoint feminism in her article on "The Social Relations of the Sexes: Methodological Implications of Women's History."

> In short, women have to be defined as women. We are the social opposite, not of a class, a caste, or of a majority, since we are a majority, but of a sex: men. We are a sex, and categorization by gender no longer implies a mothering role and subordination to men, except as a social role and relation recognized as such, as socially constructed and socially imposed.[14]

Kelly Gadol makes a clear distinction between gender and sex; whereas sex is given, "we as women are the opposite sex of an equally non-problematic one, namely men," according to Gadol, gender is socially constructed and contested. Mothering, for example, would be a socially constructed gender role for most women, in most periods of history, and in the majority of known human societies.

Postmodernist and/or poststructuralist feminist theory challenges this dichotomy between sex and gender, along with the logic of binary oppositions it creates. Judith Butler's *Gender Trouble* gives a trenchant critique of the epistemic assumptions underlying such previous forms of feminist theory. Butler writes: "Gender is not to culture as sex is to nature; gender is also the discursive/cultural means by which 'sexed nature' or a 'natural sex' is produced and established as 'prediscursive,' prior to culture, a politically neutral surface *on which* culture acts."[15] For Butler, the myth of the already sexed body is the epistemological equivalent of the myth of the given: just as the given can only be identified via a discursive framework that first allows us to name it, so too it is the culturally available codes of gender that "sexualize" a body and construct the directionality of that body's sexual desire. Writing from within the experiences of lesbian women in the women's movement, Butler's sharp critique of the distinction between sex and gender allows her to focus on how oppressive and debilitating compulsory heterosexual logic has been for some women and men. The view that not only gender but also sexuality is socially constructed allows one to enter the terrain of political contestation around issues like sexuality and sexual identity, which were hitherto considered to lie outside politics. Thus, to bring this shift in views and sensibilities to a formula: whereas standpoint feminism was obsessed with the mother and mothering, poststructuralist feminism is obsessed with sexuality and the drag queen. With this shift, however, emerge the theoretical as well as political problems of identity and difference politics.

THE DILEMMAS OF IDENTITY AND DIFFERENCE IN THEORY AND POLITICS

The principal consequence of viewing gender as well as sexuality as socially constructed is the fluidity this introduces to categories of identity.[16] Identities, personal as well as collective, are seen as "social constructions" with no basis of "givenness" in nature, anatomy, or some other anthropological essence. Such social construction, most identity and difference theorists also add, is to be understood as a process of social, cultural, and political struggle for hegemony among social groups vying with one another for the dominance of certain identity definitions over others. For example, what does "we the people" mean in the celebrated opening of the Declaration of Independence? At the time of its drafting, it meant the propertied, white male heads of households of the colonies. Women, who were disenfranchised, the African-American slave population, considered three-fifth persons by the Constitution, as well as Native Americans were phantom-like presences lying outside the invocation of the collective "we." Thus the identity of every "we" depends on a power structure; collectivities constitute themselves not only by excluding, but also by oppressing others, over and against whom they define themselves. In this sense, the identity of every "we" contains the results of collective struggles for power among groups, cultures, genders, and social classes. A "we," a collective subject, is formed by the sedimentation of such past struggles for hegemony.[17]

While the perspective opened by this thesis concerning the social construction of collective identities is extremely fruitful and significant for social and historical studies,[18] the difficulties of identity and difference politics, as well as of the theoretical research paradigms favored by such politics, ultimately derive from "the fungibility of identity."[19] In the contemporary theoretical literature on identity, one term dominates, and that term is "construction." Identities are constructed by the clash and conflict of groups. Yet "construction," which sometimes is also referred to as "constitution," is a curious term to designate a process that supposedly occurs without the subjects' willful participation and agency. In Foucauldian language, knowledge/power matrices "constitute" or "construct" us. Unlike the subject of traditional humanist discourse, in this model the subject does not exist as a locus of agency. According to Judith Butler:

> The question of locating "agency" is usually associated with the viability of the "subject," where the "subject" is understood to have some stable existence prior to the cultural field that it negotiates. Or, if the subject is culturally constructed, it is nevertheless vested with an agency, usually figured as the capacity for reflexive mediation, that remains intact regardless of its cultural imbeddedness. On such a model, "culture" and "discourse" *mire* the subject, but do not constitute that subject.[20]

Against the view that the subject is merely "mired" by discourse, Butler defends the stronger position that the subject is "constituted by discourse although not determined by it." Much exists behind this distinction. Contemporary feminist theory is bordering on incoherence if it cannot clarify a consistent and intelligible view of agency and subjectivity.[21] Distinctions between "constitution" and "determination," or "constituting" and "miring" do not clarify the question as to what views of agency and subjectivity are possible within the framework of a radically constructionist theory. If these agents retain capacities for resistance, resignificiation, or for subverting gender codes, from where do these capacities derive? What are the sources of spontaneity, creativity, and resistance in agents? In the transition from standpoint feminism to poststructuralist feminisms, we have lost the female subject. Like a script in search of an author, contemporary feminist theory has nearly effaced its own possibility.[22] Either the thesis of the radical social construction of identities is too hyperbolic and hides more than it reveals, or another theory of subjectivity, one that can explain the sources of human creativity as well as victimization and agency as well as passivity, is necessary.

This problematic status of the category of the subject is also evidenced in the way in which "race, gender, and class" are strung together as determinants of identity that guide empirical research paradigms. The question as to what understanding of the self one must presuppose to conceptualize the confluence of these identities is rarely, if ever, raised. Are these identities additive? Are they like layers of clothing that social actors can wear and remove? How are they experienced by a single individual who is herself a concrete totality uniting all of these in a single life-history? Categories of race, gender, and class are analytical distinctions at the level of theory; in any piece of social-historical-cultural research we have to show how they come together as aspects of identities of specific individuals. When we do such research, what kinds of models of life stories or narratives must we develop? Within the contemporary theoretical scene of fragmentation and multiplicity, the question of the unity of the self is hardly raised. This issue is not merely of theoretical interest; for very often these identities exist in conflict with one another. The normative demands upon the individual of race, gender, and class identities as well as of other self-constitutive dimensions may be conflictual; in fact, they may be irreconcilable. Unless feminist theory is able to develop a concept of normative agency robust enough to say something significant regarding such clashes, and which principles individuals should adopt to choose among them, it loses its theoretical bite and becomes a mindless empiricist celebration of all pluralities. The question of the subject is central for contemporary feminist theory and practice, and here is where the influence of contemporary French theory upon the politics of identity and difference shows its severe limitations.

THE POLITICS OF IDENTITY AND DIFFERENCE WITHIN THE AMERICAN WELFARE STATE

To understand the specifically American form of the politics of "identity and difference" that characterized the eighties, it is important to note some of the peculiarities and complexities of the relation of new social movements to the weak welfare state in this country.[23] The American welfare state, unlike its European counterparts, had to contend with a multinational, multiethnic, and racially divided polity. Throughout the early seventies, the American polity was faced with the dual challenge of redistributing public goods like health, education, welfare, housing, and transportation on the one hand, and of carrying out a Civil Rights agenda for the elimination of discrimination based on race, gender, ethnic, religious, and linguistic identities on the other. The most contested issues of the seventies, like busing, school desegregation, public housing, and an end to discriminatory employment practices, combined issues of redistribution with the realization of the Civil Rights agenda.

While the new politics of "post-materialist values" (Roland Inglehart) was a phenomenon observed in most capitalist welfare-states, the coming together of struggles over redistribution with Civil Rights issues was uniquely American.[24] The contemporary women's movement in the United States is an heir to this double legacy; in fact, it may be the only social movement in this country that has succeeded in uniting these agendas into a more or less coherent platform. North American women, perhaps more so than their counterparts in the rest of the world, use the legal, economic, and social means and channels of argumentation and struggle, created by the combination of the redistributionist state and the Civil Rights agenda, to further their goals.[25] From the struggle for "equal wages for equal work," to the struggle to end sexual harassment and discrimination in the work place, North American women employ both Civil Rights-type egalitarian arguments and welfare-statist redistributionist conceptions to further their cause.[26] In so doing, the contemporary women's movement enters the arena of politics as a client of the welfare state, demanding from the state and its agencies the fair and equitable distribution of certain public goods to women as a group. The logic of such demands and struggles thus pits women against other groups, like African-Americans, Mexican and other Spanish-speaking Americans, gay groups, lesbian women who pursue separatist political strategies and demands, Native Americans, differently-abled Americans, and elderly Americans, all of whom are raising similar demands for special compensation from the state, often around the same set of goods, like jobs, educational opportunities, housing, and health care benefits.

The contemporary politics of identity and difference emerges out of this multiplicity of trends, movements, organizations, and issues. Perhaps no other incident captured the historical and political difficulties of the current situation more poignantly than the Clarence Thomas and Anita Hill controversy. The controversy over Judge Thomas's confirmation to the United States Supreme Court pitted race against gender, black men against black women, white feminists against black community activists, in an endless multiplicity of identities and positionings. For the first time, the traumatic aspects of the endless multiplication of identities with their competing allegiances came to the fore. Reneging on their decade of struggle against discrimination in the workplace and sexual harassment, some feminist theorists, Catharine MacKinnon among them, rushed to the defense of race as a more central category of identity and seemed to take to heart Justice Thomas's warning that here was the "high-tech lynching of a black man" by the white media.[27]

Undoubtedly, this remains a complex, multifaceted, and difficult case in recent political memory. However, it is revealing because so many moments of identity and difference politics came to such a prominent clash around it.[28] For many women in the movement, it was not news that sexist and misogynous practices were neither race nor class specific; but faced with the possibility of being seen as opposing the appointment of a black judge to the United States Supreme Court, many feminists caved in. Instead of addressing the question raised by Anita Hill, i.e., "what kind of behavior constituted sexual harassment in the workplace?," it was asked, "which was more important to her: being a successful black professional feminist, a black diva, or a soul sister?" The Clarence Thomas and Anita Hill confrontation was a paradigmatic episode which highlighted the fungibility of identity categories: which are you—a black professional feminist or a black sister?

It is this peculiar constellation of events in recent American political history that combines redistributionism with identity and difference politics. This combination colors the contemporary struggles over gays in the military, the recognition of same-sex marriages and homosexual households (domestic partnerships), the inclusion of people with AIDS in health insurance and other benefits. The agenda of the politics of identity and difference, welfare-state redistributionism, the legacy of Civil Rights, and Affirmative Action policies come together in our current political theory and practice in conflictual and difficult ways.

I said above that the dilemmas of identity and difference politics derived from the fungibility of identity categories. Recent political controversies, including the Thomas-Hill controversy, show very well what is at stake in drawing and redrawing the lines between identity and difference. At stake are not only cultural issues of self and other identifications, but very complex issues of redistribution and state policy as well.[29] To be sure, some sought to delegitimize Anita Hill as a black woman precisely because of some normative definition of a black female as "one who stands by her man"; "only those who are like us deserve our solidarity" would be the motto here. Others reasoned that if Judge Thomas was not appointed then and there, the Bush administration would not have to nominate another black person for some time to come, on the grounds that it had tried to do so and failed in good faith. They preferred the existence of a black Supreme Court judge, even if he was potentially guilty of sexual harassment, to the existence of none. The assumption that legally defined minorities had to compete for scarce resources was itself not questioned as a principle governing public and political action.

One sees here the convergence of theoretical trends with established political options created by the North American welfare state: contemporary feminist theory proceeds from a view of the subject as a fungible construct constituted by the clash and conflict of competing identities, while the contemporary politics of the redistributionist welfare state encourage the competition among divergent groups, some of whom share overlapping membership, for a set of scarce resources. Just as the view of the subject in contemporary feminist theory borders on incoherence, so too, this model of redistributionism coupled with identity and difference politics ends in group particularisms, often with antagonistic consequences. In most major American cities, from New York to Los Angeles, urban blacks have been pitted against Hassidic Jews, North Koreans against blacks and Spanish-speaking residents, and so on. The Balkanization of urban America started some time ago and is continuing unimpeded. We desperately need a new politics of civility and solidarity, robust enough in its vision to unite those social forces torn now by fragmentation and factionalism. In this task some of the supposedly discredited and old-fashioned ideals of ethical and utopian feminism have a great role to play.

All participation in the public and political sphere presupposes some common goods, some sense of shared vision in the name of which we can act. Groups engaged in identity and difference politics are suspicious that behind appeals to communality lurks the repression and the denial of "difference." But we have to ask: the "difference" of whom from whom, and in the name of what? Creative political action does not mean repeating the injustices and divisions of the past. Creative politics expands the field of political contestation while reactivating the principles and values in the name of which such contestation takes place. The recent debate around gays in the Military is a case in point: despite the unhappy and confused compromise which the Clinton Administration reached about this issue, what made the Chiefs of Staff accept this compromise was the logic and power of anti-discrimination claims within the public sphere of the American polity. The military, as one of the last bastions of a closed community of group solidarity, continuously sets up distinctions between "them" and "us"; those who are like us and those who are different. Just as black GI's in the Second World War established the irrelevance of their race as a salient category for determining their suitability to serve in the military and thus challenged the logic of exclusion, so too, a person's sexual orientation would have to be considered irrelevant to the public performance of his or her task. Now, this compromise is unstable, precisely because it turns on distinctions between "private sexual activity" and "public demeanor," which will be extremely difficult to sustain in certain contexts. The motto, applied to gay and lesbian soldiers, "Don't ask, don't tell," basically means, "Erase your identity, who you are, and I will tolerate being with you." The really difficult political and moral step would be to move from the logic of redistributionism to the ethics of solidarity with those who are different. One should not only argue that gay people should not be discriminated against in the military, which itself is one of the fundamental redistributionist agencies in this society, providing opportunity, income, and advancement to certain social classes, but question the very definition of what constitutes "us" versus "them." Why, in fact, is the military homophobic? Is there a link between a certain form of male sexuality and the virtues considered essential for being in the military? Must military discipline rest on a suppression of erotic behavior? Are eros and militarism compatible? These are extremely difficult and subtle questions, but they can only be discussed against the background of mutual respect and solidarity among beings whose fragile identities always need sustenance.

This is the vision of a social feminism which accepts that the furthering of one's capacity for autonomous agency is only possible within the confines of a solidaristic community that sustains one's identity through mutual recognition. Opposed to the postmodernist vision of the fragmented subject is the assumption that the human subject is a fragile, needy, and dependent creature whose capacity to develop a coherent life-story out of the competing claims upon its identity must be cherished and protected. Distinct from the language of eternal contestation, conflict, and haggling over scarce resources, the primary virtue in politics is the creation of an enlarged mentality. To quote Hannah Arendt:

> The power of judgment rests on a potential agreement with others, and the thinking process which is active in judging something is not, like the thought process of pure reasoning, a dialogue between me and myself, but finds itself always and primarily, even if I am quite alone in making up my mind, in an anticipated communication with others with whom I know I must finally come to some agreement. And this enlarged way of thinking, which as judgment knows how to transcend its individual limitations, cannot function in strict isolation or solitude; it needs the presence of others "in whose place" it must think, whose perspective it must take into consideration, and without whom it never has the opportunity to operate at all.[30]

As we move into the global economic and political uncertainties of the nineties, it will be essential to exercise such an enlarged mentality, both in the domestic and the international arena. We must be ready to ask some fundamental questions again: is it obvious that the group-identity based system of social and economic redistributionism is preferable to a model of universalist social justice that indexes certain income levels rather than racial, gender, and ethnic identity as the relevant criteria for receiving certain kinds of social benefits? Would not a guaranteed annual income for the poor have saved many a welfare mother from the humiliating examination by state officials of her sexual practices and work habits? Could it have been more plausible to treat city neighborhoods as fictive collective entities to which one distributed certain benefits, like health, education, and housing collectively, rather than singling out the various groupings in the cities, and thus inadvertently contributing to the antagonism and competition raging among these groups in so many of America's cities? Identity and difference politics, whether in the essentialist version defended by MacKinnon or in the constructivist version defended by Butler, has not opened up the space for this kind of new questioning. The first kind of paradigm in feminist theory fails us by dogmatically freezing women's identity in the role of the victim; the second paradigm fails us by undermining the normative principles around which identity-transcending group solidarities must be formed. The time has come to move beyond identity politics, in the

Hegelian sense of moving beyond (*Aufheben*), that is, by learning its lessons, rejecting its excesses, and moving to a new synthesis of collective solidarities with plurally constituted identities.

NOTES

When David Trend invited me to participate in this volume originating from the symposium on radical democracy published in *Socialist Review* (vol. 23, no. 3), a version of this essay had already been prepared for other occasions. Upon reading the contents of the *Socialist Review* issue, however, I was struck by the extent to which the concerns raised in my article, in particular my misgivings about identity politics, paralleled those voiced by other authors participating in this discussion. Since some clarification of where we stand today in the United States after two decades or more of paradigm struggles within the Left is essential to the future reconstruction of any form of radical democracy, my contribution is such a stock-taking of theoretical and political developments within the North American Womens' Movements of the last two decades.

This paper was first delivered at a Symposium organized by Michigan State University on "Science, Reason, and Modern Democracy" in November 1993. It is being published here in abbreviated and revised form. A longer version of this paper will appear in a volume from Cornell University Press devoted to the Proceedings of the Science, Reason, and Modern Democracy Symposium. I would like to thank the Philosophy of Education Society for inviting me to deliver a version of this paper as its Keynote Address in April 1994. In particular, I am grateful to Michael Katz and Nicholas C. Burbules for their cooperation in making this invitation and publication possible. Several individuals have read earlier drafts of this paper: I would like to thank Theda Skocpol, Winnie Breines, and Michael Ferber for their comments and criticisms. I have also benefited greatly from the responses by Nicholas Burbules and Barbara Houston.

1. See, "Feminist Discourse, Moral Values, and the Law—A Conversation," in *Buffalo Law Review*, vol. 34, no. 1 (Winter 1985): 11–87.
2. Carol Gilligan, *In a Different Voice* (Cambridge, Mass.: Harvard University Press, 1981).
3. See, "Feminist Discourse, Moral Values, and the Law—A Conversation," in *Buffalo Law Review*, vol. 34, no. 1 (Winter 1985): 74.
4. See Claudia Card, "Women's Voices and Ethical Ideals: Must We Mean What We Say?," *Ethics*, vol. 99, no. 1 (October 1988): 125–36.
5. Card, "Women's Voices and Ethical Ideals," 74–75.
6. To characterize the differences in theoretical paradigms underlying Gilligan's and MacKinnon's feminisms is more difficult than defining the differences in their political approaches. At a certain level, MacKinnon's views of gender constitution bear affinity to poststructuralist views that regard gender as a socially and culturally constructed identity in the formation of which power plays a crucial role. She summarizes: "The position that gender is first a political hierarchy of power is, in my opinion, a feminist position" (22).

   Gilligan disagrees: "Trying to make gender fit the inequality model is the most traditional way to deal with gender, and it will not work. Gender is not exactly like social class. It is not simply a matter of dominance and subordination. There is no way to envision gender disappearing as one envisions, in utopian visions of society, class disappearing or race becoming a difference that makes no difference." (76) While Gilligan's position on gender constitution is too vague, MacKinnon's views fall into the same traps regarding identity questions as do the postmodernist constructivists.

7. James McCormick Symposium, "Feminist Discourse, Moral Values, and the Law," 69 (SUNY Buffalo, 1985).

8. For a recent collection which displays these aspects of the movement, see *Conflicts in Feminism*, ed. Marianne Hirsch and Evelyn Fox Keller (New York: Routledge, 1990).

9. See Ann Snitow, "A Gender Diary," *Conflicts In Feminism*, 9–44.

10. The term, as far as I can tell, was introduced into feminist theory by Nancy Hartsock who analyzed the possibility of building a feminist theory along the lines for Marxist theory developed by Georg Lukács in his *History and Class Consciousness for Marxist Theory Studies in Marxist Dialectics*, trans. Rodney Livingston (New York and London: Merlin Press, 1971). See Hartsock, *Money, Sex, and Power. Toward A Feminist Historical Materialism* (New York: Longman, 1983; Boston: Northeastern University Press, 1984).

11. Renate Bridenthal, Claudia Koonz, and Susan Stuard, eds. *Becoming Visible: Women in European History* (Boston: Houghton, Mifflin Company, 1987); Carol Gilligan, *In a Different Voice*; Jean Bethke Elshtain, *Public Man. Private Women* (Princeton, NJ: Princeton University Press, 1981).

12. Linda Nicholson and Nancy Fraser, "Social Criticism without Philosophy: An Encounter Between Feminism and Postmodernism," in *Feminism and Postmodernism*, ed. Linda Nicholson (New York: Routledge, 1990), 33.

13. I thank Barbara Houston and Marilyn Frye for conversations that helped me see that there were also many other women raising this kind of political objection within the women's movement, but whose theoretical commitments lay far from postmodernism. Nonetheless, the tendencies depicted here also existed, although they may not have been as dominant as I initially thought.

14. Joan Kelly Gadol, "The Social Relations of the Sexes: Methodological Implications of Women's History," in *Women, History and Theory* (Chicago: University of Chicago Press, 1986), 6.

15. Judith Butler, *Gender Trouble* (New York: Routledge, 1990), 7.

16. Judith Butler's conclusion to *Gender Trouble* (142–149) spells these issues out provocatively.

17. For a further elaboration of the political and theoretical implications of questioning identity, see my "Democracy and Difference. The Metapolitics of Lyotard and Derrida," *The Journal of Political Philosophy*, vol. 2, no. 1 (January 1994): 1–23.

18. For some recent examples of the utilization of these insights in the context of post-colonial studies, cf. Gyan Prakash, "Postcolonial Criticism and Indian Historiography," *Social Text*, vol. 10. nos. 2, 3 (1992): 8–18; Chandra Talpade Mohanty, "Feminist Encounters: Locating the Politics of Experience," in *Destabilizing Theory*, eds. Michelle Barret and Anne Phillips (Cambridge, UK: Polity Press, 1992), 74–92.

19. The *Oxford English Dictionary* defines "fungible" as "taking the place" and "fulfilling the office of" (Oxford: Oxford University Press, 1982 compact edition), 606. Identity categories are thus, in principle, replaceable, substitutable through others.

20. Butler, *Gender Trouble*, 143.

21. In addition to my reflections on this issue in "Feminism and the Question of Postmodernism," in Benhabib, *Situating the Self: Gender, Community, and Postmodernism in Contemporary Ethics* (New York: Routledge, 1992), 203–242, see "Subjectivity, Historiography and Politics. Reflections on the 'Feminism/Postmodernism' Exchange," in Seyla Benhabib, Judith Butler, Drucilla Cornel, and Nancy Fraser, *Feminist Contentions: A Philosophical Exchange* (New York: Routledge, 1994), 107–127.

22. Linda Alcoff drew attention to some of the difficulties of contemporary feminist theory with her early article, "Cultural Feminism Versus Post-Structuralism:The Identity Crisis in Feminist Theory," *Signs:A Journal of Women in Culture and Society*, vol. 13, no. 31 (Spring 1988): 405–436.

23. In *The Cultural Contradictions of Capitalism* (New York: Harper and Row, 1977), Daniel Bell spoke of the "entitlement" revolution and the clash of competing groups as being an inevitable product of welfare state capitalism. In presenting this development as if it were the consequence of false cultural and moral ideals, however, he neglected to address issues of distributive and compensatory justice, which the welfare state also had to resolve when confronted with the claims of hitherto oppressed and socially disadvantaged groups. E.J. Dionne, Jr., in *Why Americans Hate Politics* (New York: Basic Books, 1991), discusses these issues as they affected the fate of the Democratic Party in the last twenty years.

24. Cf. Mary Feinsod Katzenstein and Carol McClurg Mueller, *The Women's Movements in the United States and Western Europe: Consciousness, Political Opportunity, and Public Policy* (Philadelphia: Pennsylvania University Press, 1987).

25. See Joyce Gelb, *Feminism and Politics: A Comparative Perspective* (Berkeley: University of California press, 1989). I would like to thank Theda Skocpol for bringing to my attention the sources cited in this and the preceding footnote.

26. For a critical discussion of how some of these issues affect feminist theory and politics, see Nancy Fraser, "Women, Welfare, and the Politics of Need Interpretation," and "Struggle Over Needs: Outline of a Socialist-Feminist Critical Theory of Late Capitalist Political Culture," in *Unruly Practices. Power, Discourse, and Gender in Contemporary Social Theory* (London: Polity Press, 1989).

27. See, "Roundtable: Doubting Thomas," in *Tikkun* 6, no. 6 (1992): 23–27.

28. For a trenchant analysis of some of the cultural and political "positionings" involved, see Nancy Fraser, "Sex, Lies, and the Public Sphere: Some Reflections on the Confirmation of Clarence Thomas," *Critical Inquiry* (Spring 1992): 595–612, cf.Toni Morrison, ed. *Race-ing Justice, Engender-ing Power* (New York: Pantheon Books, 1992).

29. A lot more attention needs to be paid in feminist theory and practice to the way the welfare state, while not creating the identities of social groups, definitely encourages their formation along certain lines of identity-related grievances and precludes their development along others. A brief look at the United States's northern neighbor, Canada, for example, shows that Canadian governments have been more socially democratic in their distribution of economic and social benefits; there, cultural identity issues, and in particular linguistic identity, occupy more prominent positions than other forms of identity politics. By contrast, initiatives to make Spanish the official second language of the United States, as placed before the Connecticut state legislature several years ago, were rapidly defeated, and did not arouse particular support or even attention from social movements groups and activists except those directly concerned. Let us ask the hypothetical question: is linguistic identity any less fundamental than gender, race, or sexual orientation? Why are some identities publicly recognized and acknowledged as legitimate criteria for being counted as a member of an oppressed group, or as a "disadvantaged minority" in the official vocabulary of the welfare state? What is the role of the state in encouraging identity politics, and in this process, what other options of social struggle and groups solidarities are being precluded?

30. Hanna Arendt, "The Crisis in Culture," in *Between Past and Future: Six Exercises in Political Thought* (New York: Meridian Books, 1961), 220–21.

CAN THE SUBALTERN VOTE?

RADICAL DEMOCRACY, DISCOURSES OF REPRESENTATION AND RIGHTS, AND QUESTIONS OF RACE

Do we have to make a subject of the whole world?

—Norma Alarcón[1]

If feminism *is* read as a decolonizing movement, allied with other decolonizing movements, this is, in a sense, to say that the Right is right when it identifies feminism as a threat to the 'American way of life.'

—Laura Kipnis[2]

I RECEIVED A LETTER FROM HILLARY RODHAM CLINTON dated September 19, 1994. She wrote asking me to vote in the November 1994 election, stating—in boldface, no less, perhaps to erase any traces of doubt—that my vote was my voice. She let me know that "the nation needs to hear" my "voice" and ended the letter by reassuring me that my vote "will make a difference." Putting aside intriguing and important questions about American liberal feminism and its nationalist underpinnings and enunciations (as well as its mailing lists which made me the recipient of such a form letter), this essay will focus on how this letter implored my participation in democracy's privileged articulation of citizenship: voting. Problematizing voting and other "rights" valorized by the democratic nation-state is the

Amarpal K. Dhaliwal

idea that democracy is not only a construct of modernity, but that it also is complicit with colonial discourses in that its idealized representations are used to argue the superiority of the West.[3] In contending that the democratic nation-state is a racial formation, it is interesting to note how "democracy" gets linked to Western liberal terms such as "freedom." This essay will also highlight the erasures that maintain the image of the United States as an ideal democracy and argue that certain erasures and exclusions are constitutive of liberal democratic nation-states.

Critical of leftist intellectual invocations of liberal principles which produce notions of "radical democracy," I identify radical democracy as a modernist concept. The alignment with modernity and Enlightenment beliefs—that is, its "ethnocentric liberal underpinnings"—are evidenced in radical democratic conceptualizations of identity, opposition, consciousness, and voice; in radical democracy's epistemological privileging of absolute categories; and in radical democracy's implicit theory of representation, its teleology of progress through modernization, and its ontological premises, including its individualism.[4] Skepticism of the claims made on behalf of radical democracy are rooted not only in how this category is frequently conceptualized as an absolute (versus relational) one; the concern is with the constitutive erasures or exclusions consolidating this category. Of interest is also the racial history of democracy and the general relationships between discourses of race, rights, representation, and democracy.

WHO WILL BE RADICAL DEMOCRACY'S "OTHER"?

> The neomodernist desire to locate the space of the margin and the absence within the text is simply to theorize again from first-world interest, to display a hysterical blindness to the fact that the periphery has forced itself upon the attention of the center.
>
> —Laura Kipnis[5]

> The question is how to keep the ethnocentric Subject from establishing itself by selectively defining an Other.
>
> —Gayatri Chakravorty Spivak[6]

Asking "How will 'radical' democracy deal with colonial legacies in ways that 'non-radical' democracy does not," I will critique this presumed alternative for its embeddedness in modernist principles about difference, identity, subjectivity, opposition, and, most notably, inclusion. Pushing inclusion, advocates of radical democracy generally see the problem as one of the implementation and realization of the ideals of modern democracies rather than the ideals and structures themselves. Chantal Mouffe, in fact, believes that radical democracy is the "only viable alternative for the Left today, and that it consists in trying to extend the principles of equality and liberty to an increasing number of social relations."[7] This belief embodies an inclusionary impulse that needs to be problematized because the privileging of inclusion politics does not account for the ways that inclusion can still oppress or fail to alter structures of domination. The inability of radical democratic inclusion politics to deal with inclusion retaining peripheralization is a key limitation, especially given that, in many liberal democratic societies, many subordinated groups have been "included" by being accorded certain formal rights like the right to vote. If inclusionary attempts often reaffirm "a hegemonic core to which the margins are added without any significant destabilization of that core" or continue to valorize the very center that is problematic to begin with, it is clear that the motivation to include needs questioning.[8] The governing assumptions or conceptual logic guiding gestures to include must be interrogated in order to grapple with oppression in the form of appropriation, commodification, fetishization, and exoticization, to name a few. Liberal discourses and their encouragement of inclusion politics do not adequately theorize "oppressive inclusion" and tend to interpret "inclusion" as a sign of "fairness" or "equality." This interpretation misses how the "other(ed)" can be included to actually craft a hegemonic self. Liberal discourses that presume to want to make everyone a "self" (through inclusion) ignore that the liberal "self" always needs and is often manufactured in opposition to the "other(ed)" (the excluded).

Theorists of radical democracy who ignore liberalism's dualist metaphysics continue to want to make everyone a "self," a citizen. Mouffe, for example, wants to "expand the sphere of applicability" and "close the widening gap between democratic theory and the turbulent events of a disordered world."[9] "What we need," suggests Mouffe, "is a hegemony of democratic values, and this requires a multiplication of democratic practices."[10] In the project to "extend" democracy, Mouffe states that what is needed is a "view of citizenship which is adequate for multi-ethnic and multi-cultural societies." Mouffe suggests that a radical democratic conception of citizenship would address the demands of what she terms "new movements." This, Mouffe contends, makes a "radical democratic perspective . . . different from the liberal one."[11] The question that remains undertheorized is: how is a radicalized democracy able to account for cultural differences in ways that (other) liberal democracies do not, especially when it retains liberal conceptions of difference? Cultural difference, in liberal discourses of "multiculturalism" or "pluralism," frequently means a simple, compatible plurality with no conflict, contestation, or contradiction, thereby ignoring Homi Bhabha's point that "cultural differences must not be understood as the free play of polarities and pluralities in the homogeneous empty time of the national community."[12]

To deal with "difference," Mouffe envisions reworking citizenship into a type of political identity responsive to the demands of "a variety of movements" and maintains that radical democracy's principles would take into account different social relations."[13] In "radicalizing" democracy, Mouffe wants to extend and deepen democracy in ways compatible with the "pluralism of modern democracy."[14] Mouffe defines radical democracy as both modern and postmodern and assumes that the "political project of modernity—the achievement of equality and freedom for all—need not be abandoned."[15] Critical of liberal notions of the universal, which Mouffe acknowledges have acted as "mechanisms of exclusion," radical democracy is posed as according importance to the particular.[16] As Mouffe puts it: "The reformulation of the democratic project in terms of radical democracy . . . demands that we acknowledge difference."[17] In addition to conceptualizing difference in liberal terms and only referring to it in the abstract and without adequate specificity, it is obvious that Mouffe is aware of the modernity of democracy. But she does not link histories of modernity to histories of colonialism.[18] This runs counter to the insights of many scholars of postcoloniality and postmodernity who are seriously concerned with modernity's historical allegiance to colonial projects. These critics question whether the terms of modernity can be utilized without reinstating or reproducing colonial discourses and the hegemony of the West.

Inderpal Grewal and Caren Kaplan, in theorizing the relationship between modernity and colonialism, for example, critique certain forms of feminism for "their willing participation in modernity with all its colonial discourses and hegemonic First World formations."[19] Challenging Western feminist alliances with modernist agendas, they argue that to support the agendas of modernity is to "misrecognize and fail to resist Western hegemonies."[20] Their discussion of postcoloniality, postmodernity, and transnational feminist theories and practices could be particularly instructive to Western feminist theorists of democracy who, while they reflect on the gendered nature of democracy's citizen-subject, through a lack of engagement with issues of race and imperialism, continue to implicitly construct this subject as ostensibly "race-neutral" (tending to mean or imply Western, white). Mouffe authorizes this Western-centered position by recommending the "remedying" of "modern conceptions of citizenship," especially the "liberal notion of citizenship founded in the idea that all individuals are born free and equal."[21] Mouffe shows knowledge of Western feminist writings which have called citizenship a "patriarchal category" constructed in "a masculine image."[22] Summarizing this body of feminist scholarship, Mouffe reiterates Carole Pateman's point that "the public realm of modern citizenship has been based on the negation of women's participation."[23]

These writers fail to account for other, simultaneous, overlapping, intersecting negations which also constitute the liberal citizen-subject. Admittedly, Mouffe does mention race and ethnicity; however, she does not sufficiently account for forms of domination related to race, geopolitical location, or nationality, to name only a few. By merely describing these categories and not theorizing them and by not also noting that exclusions based on them have constituted the modern citizen-subject, these scholars exemplify Maxine Baca Zinn et al.'s critique of feminist approaches to race, ethnicity, and nation—approaches which, as Alarcón puts it, "tack on" material about "minority women" and through their implicit standpoint epistemology, work "inherently against the interests of non-white women."[24] In claiming that the "individual" is not a universal category as liberal doctrines presume, but "is a man," these writers do not specify which man or which men and thus reify liberal feminism's essential binary of "man against woman" and its reversal to "woman against man."[25] If one assumes that femininities as well as masculinities are constructed within racial terms, it follows that one cannot invoke "woman" and "man" as essentialist, monolithic, discrete categories characterized by sameness within and difference without.[26]

The contentions that liberal theory's "purportedly gender-neutral figure is implicitly male" or that "universalism [is] modeled on the male paradigm," while they highlight important concerns, need to be much more complicated.[27] Specifically, in not sufficiently theorizing the import of race, they reproduce problematic assumptions characterizing hegemonic Western feminism. They presume, for example, the separability and autonomy of analytical categories such as gender, class, race, ethnicity, and nation, and thus are only able to generate "single-theme analyses" or "additive categories models" and "added burdens or oppressions."[28] They not only are unable to comprehend the mutual constitution of these categories, but they also fail to problematize each category. As Alarcón explains, in only dealing with one category at a time or singularly including analytical categories such as race and class, these theories tend to ignore that "one 'becomes a woman' in ways that are more complex than in simple opposition to men. In cultures in which 'asymmetric race and class relations are a central organizing principle of society,' one may also 'become a woman' in opposition to other women."[29]

While problematically not recognizing the whiteness or Western-centeredness of liberalism's "neutral" subject or only recognizing this subject's gender isolated from its other features, Western feminist political theorists have been useful in noting how gender shows up *conceptually* in liberal discourses. For example, Drucilla Cornell suggests that "to change the world in the name of democracy, we need not only to change the rights of man to include the social rights of women, but also to challenge the masculinization of the rhetoric of the ideal of politics itself."[30] These writers believe that "Liberal Enlightenment discourses were not meant to include women, and their coherence depends partially on 'our' continuing exclusion."[31] Jane Flax, who uses postmodern theories to "disrupt master-narratives of the west and the language games in which terms like 'freedom,' 'emancipation,' or 'domination' take on meaning," agrees that "The theory and practice of democratic liberalism" needs to be criticized for "taking for granted a conception of citizenship which excludes all that is traditionally female."[32] Nevertheless, these theorists fail to analyze other categories and groups democratic citizenship excludes, such as "homosexuals," as well as how democratic nation-states construct themselves through notions of racial difference and hierarchy. In so doing, these writers do not conceptualize democracy as a racial formation and do not critically note the circulation of "democracy" as a colonial discourse.

MODERN DEMOCRATIC NATIONS AND DISCOURSES OF RACE

In allotting notions of "race" or hierarchical racial difference a foundational status in modern democratic nations, it is arguable that discourses of race have been preeminent in consolidating modern democracies.[33] This implies more than the assertion that exclusions of certain racialized subjects has occurred, these exclusions are implicated not as mere absences but rather as constitutive of, perhaps even necessary for, the formation of liberal democracies. To comprehend this requires attention to the colonial context of the emergence of democracy in the United States, especially as this played out in the racial construction of liberal democracy's privileged subject—the citizen—and its privileged activity—voting. Kirstie McClure, in her discussion on the "question of rights, power, and identity in Anglo-American pluralist discourse," attempts to investigate the relation between "the subject of rights" and the "subject of modernity" and concludes that "rights claiming activities," such as the right to vote, function as a sign of "active citizenship" in the modern democratic state.[34]

Race-based exclusion (and inclusion) from citizenship—and thereby the right to vote—is an event that clarifies the racial foundation of American democracy. Struggles for civic inclusion are evident in Asian immigrant struggles for citizenship and its attendant rights, such as the right to vote. Asian Americans in the early 1900s were "denied the right to naturalization [and] could not vote. The denial of the right of naturalization to anyone other than 'free, white persons' was written in the United States Constitution" and contested heavily by many groups in the late 1800s and early 1900s.[35] What is worth noting is the *fluctuating* history of "naturalization" within which Asian immigrants who were naturalized were later denaturalized. An example of this is the case of *United States v. Bhagat Singh Thind* (1923). Thind, an immigrant to the United States from India, received his United States citizenship in 1920 and was "known for his advocating independence for India, and immigration officials looked for a pretext to deport him. The bureau of immigration took him to court in an attempt to 'denaturalize' him." The United States Supreme Court upheld the position of the federal agency, and "following the *Thind* decision, immigration officials successfully canceled the naturalization certificates of several dozen other Asian Indians" based on notions of "race" and anti-imperialist politics.[36]

Immigrant struggles for citizenship and its rights—battles whose participants have been well aware of citizenship as a racially exclusionary category and cognizant of the history of who can be and has been a citizen—are paralleled not only by African American efforts, but also by women's suffrage movements. Racial notions informed even white women's agitations for enfranchisement, as Angela Davis commented upon in her analysis of the racist arguments used by white women in the mid-1800s in the United States to obtain the right to vote. Davis sums up these arguments as the proposition that "white, native-born, educated women had far more compelling claims for suffrage than did black people and immigrants."[37]

Racist notions not only figured in the denial of citizenship and voting privileges, but also structured attempts to secure suffrage. The granting of suffrage to African American men before (white) women is explored by Davis. As she explains it, (white) women's suffrage was not in the post-Civil War political agenda, while enfranchisement of black men was; but, extending the vote to newly emancipated black men in the South did not imply that black men "were being favored over white females" as some white women's organizations held. "Black male suffrage . . . was a tactical move designed to ensure the political hegemony of the Republican party."[38]

The racism of white women's suffrage movements highlights the limits of Mouffe's conception of plurality and difference because Mouffe ignores the historical reality that the attainment of one group's rights at the expense of others is a strategy often marking attempts to obtain rights. This is evident in racist "feminists" and their attempts to bolster the class and racial privileges of elite women. Elizabeth Cady Stanton is but one example of this and was asked at the 1867 Equal Rights Convention by a black delegate whether she "opposed the extension of the vote to black men unless women were also enfranchised." Her answer reflected general feminist anxieties over black men getting the "privileges of male supremacy," according to Davis. Stanton's answer was: "I would not trust him with my rights; degraded, oppressed, himself, he would be more despotic . . . than even our Saxon rulers are. . . ."[39]

Stanton's stance, underscoring the gendered and racialized terminology of bids for democratic rights, supports McClure's point that "The political issue involved . . . is more complex than the exclusion of multiple 'others' from participatory rights."[40] McClure's use of the word "others" raises not only questions of who gets defined as "other" but also how "others" other "others;" it also reiterates that the othered are necessary for the consolidation of the rights-bearing subject and his or her community, the nation. In conjunction with citizenship and voting having a racial history, this means, again, that democracy itself is a racial formation, a point Alarcón makes in "Taking into account the historical overdetermination of (raced) ethnicities in the context of Modernist nation-building."[41]

THE MODERNITY OF RACISM/THE MODERNITY OF DEMOCRATIC NATIONS

> Racism is "part of the historical traditions of civic and liberal humanism."
>
> —Homi Bhabha[42]

Etienne Balibar, along with other writers, emphasizes the modernity of democracy as well as the modernity of racism and theorizes the relationships between race and nation, between racism and nationalism. Balibar labels nationalism as the "determining condition" of racism's production because the interior or boundaries of the nation are constructed through exteriorizing or othering certain groups in a racialized manner.[43] This can be seen in California's Proposition 187, a proposition on the 1994 ballot attempting to halt the providing of state services to "illegal immigrants." Proposition 187, also called the "Save Our State" initiative, reflects a public concern with identifying the "others" and demonstrates the state construction of authentic, true, deserving nationals against images of inauthentic "illegal aliens." The notions of the "illegal" and "legal" subject, the "alien" and the "national," and the "unnaturalized and the "naturalized" citizen-subject, highlight the conceptual Eurocentrism of the category "citizen" because, by making proficiency in English mandatory for United States citizenship, this category privileges and requires, for membership, evidence of "assimilation" to Eurocentric standards. Clearly, the "race-neutral" state demands proof of English skills for citizenship and thus demands familiarity with certain cultural/linguistic practices while discouraging others, and it thus uses ideas about "appropriate" and "inappropriate" cultural differences and practices to create the very category "citizen." This type of nationalistic social construction of race and ethnicity is referred to by Balibar as the concept of "fictive ethnicity," and he states that it is necessary for the nation.[44] "It is fictive ethnicity which makes it possible for the expression of a pre-existing unity to be seen in the state," argues Balibar. He concludes that race is in fact produced by the liberal democratic nation-state and that notions of race figure into the nation.[45]

The argument that racism is constitutive of nationalism and that discourses of race generate the nation is echoed by Wolfgang Mommsen in his analysis of the interface between imperialism and nationalism.[46] According to Mommsen, even in the 1800s, "Imperialism was generally regarded as a necessary consequence of the creation of nation-states," and European nationalist arguments for imperialist expansion were usually couched as in "the national interest."[47] Inderpal Grewal, in complicating these analyses by noting the gendered nature of colonial modernity, argues that Empire's nationalism served as an imperial discourse and theorizes the ways in which imperialism articulated itself as a nationalist discourse.[48] She, in positing modernity as a condition for nationalism and in calling democracy a nationalist discourse, observes the ways in which hegemonic versions of United States democracy get linked to freedom, liberty, equality, choice, and other liberal ideals.[49]

Grewal argues not only that "the ideology of American 'freedom' constructs United States nationalism," but that the maintenance of discourse of "Americanness" and "freedom" as synonymous is a United States nationalist discourse used to uphold the "United States as model for democratic rights around the world."[50] Analyzing the "questionable structures of First World freedom and equality," she discusses the "erasures necessary for the formation of 'freedom' and 'democracy' in the United States as well as in other First World nations."[51] "The discourse of 'freedom' is essential to the consolidation and ongoing construction of Western state power structures," Grewal argues. Critical of unproblematized usages of notions of Western "freedom," she contends that liberation conceptualized in the nationalist terms of colonial European modernity works to reconstitute its cultural superiority.[52]

The idea that the supposed "freedom" of the United States is imaged through erasures is traced by Grewal to the modern discourses of colonial travel to India in the nineteenth century, discourses that contained a notion of Britain as "free" for women by actively repressing and selectively ignoring the subordinate legal and economic status of British women at the time. This presumed "freedom," interpreted as a sign of British superiority, was manufactured by ignoring the material conditions of women's lives in Britain and was a discourse endorsed and promulgated by some British nationalist/imperialistic feminists.[53] In articulating Empire as a gendered nationalist discourse of "freedom," images of the uniform and universal "unfreedom" of Indian women, for example, was relied upon; the "unfree other" thus helped construct the "free self." Such colonial constructions continue to cohere through effacements of Western patriarchies and gender oppression in countries like the United States and serve to establish the "freedom" of the West against the "unfreedom" of the non-West.

That the colonized other was required for the colonizing self to be complete reflects the modernist metaphysics of colonial discourses. If one assumes that any given modern notion gets established in opposition to its constructed negation, what follows in reference to the modern, nationalist category of democracy is that the privileged and idealized image of democracy *requires* an image of non-democracy or anti-democracy. The imaging or representation of democracy is created by, through, and in opposition to racialized imaginations or representations of its lack. It is the weddedness of discourses of freedom to democracy and the figuration of democracy in United States nationalist discourses that is crucial to account for, given that, depending on one's social and geopolitical location, United States nationalist discourses act as United States imperialist discourses.

The ways in which discourses of democracy consolidate "Western state power structures," promote Western cultural superiority, and serve to justify economic sanctions and purportedly "democratizing" Western military invasions in non-Western contexts, demonstrates how Western countries such as the United States "own" the term or category "democracy" and use it to police or discipline countries not meeting the Western criteria.[54] In this process, democracy is often measured by standards that are not only shifting, but are often unmet by Western countries themselves. Consequently, no matter what the United States does, because it "owns" democracy (as well as other terms such as "human rights") it will appear democratic. Others will invariably fall outside democracy's prescribed boundaries. These boundaries are secured and solidified through the non-democratic or anti-democratic that the racialized "other" is continually constructed as, and they are set up and stabilized to craft an image of the United States that validates and legitimates its satisfying of its democratizing desires.

The production of the normativeness of democracy—and its privileged signifiers—is connected to its consolidation and coherence through a series of noteworthy effacements too numerous to enumerate in length but which includes interesting silences about the largely exclusionary history of the right to vote in Western democracies—the fact that in the United States certain prisoners are still denied the right to vote, as well as other ways in which the act of voting as it is currently structured cannot be duly exercised due to exigencies such as not having an address, not possessing literacy, not speaking or reading English, and so on. The fact that Britain has a monarchy in 1994 and that this is not read as antithetical to democracy in the ways socialism, for example, is, is, is indicative of the Western, especially American, lock on the term, including its definitional boundaries.

UNITED STATES DEMOCRACY: RIGHTS AND REPRESENTATION

> Government under our constitution makes American citizenship
> the highest privilege and at the same time the greatest responsi-
> bility of any citizenship in the world. The good citizen cherishes
> democratic values and bases his actions on them.
>
> —United States Department of Justice, Immigration
> and Naturalization Service[55]

"The United States has often been considered the preferred land of liberal democracy"—an important commentary to note in the face of
Chan's observation that "in a country that prides itself in being a
democracy with a government of laws . . . [its] political and legal structures" have a history of "institutionalized racism."[56] Given that the
United States constructs its "democratic" image through a series of
selective constitutive erasures, questions arise as to what the United
States does to appear "democratic." One tactic is its granting selective
"rights" to disenfranchised groups, such as the right to vote. The appeal
of modernist notions of rights to negotiate or even subvert the very
structures of modernity such as the nation-state are understandable; as
Gayatri Chakravorty Spivak puts it: "Of course, one prefers *rights* talk
because of the general inscription of the globe within the culture of
European Enlightenment."[57] However, the history of (colonial) nation-
states granting rights to assert themselves as benevolent protectors, that
is, to argue "imperialism's image as the establisher of the good society,"
is an important point to consider.[58]

The modes by which nation-states dispense "rights" to actually
bolster their own preferred images and hegemonies helps to answer
questions of ideological reconstitutions, questions which are taken up
by KumKum Sangari and Sudesh Vaid. They cite Prem Chowdry's
essay about British rulers in Haryana, India, who while they granted
rights to widows, were "anxious to discourage them from availing
those very rights."[59] British colonial discourses in India as well as
related nationalist discourses replayed this theme of according rights to
those who, within the colonial free/unfree binary, were previously
"unfree" but as bearers of "rights" are "free."

The strategy of using the "other" (particularly "saving" or "eman-
cipating" the "other") as the grounds upon which to solidify one's self
and one's political agenda is a point made by many scholars of colonialism and nationalism in India. Lata Mani examines this in her
analysis of debates about *sati* in colonial India; Kumari Jayawardena discusses this in reference to nationalist movements in Asia and their
impulses to modernize and democratize in the liberal image of
European colonial modernity.[60] Mani and Jayawardena both note the
gendered terminology of nationalisms in which women are actually
the ground used to elaborate notions of "nation." According to
Jayawardena, "Many reformers of Asia seized upon the apparent freedom of women in Western societies as the key to the advancement of
the West, and argued that 'Oriental backwardness' was partly due to
women's low status."[61] In using the status of women as the "popular

barometer of 'civilization,' many nationalist reformers took on the 'woman question.'"[62] These reformers attempted to mold women into "embodiments of [the] ideal" woman, who was seen as having education and freedom of movement, as well as other liberal rights, which were taken as the "markers of modernity, development, civilization."[63] This was also done by giving them "rights." The nationalist productions of the "Enlightened woman," who had to both negate notions of "tradition" as well as guard and reproduce these very same notions, or in essence, had to symbolize both modernity and tradition, was an attempt to make women "presentable to colonial society."[64] "Though the terminology was similar, various regions showed differences in the concept of the new woman," although all of these ideological reconstitutions were intimately linked to capitalist development and "bourgeois ideology."[65]

The granting of "rights" to actually cement state power is evident in the history of United States immigration laws and citizenship as well as in Davis's conclusion that "freeing" and "enfranchising" African Americans had more do with political expediency than concern for African Americans.[66] Exclusion from and inclusion in the United States as well as eligibility for citizenship has, in large part, been based on the economic needs and political considerations of the ruling class in the United States. This is proven by Chan's analysis of the 1965 Immigration Act which changed the pattern of immigration into the United States and dramatically increased Asian immigration. This occurrence was a development "contrary to what proponents of the Act had anticipated: they had predicted that European immigration would continue to predominate."[67] The Act, which "mollified nativist groups opposed to immigration from areas of the world other than western Europe," was passed for a number of reasons related to the United States's attempts to maintain international power. "First, in terms of foreign policy considerations in the midst of the cold war, advocates for immigration reform argued that if the United States wished to portray itself as a leader of the 'free world,' the federal government had to eliminate racial discrimination not only in all aspects of public life but also in its immigration policy." In 1963, Lyndon Johnson and Congress attempted to "reform the country's immigration laws [and] at the same time, Johnson pushed through antipoverty and civil rights programs to convince the world that the United States is indeed a land of justice and equal opportunity for all people."[68]

The nationalistic image of the United States, articulating itself in liberal terms, clearly supports attempts to "democratize" the world. This democratizing impulse knows no partisan boundaries as well, given that both Democrats and Republicans (a highly fictive dichotomy of creatively imagined difference) act on it to solidify American power internationally. This is typified by a quote from Ronald Reagan, who "in a speech in June 1981 to the British parliament, announced that the United States was about to throw its prestige and resources behind a programme launched to strengthen 'democracy throughout the world.'"[69] As Sheldon Wolin astutely observes, "Reagan made no . . . suggestion that democracy might need strengthening at home." Moreover, Reagan and other "leaders of the free world" display a remarkable and telling disinterest in the sentiments of those they plan to democratize (sometimes by bombing them). This can be seen in their apparent lack of concern for the fact that Panamanian people, when asked by *60 Minutes,* no less, about whether the George Bush-led December 29, 1989, "Operation Just Cause" had "improved or worsened" democracy, overwhelmingly replied that there was "more democracy under the military dictatorship of (Manuel) Noriega." This hints that "intervening" or "surgically striking" in the name of democracy has arguably as much, if not more, to do with approval ratings and poll standings of a United States president than with any interest in "tyranny" elsewhere. In the case of the Panamanians interviewed by *60 Minutes*'s investigative reporters, "democracy was not linked to prosperity, stability, and freedom" as United States liberal nationalists would boast.[70]

That the image of United States democracy is crafted through constitutive erasures and exclusions and that the "norm" of democracy is constructed against the "deviant" or "abnorm" of non- or anti-democracy and therefore *needs* its "opposition" means more than the contention that democracy is a politically constructed and mobilized category produced through its manufactured "opposite;" it also explains how the United States always appears democratic, which it does by defining the very term and setting its standards. Questions of who decides what counts as evidence of democracy and sets its general definitional parameters are important to pose because of the utilization of democracy as a discourse to announce Western superiority. The discursive aspects of democracy warrant consideration given the uses of representations of "democracy" to configure postcolonial United States foreign policy, for example, and the discourse of democracy's deployment to justify a post-cold war buildup of the military industrial complex. Mapping the discursive boundaries, that is, the representational politics, of the category democracy is useful in theorizing the circulation of the term and helps to account for what is done in promoting its name. United States interests in spreading democracy are important to note given what the term gets linked to (peace, stability, prosperity, freedom, capitalism, etc.) and what the perceived absence of "democracy" gets wedded to (violence, instability, deprivation, oppression, socialism or communism, etc). The United States version of democracy is also important to deconstruct because it is often packaged and marketed as the only version, the most viable version, and the supreme "universal" version; a position consolidated through ignoring its flaws.

DECONSTRUCTING REPRESENTATIVE DEMOCRACY

To me, fair play means the rules encourage everyone to play.

—Lani Guinier[71]

The manifold and complex ways in which a certain brand of "democracy" displays affinities to colonial modernity and figures into hegemonic United States nationalist discourses, and the observation that it actually sustains its superiority though historical erasures, suggests the need to deconstruct United States versions of democracy as the privileged system of governmentality. Analyzing the structural deficits or limitations of democracy can assist in dismantling United States hegemonies. These limitations include democracy's subscription to liberal notions of representation—such as the belief in representability, as well as notions of transparent representation and the possibility of representativeness.

The flaws of United States democracy surrounding issues of representation as analyzed by Lani Guinier are instructive, especially in the context of the "anti-democratic" label attached to her by many United States politicians upon her nomination in 1993 to the post of assistant attorney general in charge of the Civil Rights Division of the United States Justice Department. Despite Guinier's self-identification as a "democratic idealist," she was accused of being "anti-democratic" when it was perceived that she was critical of United States electoral politics. Muting criticisms of United States democracy to pose it as "the best" is necessary to maintain its "superiority" and its hegemony, as well as justify its imposition or universalization. Critiques of it, especially those cognizant of its history of institutionalized exclusion of non-whites, are often attacked as "anti-democratic" because they shatter the illusion of the ideal democracy necessary for United States hegemony in the "postcolonial" world.

In examining the shortcomings of representative democracy, Guinier specifically analyzes the notion of majority rule. In explaining that problems lie in majority rule itself, Guinier forwards an anti-essentialist argument by discussing the meaning voting has assumed and how "voting alone does not signal fairness" and explores ways to increase the representation of interests over "head counts." In her book, *The Tyranny of the Majority*, she critiques the concept of majority rule and notes that "representative democracy needs to take into account the interests of *both* 'winning' and 'losing' voters. There can be no fairness when majorities are fixed and permanent and when they consistently exclude and ignore minority interests."[72]

Guinier, in accounting for race as an organizing category of the democratic nation-state, suggests that "majority rule is not a reliable instrument of democracy in a racially divided society."[73] Elaborating on the relationship between majority rule and democracy and thinking through the assumption that the majority can adequately represent the minority, Guinier critiques the fixedness of the majority and majoritarianism or winner-take-all majority rule. In highlighting that democracy with majoritarianism encourages the rule of the powerful because 51 percent of the vote equals 100 percent of the power, Guinier states that, "In a racially divided society, majority rule may be perceived as majority tyranny." She analyzes procedural rules and structural problems in representative democracy with racial difference and hierarchies in mind and gives recommendations to ensure that majority rule does not become majority tyranny. This is accomplished through a restructuring of decision-making, for example. According to Guinier, "there is nothing inherent in democracy that requires a majority rule. It is a custom that works efficiently when the majority and minority are fluid, are not monolithic, and are not permanent." In fact, "other democracies frequently employ alternatives to winner-take-all majority voting."[74] Only five Western democracies, including the United States and Britain, still use "winner-take-all systems of representation."[75]

Addressing issues of tokenism, identity politics, inclusion, and essentialism, Guinier emphasizes that the rules produce "permanent minority losers."[76] Examining civil rights theories as well as national-ist and integrationist theories in African American communities, which tend to argue for electoral representation proportionate to their presence in the population and equate this with political equal-ity, Guinier notes that majority rule has gone "unquestioned as long as the majority admitted a fair number of blacks to its decision-mak-ing council." The idea underlying this concept was that only after previously excluded groups were successful within the electoral process would the white majority learn to accept black representatives as colleagues in collective governance. Guinier contends this is a problematic notion because while African Americans may vote, they do not govern.[77] Even when the minority votes, it does not mean their interests will get represented.

Guinier particularly addresses the concept of "fairness" in relation to voting and notes how the United States interprets periodic elections as a privileged sign of fairness. Linking this to liberal notions of citizen-ship, Guinier posits that liberal reformers see fairness in the ideal of universal suffrage because it "incorporates the respect due and the responsibilities owed to each citizen in a democracy. Citizenship is the ultimate reflection of individual dignity and autonomy and voting is the means for individual citizens to realize this personal and social standing. Under this theory, voters realize the fullest meaning of citizenship by the individual act of voting for representatives, who, once elected, participate on the voters' behalf in the process of self-government."[78] Within doc-trines of liberal individualism, voting is conceptualized as an individual's right to "meaningful voice."[79] This right or exercise of choice is seen as empowerment, as evidence of successful representation and non-exclu-sion. Guinier, in problematizing voting, calls for the representation of interests rather than voters, a method she contends that the current sys-tem in the United States disallows because it privileges certain groups over others. Using this to question the "inherent legitimacy of majori-tarianism democracy," she advocates a "winner-take-some-but-not-all approach" that would ensure "an invigorated electorate that participates (as opposed to spectates)."[80]

Further interrogating liberal individualism, Guinier discusses debates about individual representation versus group representation. Proposing that proponents of liberal individualism overlook the "group nature" of voting, Guinier argues that "the concept of representation necessarily applies to groups; groups of voters elect representatives, individuals do not."[81] Representation is more than the "individual rela-tionship between constituent and elected representative," according to Guinier in her analysis of the "dominant theory of representation" in the United States.[82]

Guinier delves into the history of group representation in Britain and its colonies and states that group representation was the norm, for example, for the thirteen "American" colonies. Guinier notes that

"Indeed, the word 'representation' originated as a term used by medieval jurists to describe the personification of collectivities; the spokesperson for a community was its embodiment, the bearer of its representative personhood. Even in its modern form, representation often connotes the activity of furthering the interests of an abstraction rather than of an individual. Although many liberal theorists of American democracy espouse the importance of representation of the rational individual, this claim is at odds with the historical roots of an electoral system that relies on regional rather than political units of representation."[83] Guinier, continuing her evaluation of representative democracy's procedures, also criticizes its reliance on liberal notions of power by concluding that "Politics need not be a zero-sum game."[84]

CAN THE SUBALTERN VOTE?

Proponents of democracy—radical or otherwise—miss the structural flaws of democracy and its buttressing of various colonial and neo-colonial projects. Radical democracy theorists, who in the abstract mention categories such as race and ethnicity but do not specify with any concreteness how radical democracy would deal with these social relations better than non-radical democracy has a history of doing, do not engage the racial history of democracy in sufficient specificity and detail. Democracy is a modern racial formation, meaning it is constructed within, by, and through certain notions of "race." A notable example is the exclusion of certain racialized subjects from its domain. As a product of modernity, the democratic nation-state manufactures itself through the logic of binary oppositions.

In marking the racial configuration of how democracy defines and distinguishes itself against a presumed opposite, the center of a democracy needs its imagined and constructed margins for it to cohere as a center. While the center(s) may want—or even demand—that the margin(s) emulate the center(s), that is, for the othered to become "civilized," "developed," or "democratized," such a universalizing gesture undoes its own goals and terms. As Partha Chatterjee puts it, "Nationalism . . . seeks to represent itself in the image of the Enlightenment and fails to do so. For Enlightenment itself, to assert its sovereignty as the universal ideal, needs its Other."[85] Continuing this line of reasoning, the liberal democratic nation-state produces itself not only through a selectively defined other but also through a selective erasure of aspects of the self. These erasures and exclusions mark the history of and thereby constitute the liberal democratic nation-state's privileged subject—the citizen—and its privileged right—the right to vote. Moreover, these exclusions and erasures are configured by, in, and through implicit as well as explicit notions of race. The product of these racialized exclusions and erasures—the liberal democratic nation-state—in its idealized version figures into or functions as a colonial discourse in that it argues for Western superiority or consolidates Western state powers and thus maintains the hegemony of the West.

In suggesting that "democracy"—even its more "radical" versions—currently acts as a (neo)colonial discourse by virtue of its deployment to assert Western superiority, I want to highlight the political uses and limits of the term. It is important to map "democracy's" invocation by Western powers in how such a move constructs the West and non-West, and it is imperative to map "democracy's" global circulation as a term. Attending to the meanings "democracy" takes on necessitates an analysis of the shifting and differential meanings it has as well. This is not to imply the "purity" or unchanging or static meaning of "democracy"; what needs to be encouraged are more cautious and specified usages of the term. While not suggesting its complete or total recuperability, I also do not wish to imply its inevitable, eternal weddedness to or function as a (neo)colonial discourse. What this analysis points to is the racialized history as well as appeal of "democracy" and other related liberal terms, a history that mandates attention, given the relatedness of modernist principles to imperial projects.

Noting that discourses of representation, rights, and radical democracy are debates about race, debates that presume, construct, reify, and reproduce racial difference, debates that consolidate racist positions, returns the analysis to issues of voting. The problematization of voting is not an argument to abstain from voting. Contrary to suggesting voting's meaninglessness, voting is a highly meaningful act articulating race-infused notions of citizenship and democracy. The significations voting takes on must be carefully assessed. Skepticism is needed of attempts to equate speech or voting with agency, which liberal discourses do in conceiving of voting as one's "political voice" or voting as speech.[86] Questions of speech and the "speaking subject" highlight that in the postcolonial, postfeminist, postmodern world the subaltern may be able to speak, but this does not guarantee a listener; the subaltern may be able to vote, but this does not guarantee representation.

NOTES

This essay is dedicated to the memory of my grandmother Rajbans Kaur Dhillon. I would like to thank Anthony Weaver for his support and encouragement throughout the years. Conversations with him along with Kanwarpal Dhaliwal and Jagbir Dhaliwal greatly facilitated my thinking on racism and democratic nation-states and promoted my critique and skepticism of the promises of modernity. Additionally, I am indebted to Inderpal Grewal, who played a pivotal role in my intellectual formation.

1. Norma Alarcón, "The Theoretical Subject(s) of *This Bridge Called My Back* and Anglo-American Feminism," in *Making Waves, Making Soul: Haciendo Caras*, ed. Gloria Anzaldúa (Aunt Lute Books, 1990), 361.

2. Laura Kipnis, *Ecstasy Unlimited: On Sex, Capital, Gender, and Aesthetics* (Minneapolis: University of Minnesota Press, 1993), 115.

3. I use the term "the West" not because I presume such an entity's homogeneity but because colonial discourses which are the focus of my analysis presume its homogeneity and essential difference from "the non-West."

4. Alarcón, "The Theoretical Subject(s)," 357.

5. Kipnis, *Ecstasy Unlimited*, 116.

6. Gayatri Chakravorty Spivak, "Can the Subaltern Speak?" in *Marxism and the Interpretation of Culture*, eds. Cary Nelson and Lawrence Grossberg (Urbana: University of Illinois Press, 1988), 292.

7. Chantal Mouffe, "Preface: Democratic Politics Today," in *Dimensions of Radical Democracy*, ed. Chantal Mouffe (London: Verso, 1992), 3

8. Amarpal Dhaliwal, "Responses," *Socialist Review* 23, no. 3 (1994): 95.

9. Chantal Mouffe, *The Return of the Political* (London: Verso, 1993), 15, back cover.

10. Mouffe, *The Return of the Political* (London: Verso, 1993), 18.

11. Mouffe, "Preface: Democratic Politics Today," 3, 8.

12. Homi K. Bhabha, *The Location of Culture* (New York: Routledge, 1994), 162.

13. Mouffe, "Democratic Citizenship and the Political Community," in *Dimensions of Radical Democracy*, 235, 236.

14. Mouffe, ed., *Dimensions of Radical Democracy*, back cover.

15. Mouffe, *The Return of the Political*, 12.

16. Mouffe, *The Return of the Political*, 13.

17. Mouffe, *The Return of the Political*, 13.

18. See Inderpal Grewal and Caren Kaplan, "Introduction: Transnational Feminist Practices and Questions of Postmodernity," in *Scattered Hegemonies: Postmodernity and Transnational Feminist Practices*, eds. Inderpal Grewal and Caren Kaplan (Minneapolis: University of Minnesota Press, 1994), 1–33; Grewal, "Autobiographic Subjects and Diasporic Locations: Meatless Days and Borderlands," in *Scattered Hegemonies: Postmodernity and Transnational Feminist Practices*, 231–254; and KumKum Sangari and Sudesh Vaid, "Recasting Women: An Introduction," in *Recasting Women: Essays in Indian Colonial History*, eds. KumKum Sangari and Sudesh Vaid (New Brunswick, NJ: Rutgers University Press, 1989), 1–26.

19. Grewal and Kaplan, "Transnational Feminist Practices and Questions of Postmodernity," 2.

20. Grewal and Kaplan, "Transnational Feminist Practices and Questions of Postmodernity," 2.

21. Mouffe, *The Return of the Political*, 82, 83.

22. Mouffe, *The Return of the Political*, 80, citing Carole Pateman.

23. Mouffe, *The Return of the Political*, 71.

24. See Alarcón, "The Theoretical Subject(s)," 358, 359; and Maxine Baca Zinn, Lynn Weber Cannon, Elizabeth Higginbotham, and Bonnie Thornton Dill, "The Costs of Exclusionary Practices in Women's Studies," *Signs* 11/4 (1986).

25. Cited in Chantal Mouffe, *The Return of the Political*, 13. See also Carole Pateman, "Equality, Difference, Subordination: The Politics of Motherhood and Women's Citizenship," in *Beyond Equality and Difference: Citizenship, Feminist Politics, and Female Subjectivity*, eds. Gisela Bock and Susan James (New York: Routledge, 1992), 13.

26. This is noticed in a race-unspecified manner by Mary Dietz, who, in her investigation of feminist critiques of liberal political thinkers, also chides feminist political thinkers for their gender essentialist, maternalist conceptions of citizenship. See Mary Dietz, "Context is All: Feminism and Theories of Citizenship," in *Dimensions of Radical Democracy*, 63–88.

27. Gisela Bock and Susan James, "Introduction: Contextualizing Equality and Difference," in *Beyond Equality and Difference*, 1–16, citing Pateman; Adriana Cavarero, "Equality and Sexual Difference: Amnesia in Political Thought," in *Beyond Equality and Difference*, 45.

28. See Alarcón "The Theoretical Subject(s)"; and Evelyn Nakano Glenn, "From Servitude to Service Work: Historical Continuities in the Racial Division of Paid Reproductive Labor," *Signs* 18/1 (1992).

29. Alarcón, "The Theoretical Subject(s)," 360.

30. Drucilla Cornell, *Transformations: Recollective Imagination and Sexual Difference* (New York: Routledge, 1993), 169.

31. Jane Flax, "Beyond Equality: Gender, Justice and Difference," in *Beyond Equality and Difference*, 195.

32. Flax, "Beyond Equality," 197; Flax, referring to Susan James, "The Good-Enough Citizen: Citizenship and Independence," in *Beyond Equality and Difference*, 48.

33. The relationship between democracy and notions of race is a complicated one marked by exclusion, unrecognized racial privilege, and unacknowledged racism. These points have been argued differently by a wide variety of scholars attempting to map the racial geography of liberal theories of democracy. This includes the work of Donald Grinde, who exposes "American Indian influences on European political theory" (230) and argues that ". . . the liberal ideas of the seventeenth- and eighteenth-century European philosophers were a partial reflection of Native American democratic principles" (235). Gary Okihiro is another writer who attempts to highlight the participation of people of color in the United States in the ideals and structures of liberal democracy. Okihiro contends that the "ideals of the nation emanate not from the mainstream but from the margins. . ." (ix) because the struggles for equality by oppressed groups have helped "preserve and advance the principles and ideals of democracy" (ix). Continuing, Okihiro postulates that "The margin has held the nation together." These writings are evidence that the racial history is plausibly more complicated than the mere exclusion or absence of non-white groups. But rather than a search for the origins of liberal democracy, I am interested in the political uses of the terms of liberal democratic discourses, particularly as they are employed for the political agendas of colonial modernity. See Donald A. Grinde, Jr., "Iroquois Political Theory and the Roots of American Democracy," in *Exiled in the Land of the Free: Democracy, Indian Nations, and the US Constitution*, eds. Oren Lyons, John Mohawk, Vine Deloria, Jr., Laurence Hauptman, Howard Berman, Donald Grinde, Jr., Curtis Berkey, and Robert Venables (Santa Fe, NM: Clear Light Publishers, 1992), 227–80; Gary Y. Okihiro, *Margins and Mainstreams: Asians in American History and Culture* (Seattle: University of Washington Press, 1994); and Leila Ahmed, "Feminism and Cross-Cultural Inquiry: The Terms of the Discourse in Islam," in *Coming to Terms: Feminism, Theory, Politics*, ed. Elizabeth Weed (New York: Routledge, 1989), 143–51.

34. Kirstie McClure, "On the Subject of Rights: Pluralism, Plurality and Political Identity," in *Dimensions of Radical Democracy*, 109.

35. Sucheng Chan, *Asian Americans: An Interpretive History* (Boston: Twayne Publishers, 1991), 47.

36. Chan, *Asian Americans*, 93–94.

37. Angela Davis, *Women, Race, and Class* (NY: Vintage Books, 1981), 71.

38. Davis, *Women, Race, and Class*, 74, 75.

39. Davis, *Women, Race, and Class*, 75.

40. McClure, "On the Subject of Rights," 111.

41. Norma Alarcón, Ethnic Studies 200 syllabus, Fall 1994, University of California, Berkeley.

42. Bhabha, *The Location of Culture*, 250.

43. Etienne Balibar, "Racism and Nationalism," in *Race, Nation, Class: Ambiguous Identities*, eds. Etienne Balibar and Immanuel Wallerstein (London: Verso, 1991), 37.

44. Etienne Balibar, "The Nation Form: History and Ideology," in *Race, Nation, Class*, 96.

45. Balibar, 62.

46. Wolfgang J. Mommsen, *Theories of Imperialism*, trans. P. S. Falla (New York: Random House, 1980).

47. Mommsen, 6–7; Inderpal Grewal, *Home and Harem: Nation, Gender, Empire, and the Culture of Travel* (Durham, NC: Duke University Press, forthcoming 1995).

48. Grewal, *Home and Harem*.

49. Inderpal Grewal, "Reading and Writing the South Asian Diaspora: Feminism and Nationalism in North America," in *Our Feet Walk the Sky: Women of the South Asian Diaspora,* eds. Women of South Asian Descent Collective (San Francisco: Aunt Lute Books, 1993), 226–236.

50. Grewal, "Reading and Writing the South Asian Diaspora," 226.

51. Grewal, "Reading and Writing the South Asian Diaspora," 227, 226.

52. Grewal, "Reading and Writing the South Asian Diaspora," 226.

53. Grewal, *Home and Harem*.

54. Grewal, "Reading and Writing the South Asian Diaspora," 226.

55. United States Department of Justice, Immigration and Naturalization Service, *A Welcome to USA Citizenship,* revised booklet (October 1988), 3, 7.

56. Mouffe, *The Return of the Political,* 23; Chan, "Asian Americans," 61.

57. Gayatri Chakravorty Spivak, "French Feminism Revisited: Ethics and Politics," in *Feminists Theorize the Political,* eds. Judith Butler and Joan Scott (New York: Routledge, 1992), 64.

58. Spivak, "French Feminism Revisited," 299.

59. Prem Chowdry, "Customs in a Peasant Economy: Women in Colonial Haryana," in *Recasting Women: Essays in Indian Colonial History,* eds. KumKum Sangari and Sudesh Vaid (New Brunswick, NJ: Rutgers University Press, 1989), 302–36, cited by Sangari and Vaid, 7.

60. Lata Mani, "Contentious Traditions: The Debate on Sati in Colonial India," in *The Nature and Context of Minority Discourse,* eds. Abdul R. JanMohamed and David Lloyd (New York: Oxford University Press, 1990), 319–356; Kumari Jayawardena, *Feminism and Nationalism in the Third World* (London: Zed Books, 1986).

61. Jayawardena, *Feminism and Nationalism,* 11.

62. Jayawardena, *Feminism and Nationalism,* 11.

63. Jayawardena, *Feminism and Nationalism,* 12.

64. Jayawardena, *Feminism and Nationalism,* 12.

65. Jayawardena, *Feminism and Nationalism,* 15.

66. Davis, *Women, Race, and Class,* 75.

67. Chan, *Asian Americans,* 145, citing David Reimers.

68. Chan, *Asian Americans,* 145–146.

69. Sheldon Wolin, "What Revolutionary Action Means Today," in *Dimensions of Radical Democracy,* 241.

70. *60 Minutes,* CBS television, September 18, 1994.

71. Lani Guinier, *The Tyranny of the Majority: Fundamental Fairness in Representative Democracy* (New York: The Free Press, 1994), 1.

72. Guinier, *The Tyranny of the Majority,* jacket.

73. Guinier, *The Tyranny of the Majority,* xvi.

74. Guinier, *The Tyranny of the Majority,* 3.

75. Guinier, *The Tyranny of the Majority,* 17, 18.

75. Guinier, *The Tyranny of the Majority,* 18.

76. Guinier, *The Tyranny of the Majority,* 43, 53.

77. Guinier, *The Tyranny of the Majority,* 53, 123.

78. Guinier, *The Tyranny of the Majority,* 124.

79. Guinier, *The Tyranny of the Majority,* 93.

80. Guinier, *The Tyranny of the Majority,* 94, 112.

81. Guinier, *The Tyranny of the Majority,* 127.

82. Guinier, *The Tyranny of the Majority*, 119.

83. Guinier, *The Tyranny of the Majority*, 128.

84. Guinier, *The Tyranny of the Majority*, 153.

85. Partha Chatterjee, *Nationalist Thought and the Colonial World: A Derivative Discourse* (London: Zed, 1986), 17.

86. For analyses of the meanings and possibilities of "speech," see Gayatri Chakravorty Spivak, "Can the Subaltern Speak?," 271–313; Trinh T. Minh-ha, "Not Like/Like You: Post-Colonial Women and Interlocking Questions of Identity And Difference," *Inscriptions* 3/4 (1988): 71–77; and Kamala Visweswaran, *Fictions of Feminist Ethnography* (Minneapolis: University of Minnesota Press, 1994).

TAKING IT
TO THE STREETS

RADICAL DEMOCRACY
AND RADICALIZING THEORY

J. PETER EUBEN

Adam Krzeminski: What remains after Socialism?

Jürgen Habermas: Radical Democracy.

Adam Michnik: I entirely agree.[1]

1

WITH ONLY SLIGHT EXAGGERATION ONE COULD SAY that this exchange would sound peculiar to most American academics. Such praise of radical democracy has little political or theoretical echo here. Even when it does, adherents are quick to emphasize two facts to prove that their radicalism and their democracy are realistic. The first is that the literal Greek meaning of democracy—where the people rule and govern themselves and citizens share power and initiate action—is hopelessly nostalgic, dangerously utopian, anti-modern, anti-liberal, and insufficiently attentive to the compromised state of all radical proposals in the wake of totalitarianism. If the history of the past two hundred years proves anything, it is the importance of rights, proceduralism, constitutional guarantees, and the danger of "fundamentalist projects" like radical democracy, projects which are hostile to structural differentiation and social pluralism and attached to a vision of community based on a single conception of the good life.[2] But even if one wants "the people" to rule, who are they? With the Marxist project in disrepute and post-Fordist capitalism ascendant, they can hardly be identified with the proletariat. And given the post-modernist insistence that every "we" or "us" must be problematized, notions such as the "ordinary citizen" or "the people" seem impossibly abstract and reductive.

The second fact is that, whatever we think of Marxism or identity politics, the sins of nostalgia and utopianism are compounded if one turns to Classical Athens as a point of departure and reference. While sympathetic to the rediscovery of citizenship, Chantal Mouffe warns against going "back to a pre-modern conception of the political." "We need," she continues, "to be alert to the dangers of nostalgia for the Greek *polis* and Gemeinschaft types of community."[3] It is not merely the enormous differences in scale and complexity that make Athenian democracy suspect as a vantage point by which to illuminate contemporary democracy; it is also its exclusion of women from the public realm, its reliance on slaves and resident aliens, and its imperialist adventures. If the premodernism of *polis* makes references to Athenian democracy seem quixotic, the glaringly undemocratic features of it make such an appeal perverse.

These are salutary warnings against yet another version of *polis* envy and Hellenic romanticism. Nostalgia and utopianism are too often distractions and a ground for self-righteous dismissal of the complexities or corruptions of one's own time. Still, it is worth remembering that the Greek origin of nostalgia (from *nostos* and *algos*) means feeling the pain of loss or grieving over the separation from home and place, a not unfamiliar feeling in an age so preoccupied with metaphysical and physical homelessness. And it is worth recalling that the idea of Utopia (meaning Noplace), as coined by Thomas More, was not meant as a blueprint, but as a vantage point from which the moral complacency, political vanity, and hypocrisy of his age could be revealed and ridiculed.

Liberal rights and constitutional guarantees have been and can be a means for advancing democracy, as new groups claim access to rights already declared or new rights are demanded in social relations previously regarded as "naturally" hierarchical, such as those concerned with race or gender.[4] But there are good political and historical reasons to be skeptical of the sufficiency and efficacy of rights in the absence of a vigorous culture of civic activism and democratized power. Without such activism and sharing of power, social, economic, and cultural inequalities erode if not undercut formally guaranteed rights, such as the right to a fair trial. Moreover, without providing democratic content to rights they can be used for anti-democratic ends, not so much by the democratic majorities so feared by liberal and conservative elites as by legislative and administrative rulings inspired by single issue minorities using political and legal means to deprive other citizens of rights or restrict their scope, as is the case in the rights to abortion, sexual freedom, and privacy from invasive surveillance.[5]

Even when rights do what they are supposed to do, guarantee a form of protection and freedom beyond the ordinary reach of legislative and executive power, they do so more because of the success of liberal political education in creating a sustaining culture, than because of particular institutional arrangements like the separation of powers or the existence of a bill of rights. "There is no norm or norms," Cornelius Castoriadis writes, "which would not itself be a historical creation. And there is no way of eliminating the risks of collective hubris."[6]

It is also true that, in certain respects at least, Athenian society was less differentiated than our own, though this is often exaggerated as a convenient way of delegitimating Athenian democracy as a point from which to question the democratic credentials of liberalism. In addition, focusing on the homogeneity of Athens tends to obscure our own homogeneity and the anti-democratic forms social differentiation can take. It is arguable that the culture of late twentieth century capitalism is a more homogenizing force than our preoccupations with diversity lead us to believe. In recent years America has grown more and more inegalitarian, more divided by extremes of wealth and poverty, education and ignorance, more systematically dominated by corporate power, more systemically corrupt, more retarded by a mass media that fosters political immaturity, and more openly ruled by elites bent on appropriating the conduct, knowledge, and procedures of public life. Insofar as this represents a closing down of public spaces and a narrowing of matters brought before the people, to the degree that more and more of political life is being claimed as the eminent domain of professional experts and professors who reappropriate knowledge while forming a caste of initiates, it precisely reverses the democratization of power that defined the evolution of Athenian democracy.[7]

2

While praise of radical democracy is strange to most academics and recourse to Athenian democracy is suspect even to those for whom it is not, the possibility that philosophers should be in the streets, either literally or metaphorically in the language they use as a way of engaging in dialogue with ordinary citizens, is even more so. Philosophy has become an academic subject; taught in the academy by people with academic degrees, in a technical esoteric language one might call "academese." It is a course one takes or a subject one teaches, not an activity one does in order to make sense of life or the world.

But I want to return to Athens and to the Socrates of Plato's *Apology* as a point of departure for thinking about the radicalizing of theory and its relationship to radical democracy.[8] At a minimum, how Socrates lived, as well as the particular emphasis he put on interrogating those with political and cultural power, helps us look more critically at the role universities play in certifying professionals and in sustaining a culture of expertise at the expense of democratic culture that demands experts and professionals be accountable to the people. More substantially, recourse to where Socrates did philosophy (in the streets), and with whom (everyone), might provide a way of thinking about the democratizing of philosophy.

This argument concerns not only radical democracy and radicalizing theory but the relationship between them, first in Athens and then in America. To begin with, it is necessary to indicate the ways

Athenian democratic practices anticipate, inspire, and make possible certain aspects of Socratic political philosophy. This allows the possibility of showing how a democratic practice became incorporated into Socrates's philosophical activity, and looking at even those dialogues (like the *Gorgias* and *Republic*) that are explicitly critical of democracy will reveal how democratic culture remains a subtext of these critiques.

3

It is an odd and depressing fact that, while Athens *may* have been the cradle of democratic politics and culture, it was *certainly* the cradle of anti-democratic political theory. If there is any truth to the idea that founding assumptions constitute a tradition which is sustained throughout disparate historical articulations, and to Alfred North Whitehead's claim that philosophy is a series of footnotes on Plato, then there are good reasons for democrats to be suspicious of that founding, for multiculturalists to wonder about the politics of an education based on classic texts, and for post-modernists to believe that their critique of totalizing theory as initiated by Plato is an emancipatory gesture (however much they disavow such an aim).

One could of course construct a democratic theory out of various fragments in classical texts: Pericles' Funeral Oration in Thucydides, moments in Plato's *Statesmen* and *Laws* that have favorable things to say about democracy, and various passages in Aristotle (such as his praise of collective wisdom or recognition that in some respects the idea of citizenship is most fully realized in a democracy). But these are only fragments in works which are generally hostile to democratic institutions and culture.

If the absence of any theoretical defense of democracy in Athens is a fact, what are we to make of it? What does it suggest, not merely about the relationship between classical political theory and Athenian democracy but about the possible relationship between political theory or philosophy and radical democracy here and now?

One possible reason why no democratic theory existed in Athens was the class bias of the philosophers. This explains the polemicism and perverseness of Plato's attack on democracy, which goes out of its way to make the worst rather than the best case for what it criticizes. But even leaving aside the question of whether the dialogues present us with propositions endorsed by Plato, Socrates's argument in the *Republic* that status, wealth, birth, and connections disqualify one from power is unlikely to have found favor with many Athenian aristocrats or oligarchs.

Another possible reason why we have no theoretical defense of democracy in ancient Athens is that it would have been otiose. Why bother to argue for democratic practices, institutions, and ideology when they were the overwhelming fact of everyday life. This is not to say that the Athenians lacked pre-theoretical articulations of democracy as found in drama and oratory. Indeed, it is very likely that Plato was responding to popular ideology as found in rhetoric and theater rather than to other elite intellectuals. But then why no theoretical defense of democracy once the theoretical criticisms emerged? Is there no great democratic theorist because democratic theorizing, to be democratic, cannot be singular,[9] just as radical democrats should be suspicious of a preoccupation with leadership since citizens should themselves be leaders and initiators rather than passive followers? Is it perhaps the case that radical democracy "is the one political state that requires no argument for its legitimation" because the need for theory begins only when power is placed somewhere other than with the people?[10]

A third possible reason why no theoretical defense of radical democracy emerged in Athens is that there exists a necessary antagonism between democracy and theorizing regardless of the content of that theory. There are two different approaches to this argument; one that begins with the character of democracy, the other with the character of theory or philosophy.

In a recent essay, Sheldon Wolin argues that democracy is aggressively anti-organizational, suspicious of institutional forms and persistently self-transformative.[11] Precisely the aspect of democracy liberal and conservative critics have regarded as defects (its rebelliousness, episodic quality, suspicion of form and hierarchy, and transgressions of boundaries, orders, and definitions) he sees as definitive of Athenian democracy and revelatory of our attenuated commitment to it. Wolin takes aspects of Plato's critique of democracy, which he finds echoed in ostensibly democratic thinkers of our time, and revises its valences, thus creating an "Athenian" theoretical defense of democracy.

Philosophy on the other hand seems unavoidably committed to form and order, to integration and consistency, both in its own mapping of the world and in the world it maps. If true, then Thomas Hobbes's proposal that his method was not only a way of understanding politics but a paradigm for its organization, says explicitly what is implicit in the very enterprise of philosophy.

There is something to this claim and the tension between philosophy and democracy it portrays. Some such belief may underlie the post-modernist critique of "grand" theory[12] and point to the ways in which the *Republic* aims to make the world safe for philosophy just as some contemporary American critics of democracy are intent on making the world safe for the academy. And it points to the sense in which democracy is, as Claude LeFort puts it, "the historical society par excellence" because "its very form welcomes and preserves indeterminacy" as opposed to totalitarian regimes whose efforts to create a new man[13] presume an understanding of its own organization so certain that it can claim to be "a society without history."[14] The democratization of power that defines radical democracy may well presuppose such indeterminacy.

But what is arresting and provocative about Athenian democracy is the way it created institutions of self-critique, forms for transformation and defined spaces to sustain indeterminacy, all of which provided a ground and example for Socratic political philosophy.[15] What is arresting about a Platonic dialogue like the *Republic* is how much its irony, playfulness, and paradoxes make it an exemplar of dispersive, even collective theorizing rather than a paradigm of totalizing theory. Plato is more a ventriloquist than someone speaking in a single voice, and the dialogue goes out of its way to warn readers *not* to accept as conclusive the conclusions the conversation reaches.

The second approach, represented by Michael Walzer, suggests that there is a necessary opposition between philosophy (including political philosophy) and democracy[16] because philosophers are committed to truth, reason, and values that are universal rather than particular or local. Thus philosophers must dissociate themselves from the common ideas and ideals of their fellow citizens if only, like ancient legislators, to refound the community. Only by seeking the original position or ideal speech situation can the deepest and most general questions about the meaning and purpose of political associations and the appropriate structures for political communities as a whole (rather than in particular) be addressed.

It follows that philosophical validation and political authorization are two entirely different things and belong to two entirely different spheres of activity. Philosophers reason in a world they inhabit alone or that is full of their own speculations; citizens think in a world of opinion peopled by many speeches and speakers. For the philosopher, the result of her reasoning becomes a political and moral touchstone by which to judge the rightness of what the people do and how they live, and the people do not have a right to act wrongly. But in a democracy they do, and the right to decide takes precedence over making the right decisions, which is why who participates in a decision is as important as what is decided. For the philosopher, political action must be ontologically grounded, and for political knowledge to really be knowledge it must be universal and singular. Yet political "knowledge" is plural and parochial, shifting and unstable, less the product of orderly design than historical negotiation, intrigue, and contestations of power, much like democracy itself.

Given this incompatibility between philosophical validation and political authorization, democracy "has no claims in the philosophical realm and philosophers have no special rights in the political community. In the world of opinion, truth is indeed another opinion and the philosopher is only another opinion maker."[17]

Walzer is right to warn against any simplistic identity of philosophy and democratic politics. And he is right to suggest that politics demands action and closure the way philosophical disagreement does not. Socrates after all engaged in philosophical dialogue in the streets, not in the assembly, saying that if he had he would have been killed earlier, doing little good for himself or his compatriots. But I do think democracy has a special claim on philosophy, a claim that is at once historical, intellectual, and political. And if philosophers have no special rights in the political community, they still have obligations to it, particularly if it is a democratic community. The question of course is how philosophers are to fulfill those obligations democratically. How does one determine whether a philosophical critique of democracy aims at restoring it to its animating principles, pushing it to realize its best possibilities, or whether the critique masks anti-democratic contempt for the people. This is no simple matter given the number of "friends" of democracy who think it essential to save the people from themselves.

Nor is it a given that in the world of opinion the philosopher's opinion is just one among many, though it is surely never the only one or even the best one. If opinion, including political opinion, is defended by reasons and arguments as well as by appeals to sentiment and history, and if the practice of giving reasons and arguments to support opinion is itself part of that history, then philosophy becomes an elaboration of citizenship rather than something opposed to it.

Yet all this is somewhat besides the point if the philosophical impulse can be found in Socrates's claim that the unexamined life is not worth living (a claim that is both true and a serious exaggeration). For then it is not the opinion of the philosopher that has priority but his injunction to think and the way he is thoughtful.[18] It is true that Socrates had definite views—that virtue is knowledge, that it is better to suffer injustice than commit it. But the question is whether it was these views that made him a philosopher or whether it was the way he thought views about such subjects should be taught and learned that did so.[19]

4

My first example of a democratic practice Socrates philosophizes is accountability. Before any official was able to take office he was subject to a scrutiny, or *dokimasia*, by a jury of citizens chosen by lot. (Since all Athenian citizens were sometimes officials and would certainly be on many such juries, this is an instance of the people scrutinizing themselves.) The preliminary exam was intended to establish that an individual was a citizen who had fulfilled his financial, military, and social responsibilities.[20] The scrutiny was mostly pro forma. But in times of intense political rivalry, as in the aftermath of the oligarchic revolutions, it became more significant, broad-ranging, and probing. In these circumstances a candidate might be asked to give an account of his political commitments as a whole and defend the life he had been leading.

At the end of their year in office the same officials were subject to yet another examination, the *euthu nai*,[21] where they submitted their financial accounts to ten auditors and were subjected to a public hearing before examiners if any citizen made a complaint about any aspect of their performance.

These demands for accountability were part of the democratization of power that accompanied the development of the democratic *polis*. The emergence of a public realm where practices were openly arrived at was part of the progressive appropriation by the community as a whole of the conduct, knowledge, and procedures that had been the exclusive prerogatives of king and nobles.[22] As access to the spiritual world previously reserved for warriors and priests widened, knowledge and values became part of a common public culture, and so subject to criticism, contest, and scrutiny. Laws had to be justified, leaders had to give reasons for their decisions, and the exercise of power had to be defended in terms of the publicly acknowledged and continually debated ends of the political community as a whole. Initially democratization meant the accountability of leaders to the led. But as it progressed and the people became actors themselves, they came to hold each other accountable. In this they realized the principle implicit in the Athenian law that anyone who failed to take sides in a factional dispute would lose his membership in the city because the preservation of a just order was the responsibility of every citizen.

"It is not easy," Theodorus says about Socrates in Plato's *Theatetus*, "for anyone to sit beside you and not be forced to give an account[23] of himself" [169A]. We hear a fuller description of this in the *Apology* where Socrates tells how he engages politicians, poets, and artisans to discover what it is they know as opposed to what they think they know, and whether they know how important their knowledge is in the living of a life. In these exchanges he pushes people to give an account of their lives, to see what they see through and to offer reasons for what they do unthinkingly. But he does more than that; he gives an account of *his* life, indicating how difficult, dangerous, *and* necessary a thinking life is. Socrates's insistence that especially those with political and cultural power be made to give an account of their lives is an elaboration of a democratic practice he is taking more seriously than those who claim to be friends of democracy.

The paradox in all this is that Socrates is exemplifying what he is criticizing; he is being a democrat while chastising democracy. Perhaps that explains his exaggerated deference to the laws of the city in the *Crito*.[24] Perhaps he understands that what he criticizes, how he criticizes it, and even the fact that he criticizes at all, he owes to a democratic community that provides space for self-critique and self-transformation.

My second example involves the notion of *isonomia*, political equality. *Isonomia* was the slogan of Athenian democracy. Insofar as it implied an abstraction from concrete social and economic inequalities[25] absent in oligarchies where inequalities coincided, it involved an idealization, a distinction between the essential and incidental that also animates philosophy.[26] Similarly, *isonomia*'s presumption that decisions reached and disagreements resolved would be done so by voting rather than by force or the unquestioned standing of the rich and well born is echoed in Socrates's commitment to dialogue, accountability, and reasoning. Finally, political equality presumed that the democratization of power distinctive to Athens would bring with it the democratization of responsibility and wisdom; that political participation was itself the basis of political education; and that such virtues as lawfulness were primarily political in the sense that they depended upon the sense of restraint and obligation attendant on the actual sharing of power.

Socrates is critical of these claims about power, responsibility, and wisdom. The question is whether his criticisms constitute a rejection of radical democracy or are an admonishment to his compatriots to recognize what is necessary for these claims to be plausible and practical. Certainly he has no more patience with majority rule as a determination of right action than he has with wealth status or physical prowess. But it's important not to equate majority rule with Athenian democracy, both because voting came only after extensive debate and deliberation in a number of formal and informal settings—law courts, council, *demes*, agora—and because different majorities constituted on different occasions and times could reconsider a decision or law. Thus the *graphe paranomon* (literally an accusation of unlawfulness) allowed a citizen to bring a case against someone whose proposed law had been passed by the assembly. If convicted, the person could suffer severe penalties, and the law would be annulled, which meant that though a citizen could propose any law he pleased, there were good reasons to think carefully about it first. Since the proposed law would be judged by a court of considerable size (at least 501, sometimes 1001 or even 1501 citizens), drawn by lot, one could say that the *demos* was appealing from the whole body of citizens to a large random sample of the same body. Thus the people acting in a different guise were a court of appeal that could correct democratic excesses. The solution to the problems of democracy was more democracy not less.[27]

But all this presupposes a capacity for independent judgment Socrates thinks problematic in contemporary Athenian practice. If the demands of democratic citizenship are to be honored, the people must think about what they are doing, and if they do not, democracy cannot be defended. This is not so much a rejection of radical democracy as an argument about the kind of culture and intelligence it requires. Socrates may well be faulted for his intellectualism, and it may be true that his demanding ideas of democratic citizenship can too easily become (as perhaps it did for Plato) an indictment of democracy's possibility. But I do not think this makes Socrates anti-democratic, nor, more importantly, that his idea of thoughtfulness is any the less crucial for the education of contemporary democratic citizens.

My third example of a radically democratic practice philosophized by Socrates and Plato is drama. The "war" between poetry and philosophy has become a staple of Platonic criticism. But I think the relationship is more complicated because I think philosophy and drama analogous projects, and because I think "the philosopher," in this case Plato's Socrates (and perhaps Plato himself), drew on precisely the history and sentiments of Athenian intellectual culture represented in drama.

Few people think of drama as a public institution and democratic practice as the Athenians did. In Athens, drama was performed in public, by the public, and concentrated on public issues and themes, ranging from particular political actions, such as challenging Spartan hegemony in Greece or assuming an empire, to more structural considerations, such as the dominance of city over household and the democratization of power. Tragedy in particular "problematized" the cultural accommodations and social inequalities upon which the democracy rested. It did this not only by dramatizing the fate of "marginalized" groups but by its inclusion of women and perhaps slaves in the audience in contrast to their exclusion in conventionally defined political institutions.[28] In making the half-invisible particulars of everyday life visible as a form of life, by putting the actions of a democracy on stage before the citizenry who had decided upon them, tragedy provided a time and place to interrogate the forms, practices, and boundaries that defined the *polis*. Moreover, the wisdom provided by the experience of theater justified reliance on selection by lot and rotation in office, which presumed that ordinary men were capable of responsibly exercising power. The theatrical distance from the moment of decision provided a more "theoretical" understanding of events than was possible in the Assembly, Council, or courts. Given all this, it is not surprising that the Greek word *didaskalia* means both teaching and education as well as rehearsing a play.

Comedy did something similar by pilloring the most powerful intellectual and political figures in the community, such as Kleon and Socrates, much as the latter did in more subdued ways in the *Apology*.[29] Together with tragedy, comedy comprised a democratic tradition of self-reflection and self-criticism, one that Socrates could rely on as a shared cultural experience.

5

Even if the argument about the connections between Athenian democracy and Socratic political philosophy is persuasive, of what possible interest and use is it for understanding the contemporary connections between radical democracy and philosophy? Clearly it cannot be a matter of application or prescriptions. Rather, it is a matter of introducing another voice into the conversations opened up by the collapse of communism and the disarray of Marxism. It is a voice less concerned with conclusions and decisions than with provocations, though the need is recognized for theorists to address political practice, and concrete implications do result from asking questions.

This voice is used to ask three questions. The first is, what difference would it make for how we think and what we do as academics, teachers, and citizens if we took Socrates, as portrayed here, as a model of a philosopher/citizen in a democracy? Socrates seeks to promote the independent judgment of his fellow citizens as a necessary condition for the success of radical democracy. Citizens could and should be able to speak freely and effectively to power and exercise it responsibly themselves. They should know how to give an account of their lives, why and how to demand such accounts from cultural and political elites, and, what is perhaps more essential, know why they must hold each other to account.

If we took Socrates seriously as a teacher, citizen, and philosopher, we might need to be more willing to venture into the streets of our cities, if not literally then metaphorically, engaging in arguments and conversations with our fellow citizens about the shared responsibilities of power in a language they understand. Only then could we be students of our students and so be better teachers of them. Speaking in a less technical language (a language we use even as we critique the invasion of technique into "the life world") could ground our arguments. Aristophanes illustrates this practice in a caricature of Socrates sitting high up in a basket studying the heavens, while his students with their behinds in the air and noses on the ground take a double major in astronomy and geology.

If we take Socrates seriously, political education in a democracy must be done democratically. It is this problem that worries Walzer when he warns that philosophers have no special privileges in a democratic polity and leads Hannah Arendt to insist that "political education" is a dangerous conflation of activities and forms of authority.[30] While education implies a hierarchy between teacher and student or parent and teacher, politics presupposes the equality of political adults. This is a useful warning against vanguardism and the pretensions of what Foucault calls "general intellectuals."[31] But it is not conclusive if democratic political education is done democratically, if it is democratic in text and subtext, in substance and process. For Socrates, that requires "genuine" dialogue rather than a covert monologue. But since dialogues involve complex negotiations of power at the moment of a dialogue's establishment and re-negotiations thereafter, "real" dialogue is only possible when philosophers converse with and are part of an activist citizenry able to talk freely to power because it exercises it and understands its dynamics.

The second question asks, what is involved if we take this (very selective) portrait of Athenian democracy seriously? One thing we might recognize is people doing familiar things differently; another is that the institutional arrangements, practices, and arguments we label democratic, Athenians would label oligarchic. Unlike virtually all of Western history when democracy was a term of abuse, everyone in our time claims to be a democrat and every nation claims to be a democracy. Yet at the same time democracy has emerged as the criteria of legitimacy; John Dunn calls it "the moral Esperanto of the present nation-state system."[32] It is devalued in practice or so attenuated in theory as to be unrecognizable as a distinctive form of politics and culture. Thus one powerful theoretical tradition continues to follow Schumpeter in regarding democracy as the least bad mechanism for assuring a minimum accountability of the rulers to the ruled. In these terms, a nation is democratic if political parties compete for votes as corporations do for buyers. What matters is not what rulers do with the power they get through periodic elections, but the way they acquire it in the first place.[33] This "democratic revisionism," as it was called, points to a truth more obvious now than in 1943, when Schumpeter wrote *Capitalism, Socialism, and Democracy*. It is even more apparent now than in the early 1960s when a number of American political scientists took over some of Schumpeter's specific arguments and most of his attitude toward democratic politics: that the very nature of the modern state precludes more than token accountability,[34] involves a minimalist commitment to political equality, and is actively opposed to the dispersal of power and responsibility.

Even if the state is too dependent upon bureaucracy and routinization, too reliant upon professional expertise, too defined by centralized power, and too easily coopted by elites intent on minimizing citizen participation except as a mode of legitimation, we cannot ignore the state or be indifferent to the moments and places in which it can be democratized. On the level of the nation-state, liberal values, institutions, and procedures have a crucial role insofar as they restrain the state from usurping or monopolizing public spaces and speech. We must be cautiously and skeptically attentive to the state and to the common good it proclaims as long as it both frames civil society and occupies a space within it, as long as it has a role in fixing the boundaries and conditions and is the basis of rules of how its citizens associate.[35]

But if we value radical democracy, if we value mutual accountability, political equality, responsibility, and lawfulness, if we value politically educated citizens, we must look below the state level in order to find ways and places to maximize the democratization of power. There is a shared sense that the state will not do and is not doing what needs to be done, whether it be the politics of everyday life described by Michnik in his *Letters from Prison*; feminist concerns with the play of power in families, private life, and definitions of gender and sexuality; Habermasian concerns with civil society; or "communitarian" concern with localism or post-modernist redefinitions of agency and sites of resistance. The state is both too small to deal with international capitalism and potential environmental disasters and too large to provide the opportunities for radical democracy. In such a context, democratic Athens may be a useful interlocutor.

The third question concerns the connection between radical democracy and radicalizing theory. To insist that Socratic political philosophy, as we see or hear about it in the *Apology*, and Athenian radical democracy are part of the same discourse raises a general question about the connection between ways of knowing, definitions of who the knowers are and how they can be recognized on the one hand, and of the world they constitute as knowable and seek to know on the other. More specifically, it raises the contemporary question about the relationship between the bureaucratic state, technological society, and academic discourse as exemplified by political theory and philosophy. A theory that adopts the same notion of rationality as the structure it studies helps that structure operate rather than effects a theoretical distance from it. Using or imitating the entrenched language of power and authority to study democratic politics may well reify that authority and power while muting the very possibility of radical critique.[36] The 1976 Report to the Trilateral Commission implicitly acknowledged these connections when it linked an "adversary culture" created by "value-oriented intellectuals," critiques of authority and power, suspicion of rationality, and the dangers of overeducation to the rise of democratic activism.

Socrates used entrenched language against entrenched power by elaborating democratic practices into a challenge to democracy's own ideological hegemony. He did this in the service of democracy even where he criticized it, which is one reason why he can claim that his calling people to account is a sign of his patriotism. His way of doing philosophy was grounded in history and sentiment, but it was a democratic history and sentiment. It was this history and sentiment that provided impetus and substance to his radical claim that the unexamined life was not worth living. If his contemporaries had regarded such a claim as simply absurd or unintelligible he could not have caused the trouble he did, and they, in turn, would have had no reason to silence him. It was because they could recognize the power in his imperative and had to confront the disparity his questioning provoked between how they lived and how they liked to see themselves as living that they found him so annoying.[37]

On the one hand, Socrates's insistence that we "think" and be thoughtful seems vague and thin. After all, this radical thinker never directly challenged the subordinate status of women or the existence of slaves, never offered a structural analysis of class (as Aristotle did), and never recognized the force of what we would call material conditions.[38] But on the other hand, his supposition—implied by his being in the streets talking to all he met, especially his fellow citizens—that philosophical reflection should be an aspect of democratic citizenship, is too intellectualist, too close to turning the *agora* into a classroom, too moralistic and insufficiently political. Indeed his refusal to participate in the assembly may represent a recognition that philosophical dialogue has no place in political debates where action must be the outcome. But the *agora* is a public space and so Socrates is engaged in public discourse even if it is not political debate narrowly understood.[39] Perhaps the analogy here is with the way citizens brought the experience of theater to the deliberations of the assembly and the experience of sharing power in the assembly, courts, and councils to the theater. Perhaps that is what Socrates hoped: that people would bring the critical thoughtfulness and independence philosophy makes possible to their politics. It is not that every citizen should be a philosopher, a prescription certain to generate tragedy and comedy, but that every citizen be capable of having philosophical moments where the parochialism of commitments that might otherwise be necessary for living an historically rooted life become problematic.

In the end Socrates does not offer a theory of democracy but the possibility of democratic theorizing or philosophizing. If this approach appears too thin or too demanding, and the political education necessary for it too involved and time consuming to constitute it as a way of improving democracy, it may be impossible to consider the alternative.

NOTES

1. "'More Humility, Fewer Illusions'—A talk between Adam Michnik and Jürgen Habermas," *The New York Review of Books*, 24 March, 1994, 26. See the debate around Stanley Aronowitz's "The Situation of the Left in the United States," in *The Socialist Review* issue on *Radical Democracy*, vol. 23, no. 3 (1994). See especially Aronowitz's definition of radical democracy, 268.

2. This argument is made by Jean L. Cohen and Andrew Arato in *Civil Society and Political Theory* (Cambridge, MA: MIT Press, 1992).

3. In the Introduction of Chantal Mouffe, ed., *Dimensions of Radical Democracy* (London and New York: Verso, 1992), 5. This book represents an exception to my generalization (though by no means all the essays in it are sympathetic to what I am calling radical democracy). See also the concluding chapter (written with Ernesto Laclau) of Chantal Mouffe's *Hegemony and Socialist Strategy: Towards a Radical Democratic Politics* (London and New York: Verso, 1985).

4. For the democratic potential of rights, see Mouffe's essay, "Democratic Citizenship and the Political Community," in her *Dimensions of Radical Democracy*, especially 226–27. For why a vigorous civic culture is necessary for rights to do what liberals want them to, see Steven Lukes's discussion of "the third dimension of power" in his *Power: A Radical View* (London: Macmillan, 1974).

5. See Sheldon S. Wolin, "What Revolutionary Action Means Today," in *Democracy* (Fall 1982): 17, 28.

6. Cornelius Castoriadis, "The Greek Polis and the Creation of Democracy,"

in *Philosophy, Politics, Autonomy*, ed. David Ames Curtis (New York: Oxford University Press, 1991), 115, 116.

7. For the critique, see Wolin, "Revolutionary Action Now." For the way that critique inverts the evolution of Athenian democracy, see Jean-Pierre Vernant, *The Origins of Greek Thought* (Ithaca, NY: Cornell University Press, 1982), 47–48, 51–52.

8. I am of course aware of the irony of arguing that there is an affinity between Socrates and the city that killed him (despite his claim that what he did and demanded was of the greatest benefit to its democracy). But there is another side to the story of Socrates's death and the hostility between philosophy and democracy it is thought to conclusively demonstrate. There is evidence (in the *Apology* and *Crito*) that Socrates provoked his trial and punishment, that he was surprised by the closeness of the vote given his provocations, and that he refused exile and fleeing because he wanted to continue challenging the Athenians after his death as he had done in his life. I have argued this at length in Chapter 7 of *The Tragedy of Political Theory* (Princeton, NJ: Princeton University Press, 1990).

9. Rousseau is an obvious though contested candidate, and George Kateb has made a powerful and ingenious case for Emerson in *The Inner Ocean*. As John Dunn points out, the articulation of a democratic theoretical vision emerged along with the suspicion that such a life might be impossible in practice. See his *Western Political Theory in the Face of the Future* (New York: Cambridge University Press, 1993), 192.

10. Douglas Lummis, "The Radicalism of Democracy in Democracy," (Fall 1982): 12. He goes on: "If you are going to give power to the philosophers, the Prince, the elected, or to the party central committee, you have to explain why. In the case of placing power with the people, no such argument is required. An explanation may be required of why such a situation will be safe, efficient, lasting, or a source of wise decisions, but not why it is legitimate."

11. In Sheldon Wolin, "Norm and Form" and "The Constitutionalizing of Democracy," in Euben, Wallach, and Ober, *Athenian Political Thought and the Reconstitution of American Democracy* (Ithaca: Cornell University Press, 1994).

12. It is, of course, a relentlessly theoretical critique of theory.

13. This is one reason to be suspicious of the American conservative agenda of re-creating students like those supposedly deferential ones of the 1950s or the radical agenda of creating the new politically correct ones of the 1990s.

14. Claude Lefort, *Democracy and Political Theory* (Minneapolis: University of Minnesota Press, 1988), 16.

15. I do not want to exaggerate. It is not clear how much difference this tradition meant for concrete political action; how much things changed because of it. Interrogating one's cultural accommodations or established hierarchies does not mean you will modify let alone dismantle them. One could even argue that by providing a controlled release of such problematizing, institutions like drama did the opposite. For a number of reasons I do not think this the case, but the evidence is not conclusive.

16. Walzer's argument appears in "Philosophy and Democracy," in *What Should Political Theory Be Now?*, ed. John S. Nelson (Albany: SUNY Press, 1983), 75–99.

17. Walzer, "Philosophy and Democracy," 79.

18. I mean "thoughtful" in the way Hannah Arendt does in her discussion of Eichmann in *Jerusalem: A Report on the Banality of Evil*, revised and enlarged edition (New York: Viking Press, 1964) and in her later reflections on

Eichmann in *Thinking*, Volume I of *The Life of the Mind* (London: Secker and Warburg, 1978), 3–5.

19. In the end I do not think this distinction sustainable for Socrates or in general.

20. The fullest ancient account of the preliminary scrutiny is in Aristotle's Ath, Pol 55–59. For two different views of its range and significance see Mogen Herman Hansen, *The Athenian Democracy in the Age of Demosthenes* (Oxford: Basil Blackwell, 1991), 218–224 (which includes a discussion of the *euthu nai*) and R. K. Sinclair, *Democracy and Participation in Athens* (Cambridge: Cambridge University Press, 1988), 77–78. As usual the most encyclopedic consideration can be found in Martin Ostwald, *From Popular Sovereignty to the Sovereignty of Law* (Berkeley and Los Angeles: University of California Press), 43–51.

21. On *euthu nai*, see Ostwald, *From Popular Sovereignty,* 12–13, 55–60, 71–78; Sinclair, *Democracy and Participation in Athens,* 72–79, 174–75; Hansen and Jean Pierre Vernant, *The Origins of Greek Thought,* 51–52.

22. See the discussion in Chapters 3 and 4 of Vernant.

23. The phrase Socrates uses, *logon didonai*, means to "give an account" in a technical sense of rending a financial account or audit. So when in the *Apology* Socrates tries to shame the Athenians for caring more for their wealth than for their soul, the philosophical co-optation of such a material, technical term was a profound challenge and expansion.

24. His argument suggests that radical critics of democracy have special obligations to the city they criticize; that his deference here (he literally calls himself a slave to the laws) has everything to do with his refusal (in the *Apology*) to accept silencing even when enjoined by law.

25. But there were severe limits on what sort of social and economic inequalities were allowable (for citizens). These limits were ideological, as Ober has argued in *Mass and Elites in Democratic Athens: Rhetoric, Ideology, and the Power of the People* (Princeton: Princeton University Press, 1989), as well as economic (the responsibilities for outfitting triremes, producing plays, etc.). Ober argues that democratic ideology mediated the reality of social inequalities and the goal of political equality, thus arbitrating class tensions that would otherwise have led to destructive civil wars.

26. See the discussion in Dunn, *Western Political Theory in the Face of the Future*, Chapter 1.

27. See the discussion in Castoriadis, 116–17. Consistent with his view of democracy as aggressively anti-institutional, Wolin regards such practices as anti-democratic. See "Norm and Form," in Euben, Wallach, and Ober, *Athenian Political Thought.*

28. I have made the argument that tragedy is a political institution in my *Introduction to Greek Tragedy and Political Theory* (Berkeley and Los Angeles: University of California Press, 1986), and Chapter II of *The Tragedy of Political Theory.*

29. Comedy also presented "structural" challenges to the democracy within which it was institutionalized. In the play *Women in the Assembly*, Aristophanes asks whether Athenian women could be constituted male if the supposedly all-powerful Assembly voted for it. If the *demos* could constitute political realities by legal enactment, could they also "deconstruct" the natural world in which men alone were empowered political agents? What was the limit to human power and what was the status of "natural"? See Ober, "How to Criticize Democracy in Late 5th and Early 6th Century Athens," in Euben, Wallach, and Ober, *Athenian Political Thought.*

30. Hannah Arendt, "The Crisis in Education," in *Between Past and Future: Eight Exercises in Political Thought* (New York: Penguin Books, 1983).

31. See "Intellectuals and Power: A Conversation between Michel Foucault and Gilles Deleuze," in *Language, Counter-Memory, Practice: Selected Essays and Interviews by Michel Foucault*, ed. Donald F. Bouchard (Ithaca: Cornell University Press, 1977), 205, 217.

32. Dunn, *Western Political Theory*, 2.

33. See Joseph Schumpeter, *Capitalism, Socialism and Democracy* (London: Allen and Unwin, 1943), and Dunn, *Western Political Theory*, 26.

34. As part of what she calls an "immanent critique" of liberalism, Mouffe urges that radical democrats not proclaim "the ideological and illusory character of so-called 'formal bourgeois democracy,'" but take liberal principles literally, thereby forcing "liberal democratic societies to be accountable for their professed ideals" (*Dimensions of Radical Democracy*, 2). But accountable to whom and in what ways? If liberalism promotes a citizenry unable to hold others accountable or indifferent to the need, it is not clear what the argument means.

35. This is Michael Walzer's argument in "The Civil Society Argument," in *Dimensions of Radical Democracy*, 89, 107. The theoretical scaffolding for his argument here appears in *Spheres of Justice: A Defense of Pluralism and Equality* (New York: Oxford University Press, 1983).

36. Michael Shapiro, "Politicizing Ulysses: Rationalistic, Critical and Genealogical Commentaries," in *Reading the Postmodern Polity: Political Theory as Textual Practice* (Minneapolis: University of Minnesota Press), 29.

37. So, in the *Apology*, Socrates contrasts the Athenian self-presentation as a free people and their expectation that defendants grovel before juries at their trial.

38. Even worse, he has been accused (by I. F. Stone for one) of being a proto-oligarch partly responsible for the right-wing coups of 411 and 404 BCE. But Socrates did offer a critique of imperialism and the hyper-masculinism of the heroic ethic and, depending upon how one reads dialogues like the *Meno*, *Symposium*, and *Republic*, thought slaves could think, women were the greatest teachers of *eros*, and women could rule. Finally, the evidence for Socrates's responsibility for the conservative reaction is problematic at best, and Stone's reading of the dialogues as evidence for it is painfully literal-minded.

39. As Havel, Michnik, and other dissidents have argued, under a corrupt regime politics goes on outside the realm of the state.

2

DEBATING RADICAL POLITICS IN THE UNITED STATES

6

TOWARDS RADICALISM

THE DEATH AND REBIRTH OF THE AMERICAN LEFT

PROLOGUE

CHICAGO TRIBUNE EDITORIAL WRITER CLARENCE PAGE
stated the obvious on NPR's *Weekend Edition* for December
11, 1994 that many of the slogans and programs of the
Republican midterm election victory, such as the empowering of people to take control over their own lives, were
borrowed from the 1960s left. Since the 1960s, as the left
moved toward statism and became virtually identical with the
Great Society, the conservatives have captured the ideological
spaces of freedom, localism, and individual liberty. The main
thesis of this chapter is that the disaster visited upon the left
over the past two decades is a product not of the rejection of its
broad social, political, and economic agenda, but the result of the
left's betrayal of its own ideology and program.

Bill Clinton rode to office because of a split in conservative
ranks. This victory was helped along by Ross Perot who ran as an
independent conservative committed to reversing the fifty-year-old

STANLEY ARONOWITZ

bipartisan foreign policy and siphoned off enough of the vote to defeat George Bush, the quintessential internationalist. Clinton also benefitted from the division between the Christian right and mainstream Republicans who despite their rhetorical obedience to the right's social views were less than enthusiastic about repealing abortion rights and blocking gay and lesbian rights. Clinton won with a plurality, 43% of the vote, somewhat more than the remainder of the Democrats' traditional liberal constituency. Apart from personality glitches (most of which concern the extent to which he remains, in his odd way, a child of the sixties), Clinton was able to fulfill many of his budget and deficit reduction promises in the first two years of his presidency but could not fulfill his social agenda to end discrimination against gays and lesbians in the military, or to enact a universal health care plan. The abject failure of the health plan in the Democratic 93rd Congress was, undoubtedly, Clinton's most dramatic defeat and undermined the viability of his administration.

The administration claimed to have improved United States economic performance. Gross Domestic Product began to significantly increase in late 1993, and new jobs were generated. But most voters did not give Clinton credit for the economic upturn because it did not alleviate the general perception that any improvements were, at best, only temporary. In 1994, the Democrats lost control of Congress because the first Democratic administration in twelve years failed to lower popular anxieties concerning the future. Everyone knew that the new jobs were lousy and that even in the midst of "recovery," thousands of good jobs were being eliminated every week by technological changes, mergers, acquisitions, and plant closings.

As much as the neo-liberals, the popular left representing unions, ecology, black freedom, and women's movements, was decisively beaten in the mid-term elections, this essay will argue that this is the culmination of a trend that began in the late 1960s. One of its salient features is the extent to which New Left critiques of the social welfare state have become staples of right-wing rhetoric. The early New Left harbored both anarchistic and Jeffersonian impulses. In the name of participatory democracy, the New Left excoriated welfare bureaucracies for encouraging dependency; demanded decentralization and democratization of government services through community control of the police and other institutions ostensibly serving poor people; and attacked the modern multiversity for massifying education and the public schools for miseducating children. In the wake of the left's abandonment of these ideas, conservatives have been pleased to appropriate them, just as the left's critique of liberal democracy became grist for fascism's ideological mill in the 1920s and 1930s. Once again, we can observe a frontal assault on representative institutions in United States politics. The right's successful use of the referendum and initiative—a democratic reform of the early twentieth century—is a symptom of a new crisis of the liberal state.[1] As before, the widespread support for direct voter preferences on public issues signifies a deep distrust of the permanent government—this time held by Democrats, but earlier a Republican monopoly.

Many of these initiatives have concerned tax policy. Since the late 1970s, voters have generally approved propositions that would set spending limits and restrict legislative taxing powers. After World War II, it was the labor movement and other organizations of the popular left that complained about the tax burden on working people. Their criticisms were ultimately muted by the cold war, when military expenditures became an important element of prosperity, including a relatively painless conversion to "peacetime" production. Of course, in contradistinction to the right libertarians who, in recent years, have called for the abolition of the income tax, social justice movements have traditionally sought to eliminate or sharply curtail regressive taxes, such as those on real estate and retail sales, and make the income tax more progressive, that is, make taxes a mechanism for redistributive justice. As rightist attacks on the social wage have intensified since the 1980s, the left has felt obliged to defend even its most regressive features, such as the existing tax structure, bond issues to improve education, and the welfare system. This reversal makes the left appear to be establishmentarian, a posture that fuels the paradoxical image of conservatism as a rebellion against the status quo.

The decline of the left in United States politics is also linked to international developments, particularly in Europe where a wave of economic liberalism, nationalism, and ideological conservatism has resulted in defeats for the left parties of governments. Even when, after communism's collapse, socialists win elections in Eastern Europe as well as western Europe, they are increasingly unable to deliver even the most modest social gains, let alone anything approaching full employment, a staple of the stalinist regime.

The situation in the United States is characterized by the depth of the decline of proto-social-democratic reformism, the virulence of anti-immigrant nationalism, and the left's defensive even if somewhat successful struggle over the social issues of abortion and sexual freedom. In the new global environment, the capitalist democratic state is simply incapable of delivering much except its own demise. Many believe the more it spends of their money, the worse it gets. Perhaps the most sweeping of right wing ideological successes was to have pitted the traditional working class, itself in the process of decomposition and recomposition, against the poor. Contrary to overwhelming evidence that most of the poor are employed, many believe that poverty is linked exclusively to joblessness. And there is some suspicion that the major beneficiary of big government is not big business, but those on the public payroll and its putative welfare clients. The left has offered neither a plausible explanation for this perception nor has it persuaded most people that simply fighting harder for the same old things will change circumstances. Even where the social justice agenda has some popular base, many of its constituents, with the outstanding exception of pensioners, have lost hope that anything can be done.[2] The ebbing of hope, perhaps more than any other factor, accounts for the relative ease with which both Democrats and Republicans have dismantled the welfare state.

1

In our collective penchant for periodization, some writers have ascribed the new epoch of simultaneous capitalist global economic hegemony and right-wing political ascendancy to the collapse of Communism after 1989. Indeed, from the perspective of the post-colonial countries, for instance, the disappearance of the Soviet Union has been a near disaster. Since the cold war is no longer the defining framework of international relations, most states wishing to enter the path of industrial development have no alternative but to seek American approbation in order to obtain funds from the World Bank.

But this scenario does not explain the *conditions of possibility* for the current state of affairs. While it may seem excessive to declare a single event responsible for epochal shifts, there is considerable evidence that the world-wide recession, which began in 1973, was signalled by consumer gas shortages and followed by the dramatic rise of oil prices.[3] This event was itself prepared for by a series of developments, particularly the early signs of global economic restructuration through transnational corporations and the growing American dominance of commodity and capital markets worldwide. Under these conditions, the politics of hope represented, however incompletely, by the liberal wing of the Democratic Party gave way to a new, cynical politics of decline led by the right.[4] In this new political environment, both political parties share the same vision, differing only on the *means* to impose austerity on a recalcitrant population.[5] Of course, in the game of austerity budgets, the Democrats in America and the Socialists and the Laborites in Europe are always at a disadvantage; if voters are prepared to buy the deal of less social welfare and more state repression, they would rather support the real thing. While the electoral left parties are absolutely necessary as instruments of persuasion, their ability to ruthlessly follow through is constrained by the inevitable refusal of large fractions of their constituency to go along with austerity indefinitely, especially reductions of the social wage.[6]

The landslide re-election of Richard Nixon in 1972 against challenger George McGovern and the election of Margaret Thatcher seven years later in the United Kingdom mark a new era of what can be described as post-keynesian, post-welfare, ideological politics. In contrast to the consensus conservative and liberal/social-democratic governments of the immediate post-war period where class conflict, however fierce, was successfully contained within a fairly narrow spectrum of issues, the last two decades of openly rightist government policies have witnessed precisely that which has always been denied by progressive reason: the recurrence of economic liberalism in which the poor—native born as well as immigrants—are subject to a series of repressive measures based on high moral strictures. Chief among these measures is that the rule of law and hard work are universal obligations; in the Anglo-American world, many of the hard won gains of labor were rolled back under the slogan of making industry "competitive." Those prone to resist these measures are labeled spoilers by the forces of the new world economic (dis)order who remind us that "realism" dictates compromise and retreat. And, perhaps in utter despair, a considerable fraction of trade union and social movement leaderships have surrendered to realism as their last, best chance to survive (at least in the short run).[7]

In contrast to the prior regime of regulation with its fordist labor relations, some writers, notably Lash and Urry and Claus Offe have named this the era of "disorganized" capitalism.[8] Although the distinction may be overly schematic, there can be no dispute that many of the main features of the post-war state interventions have been dismantled. These include business-oriented regulation policies of banks, government subsidies for smaller business investment through lower interest rates, and substantial public investments in education and training. In the United States, environmental and occupational health and safety regulation remains largely intact, except for enforcement, a ploy which, to a large degree, effectively nullifies the law.

And, of course, the religion of free trade reigns. The successful conclusion of GATT and NAFTA negotiations signal the erosion of the remnant of commodity quotas and other economic protections supported by national capital and the labor movement. Once confined to low-technology industries such as textiles and apparel, the war of labor against itself has been re-introduced on a global scale. The virtual end of protectionism will hurt workers in the most industrially developed countries for a time, but in the long run these agreements are likely to close the gap between the rich and poor nations, possibly leading to the first truly international workers movement(s).

These dramatic changes may be understood in terms of the end of a long cycle that definitively ended sometime in the late 1960s, especially when it became clear that the Vietnam War would end, thereby lifting the mask from the state's already festering legitimation crisis. In the context, the war was a detour of developments that could have surfaced much earlier. In nearly every year since 1973, there has been a drop in real wages, even as family income rose, largely due to the entrance of millions of women into the low-wage service sector but also to the weakness of the United States labor movement. There is a growing trend toward part-time, contingent jobs leading, in the phrase coined by economic experts, to the proliferation of "disposable" workers. The working poor expands as sections of the most stable fractions of the working class, now displaced from the old monopoly-sector production industries, compete for low-wage and seasonal employment. This pushes the working poor further down or entirely out of the paid labor force.

Everywhere in the world, governments—Communist no less than others—scramble to sell state-owned enterprises and remove regulations such as labor and health codes, trade restrictions and taxes, but defend crushing or marginalizing dissent on the ground that such liberties may endanger the investment climate. The Russian government has gone so far as to auction its awesome physics and biology establishment to private investors, thus insuring that its future as an independent state will be compromised. Meanwhile, after three years of the new capitalist freedom, the recent electoral victories of the former communists—some of which have formed nationalist blocs and others, democratic socialist parties—attest to the loyalty that large sections of the population retain for the most desirable features of state socialist regimes: the provision of health, education, and income guarantees. Yet, even where the social justice left comes to power as in Poland and Hungary, it is not clear that it can restore job and income guarantees or even free health care and education, especially in the wake of the utter economic destruction these countries suffered and their eagerness, despite all, to lure foreign capital.

Concomitant with the political and economic transformations, we can observe profound discursive shifts under the sign of changed social and economic *perception*. In many countries there is no principled validation of public goods, except on ecological grounds. On the contrary, the watchword of public policy is to manage the terms of privatization. Responding to the general business demands for reduced government spending to balance the budget and thereby release capital for private investment, social darwinist discourse in education and health has risen sharply in the United States. Since the dominant view is that there is too much government, many now believe that infusions of money for badly deteriorating public schools, public hospitals, and other health services for the poor is simply a bad investment. According to current conservative wisdom, if the poor are genetically or culturally incapable of acquiring "cognitive" skills, why waste taxpayers' money on schooling? (Taxpayers are always a code for the middle class property owner.) Hence the overwhelming tendency, especially in cities with substantial black, latino, and Asian populations, to fulfill tax reduction and budget balancing mandates by radically cutting school budgets, thereby reducing the classroom to an aging vat. As Jerry Watts argues, the real meaning of the recent intelligence controversy raised by Richard Herrnstein and Charles Murray's *The Bell Curve* is the impetus to naturalize black oppression by denying their victim status.[9] In this analysis, the question is not one of equality; the issue is whether the larger society retains the institutional responsibility to deal with racism.

If this concatenation between the larger right-wing political agenda, economic restructuration, and the reappearance of the discourse of social darwinism is too functionalist for dialectical taste, one can ascribe the link to conjuncture, elective affinity, or even coincidence. Yet, we are entitled to suspect there is more than an accidental connection between the brutal attack on urban services and the rise of new "scientific evidence" of black inferiority. From Allan Bloom's *Closing of the American Mind* to *The Bell Curve* we have witnessed no end of racialized rationalizations for dumping the cities. As always, the liberals drag out science to refute arguments whose scientific fallibility is beside the point. As always, a public seared with insecurity and fear is not prone to be confused by "facts."

Given the ideological and political weakness of the labor movement and the shaky post-war social compact in the United States, breaking an agreement according to which workers gave their unflagging loyalty to American capitalism and its international policies in return for a corporatist version of the social welfare state was a relatively easy task. The strategy, whether explicit or not, was to conquer the intellectual terrain by establishing a new common sense. In addition to reviving ideologies that legitimate inequality, there developed a "new" economic wisdom. This entailed the simultaneous attack on Keynesianism, the prevailing economic doctrine of the regulation era. Discrediting the idea of government interventionism was combined with reasserting monetarism and with a spruced-up version of the once derided smithian doctrine of market-driven social and economic policy.

Henceforth, state intervention was to be confined to measures such as regulating interest rates and the money supply—steering mechanisms, which economists believe are both relatively weak intrusions but reduce the threat of inflation (read reduce wage increases). Under most circumstances, government investment, either in production or in the social wage, is strictly eschewed as an unwarranted interference with free trade in labor and goods. Theoretically, the doctrine opposes social welfare, including social security, except as a voluntary private insurance program. Minimum wages and maximum hours legislation are said to restrain free markets and especially discourage investment and employers from hiring workers, and nearly all forms of business regulation are rejected on the same grounds.

The new mantra of economic policy is that growth depends on limiting public services to the bare essentials and reducing and balancing government budgets, even through a constitutional amendment. Once consigned to the precincts of light entertainment, the so-called "Chicago school," whose theories and prescriptions during the regulation era were taken almost as seriously as those of the marxists, suddenly grabbed the spotlight. Milton Friedman and his accolytes were regular guests on news and public affairs television, and by the early 1970s, their views rapidly occupied the political mainstream. Friedman's conflation of capitalism with freedom and socialism with totalitarianism while by no means new became the veritable slogan of economists and policy-makers regardless of party.

The obligation to provide full employment no longer governs state policy. In fact, in an environment where social protest has been effectively contained or channeled into "apathy" and all major commodities must compete on a global scale, full employment is no longer considered desirable by many economists and policy-makers, because, they argue, it tends to produce inflationary pressures by raising wages, reducing profits, and bridling investment.[10]

The fundamental commitment of the Clinton administration, like Jimmy Carter's in the late 1970s, to the neo-classical paradigm helps explain why, in addition to the palpable erosion of national economic sovereignty and despite Democratic congressional majorities, neither presidency was able to extend the social welfare state. Assuming good faith, the problem for the "new" Democrats is that since they are sincerely persuaded that every increment in government intervention must justify itself in fiscal and market terms, they have rigorously excluded any *decommodified* health, welfare, or labor policy. Consequently, in response to the soaring costs and diminishing coverage offered by existing private health care plans, the administration refused to propose a plan patterned after those of Canada, Britain, or France in which the government is the sole insurer. Rather, in true neo-classical fashion the Clintons placed universal health care squarely in the hands of the private health insurance industry. In order to achieve cost containment, the ostensible chief goal, Clinton also proposed to regulate prices by establishing a schedule of benefits and allowable fees calibrated to employer- and individual-paid premiums.

The plan was incoherent because the regulation feature violated the principle of market-driven programs. The question could be raised:

if Clinton was sensitive to the market, why did he re-impose regulation? Hesitant to criticize Clinton's flawed approach, the left put forth its own "Canadian-style" plan without taking it seriously. For, in order to advance decommodified health care it would have had to decimate, intellectually as well as politically, the illogicality of the Clinton proposal. Since the left remains tied to even this frail, ideologically compromised shell of a liberal regime, its own position was drowned out in the debate as the Clinton plan bit the dust.

The second element of the discursive reaction is to tar Clinton with the brush of the 1960s counterculture. The Christian and conventional Right have claimed that Clinton is really a cultural radical—in House Speaker Newt Gingrich's felicitous phrase, a "countercultural McGovernik"—hiding behind a human rights veneer. While, at the policy level, Clinton's debt to the counterculture is fairly obscure, his earlier history of anti-war protest, but even more his iconography (a love for rock and roll; openness to lesbian and gay rights; his nomination and betrayal of two black women, Lani Guinier and Joycelyn Elders; and so on) belie his New Democrat self-presentation. As his retreat from the campaign pledge to end military discrimination against gays clearly revealed, Clinton was unable to sustain, beyond support for abortion, any of the precepts of social liberalism. Included in this is his open-throated support for some of the draconian measures of the Crime Bill, especially the pledge to build more prisons and extend the death penalty. Yet, these overt indications of conservatism did not succeed in washing away the lingering conservative or liberal doubt concerning the President's "true" motives. The absence of a *public discourse* in defense of substantive social and cultural freedom provided the Right with an open field to shape the debate.

Despite considerable public support for abortion and sexual freedom, the social liberals and radicals have plainly lost the initiative by trying to wrap themselves in family values and presenting their socially liberal views in terms of human rights. It would be difficult to find a single pro-sexual freedom politician or feminist activist. Speaking an ACLU-type rhetoric, they have backed away from the political and cultural perspectives of early feminism and the counterculture that vigorously promoted sexual freedom; on the contrary, many intellectuals and activists are apologetic and defensive about their own erstwhile involvement or sympathy with cultural radical movements. Many feminists and gay and lesbian activists are silent in the wake of Clinton's retreats. Given the fragility of the administration, they have been unwilling to add comfort to the right's attacks. Since there is neither intellectual nor organizational energy for building a new political force, the social and cultural radicals, no less than the social justice left, is largely unarmed.

Finally, the labor movement and other elements of the social justice left have been unable to stem the hemorrhaging of the traditional social wage, let alone defend collective bargaining and labor's right to organize. The exceptions indicate a new direction, especially the dramatic General Motors strike of 1994 in Flint, Michigan when in protest against forced overtime workers demanded and won new hiring. This policy subsequently spread to many of the company's plants after more General Motors workers decided that "they had to have a life" and could no longer tolerate 60–70 hour work weeks. The locus of the fight in the late 1990s is likely to shift from the national state to the corporations and to the *local* state. Unions could have offered more resistance throughout the 1980s to employer demands for concessions and might have forged an offensive legislative strategy only if they were prepared to break with the Democratic Party's increasingly conservative direction. Fearing isolation and even more profound defeats, union leadership muted its most redistributive demands, but lost anyway because most unions have ceased to be *movements* but operate as insurance companies and law firms.

These factors point to one crucial element that may help explain the left's decline. Put simply, the left—both its popular and its ideological wings—was nearly completely integrated into the regulatory era. Far from offering an alternative, much less opposition to the New Deal and its successors, the social-democratic and communist lefts were products of this era in their style of organization, the ambivalence of their social and political loyalties, and particularly in their public discourse. For most of the twentieth century, the left did not say what it meant and in crucial respects did not mean what it said, at least with respect to its fundamental beliefs. The double-voiced nature of the left public discourse was not unique to it; liberals were often caught in the contradiction between belief and policy. But, for a movement that presented itself as an alternative to the widespread perception of political discourse as empty phrases and politicians as duplicitous, the mainstream socialist and communist left was played within the rules of the game and lost its character as either opposition or alternative.

Since the New Deal, the ideological left has functioned, in Michael Harrington's phrase, as the "left-wing of the possible."[11] It was obliged to accept regulation as the framework of political combat and, in the interest of combatting the Right and most particularly fascism, sought alliances with the liberals and consciously muted its revolutionary program.

3

The decline and disappearance of the ideological left corresponds to the broad failure of Marxist politics worldwide. Everywhere, the socialist, communist, and independent left parties and movements have lost power where they have been the traditional parties of government. They have seen their substantial political bases erode, sometimes disastrously; in the United States where the socialist left has never enjoyed appreciable electoral success, it has been so marginalized in public debates that the left's existence is affirmed only by demagogic attacks by conservatives and rightists.

No less than the popular left of which it is a fraction, the ideological left was obliged to position itself within the regulatory system but did not theorize it in these terms. Rather, the rhetorical *revolutionary left*, in contrast to the democratic socialists who in the 1950s renounced revolution in favor of incremental reforms within the liberal state, elided the imperative of coming to terms with the new situation. Instead, its political strategy was indistinguishable from that of left New Dealers or socialists, while the marxist parties retained their affection for the revolutionary *phrase*.

The first elision was the doctrine that post-war economic stability was a temporary respite in the long-term tendency towards capitalism's General Crisis. For this reason, American global hegemony after World War II obliged the left and the workers movements to conduct struggles for reform and to build the "mass base" for the inevitable revolutionary moment. In 1946–47 the leader of the reconstituted Communist Party (it had been dissolved in the delirium of wartime unity), William Z. Foster, predicted a period of "sharpening class struggles" which he foresaw as the consequence of capitalism's inevitable post-war decline, a product of internal contradictions and the superiority of a growing socialist camp.[12]

Indeed, the "socialist" world and the national liberation movements it supported expanded dramatically as a consequence of imperial withdrawal in the wake of revolutionary insurgence, notably in China and Vietnam, the Red Army's intervention in Eastern Europe, and Britain's steady surrender of its empire. Recall, the immediate post-war period was marked by the simultaneous emergence of a non-aligned bloc of post-colonial Asian and African countries, but also the war-induced development of mass communist parties in France and Italy and the rise of Labor governments in the United Kingdom and Scandinavia. The Communists were, no less than the Socialists and Labor parties, resigned if not wholeheartedly committed to incremental reforms.

But, by the 1950s, the Soviet-dominated countries of Eastern Europe were experiencing their own internal problems. The 1956 uprisings in East Germany and Poland and the Hungarian revolution revealed deep cracks in the Soviet bloc. Their brutal suppression by Soviet tanks only confirmed the suspicion, first kindled during the infamous Moscow trials and repressed in the glow of wartime unity, that Communism was a new totalitarianism.[13] These events produced many defections at all leadership levels in the United States Communist Party, especially after the party apparatus ended debate over the future of the movement.[14] And, of course, the Sino-Soviet split, from which the world communist movement never recovered, undermined the Soviet claim to world revolutionary leadership, especially for many of the younger left attracted by Mao's seemingly revolutionary ideas.

By the 1970s, the economic weaknesses of the Soviet Union itself surfaced as Leonid Brezhnev actively sought accommodation with the Nixon administration to secure foodstuffs and large loans from the World Bank. This was the crucial meaning of the contemporary phrase "detente." The Soviet Union was fully prepared to abandon its intervention in the anti-imperialist struggle if the United States agreed to help its leadership mask the economic bankruptcy that plagued the country especially, but not exclusively, in agriculture. By the end of that decade, most Eastern European states were happily accepting western loans in order to bring their countries into the consumer age without the pain associated with rapid economic development.

Eugene Genovese and other pro-soviet intellectuals may have tolerated or otherwise been ignorant of the many calumnies visited by the Soviet state on peasants and dissidents, including intellectuals and even loyal Communists who dared to question the official story.[15] By the early 1960s, most young intellectuals and activists believed neither European nor Chinese socialism provided a model for the United States and the western European democracies. The Khrushchev report to the Twentieth Soviet Communist Party congress had been widely publicized; C.Wright Mills among others had advised the New Left to break from stalinism (and also its mirror image, trotskyism).[16] Although the United States Communist Party remained a force in the civil rights movement, especially in the south and some trade unions, it was believed to be ideologically and morally bankrupt. Still, the Communists were not banished from the anti-war movement because the complicity of many liberal intellectuals with McCarthyism was more of a concern. As long as the Soviet and Chinese Communists remained staunch supporters of Third World liberation movements, many intellectuals, egregiously, were loathe to openly criticize or condemn actions such as the Prague Spring, or the declaration of martial law by the Polish government in the wake of the rise of the Solidarity Labor Union, or the suppression of intellectual dissent in Cuba. This loyalty visited incalculable harm to the socialist left's reputation because it seemed to verify the charge that radicalism was identical with support for regimes that repressed freedom. To this day, many "anti-imperialist" intellectuals refuse to reevaluate their own dogmatic anticommunism.[17]

In fact, despite recent disavowals by some of its leading lights, the New Left represented the first attempt in at least two generations to propose truly radical ideas. Following the critique of revisionist historians of the New Deal as "corporate liberalism," the oppressive social welfare state, the authoritarianism of centralized government bureaucracies, and the destructiveness of the permanent war economy became favorite new left themes.[18] The New Left rejected the common sense that conflated representative democracy with the very idea of democratic participation and proposed an alternative conception of democracy that entailed community control of key institutions such as the police, welfare, and education. While by no means contemptuous of the electoral process, or even of the necessity for some representative legislative institutions, it held these to be subordinate to direct participation "in the institutions that affected the lives" of "ordinary people."

The core of the New Left's perspective entailed a critique of representation. Elected officials from both parties "represented" the corporate capitalist system to which they were committed, not the particular constituencies that sent them to local legislatures, congress, or executive offices. Hence, organizing the poor, racial minorities, students, and other unrepresented people became the main political strategy of the student-based New Left.[19] On the whole, these activities were symbolically extremely important because they called attention to the contradictions of representation—even if, except for the southern voter registration campaigns, they didn't succeed in building permanent organizations or social movements.

Intellectually, Students for a Democratic Society (SDS) and other New Left groups remained vague about which models of direct democracy could serve as benchmarks. There was no systematic examination of the early years of the soviets, no concerted effort to go back to the experience of the American and French revolutions; the Paris Commune; or the San Francisco, Seattle, and Minneapolis general strikes during the early decades of this century. Perhaps the main weakness of the New Left was its dogmatic dedication to Henry Ford's proposition that "history is bunk." Surely, the early New Left displayed a hostility to marxism which bordered on anti-intellectualism, a legacy that is still prevalent in new social movements.

SDS, other New Left groups such as Student Nonviolent Coordinating Committee (SNCC), and local organizing projects among the poor helped call attention to the defects of United States democracy as they appear from the perspective of the excluded. Especially effective was the practical assertion that America was divided into two nations: rich and poor.[20] Yet, often these groups remained blind to their own anti-democratic tendencies. In fact, the early feminist movement arose as a critique of the New Left's inconsistent adherence to its own radical principles, especially the penchant of male leaders to use women as everything from secretaries to bedmates but not to admit them into leadership positions. The appearance of the Black Panthers and the Muslims at the height of the civil rights movement's legal success attested to growing discontent with the liberals' purely formal approach to black freedom. Martin Luther King Jr., who had originally distanced himself from class issues, was finally persuaded that class as well as racial discrimination lay at the heart of black oppression. His call for a movement of the poor was quickly followed by strong support for a Memphis Sanitation Workers strike, during which he was assassinated; no doubt, for his increasing attempts to bridge race and class issues.

By the late 1960s, the anti-war forces had developed into a multitendency popular movement, which extended far beyond its initial student and pacifist base. The reason for the reemergence of political radicalism by the end of the decade is no different from that of the depression decade: a high level of mobilization and protest brings many people into an expanding circle of radical political discourse. In a word, the New Left was more than a protest movement; it was a political counterculture consisting of many tendencies including, by the late 1960s, feminism and ecological activism. Its demise is *overdetermined* by the decay of the regulation era of United States capitalism; by its own internal tensions, such as the gender and racial divisions after 1967 about which much has been written; by the internal splits in the white left with the revival of a sectarian marxist-leninist movement whose peculiarly new left style should not be confused with the older incarnations; and by the resolute refusal of the New Left to institutionalize the movement and the retreat of many movement intellectuals into the universities, a move which reflected as well as hastened the breakup.

Wini Breines has identified the major weakness of new left radicalism with its strength: its disdain of party formations or other permanent forms of political organization.[21] She has persuasively shown that the failure of the movements of the 1960s to forge a new political organization that could unite its disparate identities was by no means an historical accident. The movement's prime spirits were actively opposed to such a formation because they believed parties are inherently bureaucratic and disempower the base. The grave consequence of this "decision" has been to enframe and disarm United States radicalism during the period of globalization and political realignment. While, in retrospect, there was no possibility that the left could have overcome the complexity of factors that moved world politics to the right during the ensuing epoch, a politically coherent movement might have reduced ensuing political fragmentation and defeat.

According to the politics of populist guilt the duty of the left was to uncritically identify and support those peoples, social groups, and individuals deemed to be the most oppressed. This was a major flaw of the New Left, which today retains considerable influence in the new social movements and on their supporters. According to this view only the abject can be social and political agents.[22] All others suffer from inauthenticity and may be redeemed only by providing the resources needed by the real folks. Although the organizations of the New Left have disappeared, guilt is alive and well in and around identity politics and the still potent third-worldism that often masks itself in new slogans of globalization.

This brief moment of a mass movement of mainly radicalized youth, which succeeded in putting some spine in all radicals, was mortally wounded by the failure of the *Days of Rage* at the Democratic convention in Chicago and by the 1970 shootings at Kent State; it definitively ended by the early 1970s. Since the fragmentation and dispersal of the New Left, much of it sequestered in marxist-leninist formations, the left simply does not exist as a public presence.[23] Most telling is the defection of youth from the traditional left propositions, not merely in the electoral arena (most people aged 18 to 25 years don't vote) but also in relation to any kind of political participation. Except for a discernable group of primarily university-based young women and black, Latino, and Asian activists, there is no genuine youth movement of the left.[24] In fact, activism among young people is most visible in conservative and right-wing movements for a fairly simple reason: the right appears insurgent; the left defends the status quo. The right seems young, while liberals appear old and tired. Although this reversal may be an unintended consequence of decay, young people are not likely to be persuaded by accounts of paradox. Nor is there much evidence that radicals are prepared to do the rethinking needed to make possible even the most modest development of a youth movement. In short and on the whole, the left consists of fragments of two over-forty generations. People born after 1960 have never encountered the left because, since 1975, it has been largely absent from the national debate except in universities.

The space of the alternative and opposition, especially at the local level, is occupied by intellectuals and three major social movements: feminism, gay and lesbian movements for sexual freedom, and ecology. With few exceptions, these movements are grounded in specific identities and, for the most part, eschew efforts to combine struggles on

93

cultural issues with questions of social or class justice. Contemporary social movements have abandoned class politics for bad political but good historical reasons, not the least of which is the blindness, even hostility, of the still largest and most influential organizations of the popular left—the trade unions and the civil rights organizations—to cultural issues. If unions do not press class issues, except at the bargaining table, and show no inclination to forge alliances with social movements, why should these movements not retreat to identity politics? As for the black freedom movement, it is fair to state that it has focused on pressuring large corporations and state institutions to provide mobility for its technical and professional intellectuals rather than pressing for economic policies to alleviate the startling decline of living standards for the black majority. Recent gains for women in universities, corporations, and electoral politics have confirmed the viability of this strategy, although it can be argued that the politics of cultural identity have reached their limits with the unmitigated triumph of the right.

If the political defeats for the left are interpreted as the culmination of a long process of restructuration leading to conservative hegemony in *both* the economic and the discursive fields, there can be no future for social movements that choose to contest cultural/discursive power without addressing the question of globalization of political and economic configurations. Not only is there no significant theorizing of this question among intellectuals linked to the new social movements (except among ecologists), but many intellectuals remain adamantly opposed to raising the question of global capitalism and the changing terrain of class relations on the premise that to speak the language of political economy is to sink into some version of marxist orthodoxy. Instead, theoretical and political discourse linked to issues of sex and gender presuppose the national context and tend toward a culturalist bias.

While the experience of the last quarter century demonstrates the futility of making economistic, mechanical correlations, the absence of almost any efforts at such links, at the strategic as well as the intellectual level, may have relevance to the dead ends feminism and ecology have confronted since the late 1980s. Needless to say, the right harbors no such compunctions, for its triumph may be traced, in no small measure, to its ability to capture the high ground through economic, political, and cultural discourse that makes claims to the ethic of Freedom. Meanwhile, the left is polarized around quite separate, often hostile social justice and cultural wings, each of which rigorously attacks the other as hopelessly one-sided.[25]

One of the more dramatic examples of how the left has ignored class politics may be observed in the complicity of the ideological left, as well as social movements, in the bureaucratically-addled welfare state. Instead of elaborating an *alternative* such as guaranteed income, shorter hours, work-sharing, and the abolition of overtime based on the re-progressivization of taxes, the left shudders when conservatives raise the demand for tax and spending reductions. For the time being, let us bracket the truism that they mean to soak the middle and working classes by such proposals. However, in the past quarter century of resonant rightist attacks on "big" government, there has been no left acknowledgement that the critique of the bureaucratic state and ideas such as localism, more popular control over social institutions such as schools, and so forth are traditionally *radical* alternatives to the liberal state. Nor have any significant fractions of the left, including its press, undertaken a serious and systematic analysis of the valid basis of popular support for various tax-cutting initatives.

The left has refused to engage in a useful dialogue with proponents of tax cuts because the cuts are perceived to be directed at the social welfare state and its Great Society presuppositions. Since most workers are in hock up to their ears, they are only too receptive to suggestions that their burdens may be lighter. With some justification, the left interprets popular support for lower taxes as an expression of growing racism and sexism, and it often stops with this insight. Fearing tax cuts will result in reductions of the social wage, it has joined with liberal statists to defend existing arrangements.

The left's disappearance is due, in no small measure, to its own complicity with the underlying philosophy of the Great Society, which in the name of *compassion* has effectively transformed many citizens into clients. It is an ideological tendency that some crucial elements of the left-feminists—civil rights champions as well as laborites—are militantly statist. Such positions are clear losers on *both* practical and theoretical grounds. Left-wing antipathy to the wide support among working people for lower taxes is closely related to pervasive class guilt among activists and intellectuals. In current discourse this guilt privileges the most abject as the true political agents, regarding nearly everyone else as "privileged" and hopelessly integrated into the prevailing order.

Tacitly, many now accept the relentless barrage of misinformation that maintains capitalism has succeeded in delivering the goods to the immense majority. Perhaps this is the underlying reason for left confusion on economic questions. Have we bought the three class model proposed by liberal sociology? Is American society divided between the rich; the middle class, including most workers; and the poor? And are *income criteria* dominant in class formation?

The ranks and the leadership of popular left organizations and new social movements harbor people who have revolution or at least radical social change "in their hearts" but who, in concert with the twentieth century legacy of American radicalism, function as the left-wing or even the mainstream of social-welfare liberalism. This legacy is rooted in the transformation at the turn of the century from a swashbuckling, competitive capitalism to its "organized," "state," or "monopoly" form. The first two decades of the century were years of intense left-wing discussion and debate over the fundamental path to a new society. Its categories—electoralism versus direct action; state regulation versus decentralized democratic participation; and cultural freedom *as well as* social justice—are precisely those that were again raised in the 1960s and need to be raised again today.

In the end, the old anarchist and libertarian socialist slogan of constituting society as a "cooperative commonwealth" or, in Marx's words, "a free association" gave way to a conception of socialism whose key institutions were neither popular assemblies nor groups of producers and consumers but the institutions of a highly centralized state. These institutions include representative bodies and administrative agencies, neither of which fulfills the promise of participation for the vast majority, whatever its ideological proclivities.

In the long era of regulation, the left as a whole became habituated to a political discourse that did not express its own aspirations, nor did it delineate the relationship between the struggle for reform and social transformation. In time, even vestiges of what would commonly be called a "vision," let alone a strategy of fundamental change, were relegated to the classroom, to the dinner table, and to private imagination.

5

... political freedom, generally speaking, means the right to be a participator in government or it means nothing.

—Hannah Arendt

Neither the popular nor the ideological left is more dedicated than their right-wing adversaries to offering a new political "truth." Political discourse is typically strategic; it is determined by conditions of time and place. In effect, the left believes that politics is the continuation of war by other means, and the fundamental question is how to win? This is not conducive to creating public spaces in which alternative conceptions of politics may be debated, the only experience of which the left has had being alternative programs and positions. Since politics is defined outside of the realm of truth when taken seriously, the left can be trusted no more than its adversaries.

It is not a question of proclaiming, abstractly, an article of faith, such as the belief that capitalism is an unethical system which reproduces inequality or one that produces periodic crises. Truth-telling is not identical with the equally vacuous statement that socialism would be better. Radicals are obliged to address the overwhelming feeling of powerlessness shared by people of different economic strata and their sense of being progressively removed from having a say in their own futures. In earlier decades of this century, risk was defined by actual war. Such uncertainties are now compounded by a new sense of economic insecurity and social disaster and the pervasive fear of ecological crisis. These perceptions are widely shared and drive people to withdraw from political involvement.

What are the conditions of possibility for participatory or radical democracy? Is this concept merely a self-deception among some erstwhile socialists on the way to their inevitable acceptance of liberal, representative democracy as the sufficient and necessary condition for freedom? If this claim is to be valid, must we accept Harrington's formula for the left's strategy—the popular front without stalinism—and renounce as either unnecessary or ill-conceived the critique of bureaucratic capitalism and state socialism? To assess the results of the past twenty years exclusively in terms of the discourse of political defeat leaves out the structural transformation discussed here and a second change which, following some tendencies in political theory, may be described as a "crisis" of the liberal democratic state.

There are two distinct accounts of the crisis. One account ascribes the observable decline in participation in elections and political life to the growing powerlessness of states to deliver anything to large chunks of the population and to the emergence of global metastates. The second account makes no attempt to link economic changes to the long-term decline of participation. Instead, this line of thought focuses on the factors leading to a decline of the *public sphere*, the social space where individuals congregate to discuss and debate the issues that affect their lives. In this perspective, whether decisions are finally made by a legislative body or directly by participants is less significant than the existence of an active polity. Many who have commented in the public sphere debate stress the influence of mass media, corporate lobbies, and the demobilizing tendencies of the welfare state itself for discouraging public dialogue and participation.

In his pathbreaking works *Public Opinion* and *The Phantom Public Sphere,* Walter Lippmann calls attention to the decline of the public. Lippmann, a disillusioned Jeffersonian, concluded that participatory democracy was simply unrealistic; experts were fated to decide public issues, and the role of the electorate was confined to a check on their unwarranted power. Others, notably Arendt; the historians of the anti-federalists in the American Revolution; Kristin Ross's deft account of the aesthetics of the Paris Commune; and some contemporary political theorists such as Negt, Kluge, and Nancy Fraser have valiantly attempted to resurrect the self-governing polity as a living alternative to representation.

Arendt articulates one of the salient features of this tendency as the rigorous separation of questions of politics from two of the key features of the rise of the labor and social movements in the nineteenth and twentieth centuries: the reduction of politics to particular "interests" and the insistence that the "social question" in both its economic and cultural aspects is intrinsic to questions of political power. Arendt insists that politics is the province of free individuals, not organized social groups for whom the commonweal is a pie to be divided on the basis of superior force. Groups—crowds, mobs, demonstrators—may act to redress their collective grievances or advance their specific interests, but only individuals can speak and actually participate in the process of governance.

At first glance, Arendt's position may appear odd. How, in this world of competing interests, parties, and groups, can theory assert that the social question is a disruption of the democratic polity? The social question dominates what passes for politics in the contemporary world. As Harold Lasswell puts it, the main political question is, Who gets what and how? Arendt makes no attempt to analyze the contemporary situation. Her project is to answer the question, What are the conditions of possibility of freedom? The first approximation is to redefine governance in terms of self-determination, to insist that direct participation is the only possible condition for a democratic polity. All other issues should be left to the private sphere; that is, government governs best which only concerns itself with true public issues. Ambiguous in this discourse is the status of the economic. For Arendt, labor and by extension all economic relations are essentially animal or survival problems. If the political is defined as that sphere in which the specifically *human* is addressed, problems of production and distribution are best left to the "pre-political" private sphere, subject only to what Arendt calls "administration." (Habermas interprets these questions as extra-political since they are subject only to rational/technical solutions.) But both Arendt and Habermas have seriously misread the history of the relations of humans to nature. Arendt appears to accept the progressive domination of nature as a necessary condition for entering the realm of freedom. If one regards the domination of nature as, in part, political and not normative, then issues of science and technology no less than production problems should be subject to public discourse and to the processes of self-management.

One could interpret Arendt's prescription in another way: the class struggle, including that between men and women, black and white may be conducted outside the realm of the state. For Arendt, the only chance for genuine politics is to move the "social question" to the arena of the pre-political. Workers, women, and "minorities" would seek redress for their grievances through industrial and other extra-parliamentary forms of combat. This suggests that the left lost its way the moment it entered the struggle for state power in order to solve the social question. Apart from struggles to secure the space for social combat through civil liberties, social movements would avoid engaging in the politics of interest.

What other conditions lend themselves to the broadest and the deepest participation? Clearly, as ecologists have argued, one must address the scale of social and political organization. The argument that large-scale organizations are more efficient since they save resources turns out to be fallacious. This view is based on the primacy of the economic in the constitution of society. Economies of scale have more to do with the centralization of power than saving resources. When placed in the context of both political participation and ecological criteria, bigness turns out to be an obstacle, a negativity.

In order for a form of social organization in which each individual possesses the capacity for speech and exercises it to thrive, society must organize itself in such a way that necessary labor is subordinate, both in its significance and in its duration to free time. This includes, of course, housework and child-rearing as well as the production and distribution of goods and services. In contrast to Arendt's argument, labor should be subject to the same self-managed regime as other so-called public activities. We must reject the claims of Daniel Bell, Habermas, and Arendt that economic problems have in modern societies become essentially technical. In a regime of radical democratic participation, the exigencies of economic life may no longer drive the whole society; they are subject to political and cultural criteria.

Marx's critique that capitalist social relations entail the primacy of the economic has been taken by some of his followers as a positive, scientific law of social development. Given the fantastic growth of scientific and technological knowledge, the productive powers of labor permit us to have a practical perspective of social life not driven by economic necessity. While there are ecological scarcities, these need not imply that scarcity itself is a permanent form of life. If political priorities are set straight, scientific and technical work would be directed toward finding alternatives to fossil sources of energy; industrial technology would seek replacements for non-degradable materials; social and cultural theory would envision a concrete utopia on the basis of ecological thinking as well as political and economic ideas oriented to freedom. In short, the difficulties we experience imagining our way out of the dichotomies of ruthless global capitalism and a failed, totalitarian state socialism are neither technical nor economic. They stem from our inability to imagine the conditions of possibility of a truly free society of autonomous, yet cooperative, individuals. While Heidegger and Marcuse may have identified technological domination as a culprit, the specificity of the history of socialism itself must be reckoned as an important component of this profoundly pessimistic anti-utopianism that has gripped contemporary culture.

From this formulation, we derive contrasting conceptions of reform and political strategy. As Gorz and Mallet argued more than thirty years ago, rather than participation, the left fights for reforms that restructure power relationships. For example, following an older proposal, it would not defend the welfare state, but would demand its abolition on the basis of guaranteed income and would call for a decentralization of social services in which professionals and "clients" would share power. This perspective entails a second look at participatory management schemes at the work-place. Instead of maintaining a defensive, adversarial posture toward management proposals as unions did in the early 1980s, workers and their unions would offer counterproposals to democratize the workplace, a measure that would inevitably entail reduction of working hours, not only in order to share employment with the jobless, but also to provide time for decision-making.

Socialism as a framework has been seriously damaged by the history of the socialist movement. We must invoke an older, but really new conception of social transformation that may be designated *radical democracy*. This shift is by no means cosmetic, but neither does it signal a retreat from the earlier connotation of communism or socialism: the conception of the "social" as an *association* of producers, consumers, and a polity. Radical democracy is achievable by creating institutions of popular control in which decisions are lodged with those directly affected by them, a realignment of economy and the polity entailing the reintegration of various aspects of life within smaller regional economies and social units.

Radical democracy problematizes both the traditional, exclusive left designation of the proletariat as historical agent and the tendency to displace class politics with a politics of identity. Although writers such as Arendt are right to call our attention to the issue of freedom, admonishing us not to confuse the social question with politics itself, the insistence that the social question prevents us from addressing the truly political questions is deeply mistaken. Pluralism might inhibit repressive hegemonies or even counterhegemonies, but to separate the social question from the formation of a free polity relegates radical democratic theory to ethics. The politics of the present must be interrogated with a vision of the future capable of linking them.

The conventional activist critique is that this programmatic conclusion does not tell anyone what to do on Monday morning. Perhaps we have been overly concerned with addressing an unexamined agenda whose defensiveness is comparable to a slave morality; it is reactive, full of resentment, and utterly without hope for the future. The next left will emerge as a critique of the ideologies and programs that encumber its predecessor.

NOTES

1. The referendum and initiative was one of the many reforms proposed by turn of the century populists and progressives to combat the wholesale corruption of state and local legislatures by large corporations. Its most fervent champion was Tom Johnson, who became mayor of Cleveland, but it received its greatest impetus from the broad-based populist movements in California led, for a time, by governor Culbert Olson and the socialist writer Upton Sinclair.

2. The largest organization of senior citizens, the Association of Retired People, has 33 million members, probably the largest secular voluntary organization in the country.

3. See Stanley Aronowitz, *Food, Shelter and the American Dream* (New York: Seabury Press, 1974). The reception of this book on the left was something less than positive because it argued that the food and energy crises of the period signaled a restructuration of world capitalism that might fatally undermine the historic New Deal agenda.

4. Joel Kreiger, *Reagan, Thatcher and the Politics of Decline* (New York: Basic Books, 1986).

5. On December 15, 1994, Clinton delivered a concession speech to the American people. By announcing a "middle class bill of rights," a melange of tax cuts combined with spending cuts, the President hoped to head off the Republicans by stealing their thunder and forestalling a capital gains tax cut.

6. New York's mayor Rudolph Giuliani's passion for cutting the social wage may have come a cropper when he proposed draconian cuts in the school budget in order to balance the city's spending. As a result, some of his most ardent supporters from Staten Island and Bensonhurst, Brooklyn staged uncharacteristic protest demonstrations at City Hall.

7. As I prepared this manuscript for final submission, the Executive Director of New York's largest municipal employees union dropped the tradition of protesting against using welfare recipients to break union standards and declared his agreement with Giuliani's plan to get able-bodied adult welfare recipients to earn their checks by working in schools, parks, and other city agencies.

8. Scott Lash and John Urry, *The End of Organized Capitalism* (Madison: University of Wisconsin Press, 1989); Claus Offe, *Disorganized Capitalism* (London: Basil Blackwell, 1988).

9. In a speech (November, 1994) at CUNY Graduate Center, Jerry Watts argued, persuasively I think, that far from seeking social emancipation, the real goal of the modern civil rights movement has been to secure for blacks "victim status," a gain which obliges the larger society to recognize and compensate for black oppression.

10. The demand for full employment is still the official position of most of the popular left and nearly the entire ideological left, but it has had no *practical* value since unions and civil rights organizations successfully included

job creation within 1960s Great Society programs. It has been all downhill since then.

11. In several important books in the 1970s, the socialist leader Michael Harrington foresaw a major political realignment in United States politics, predicated on the growth of the left-liberal coalition. Conservative Democrats and the Republican Party would join together to oppose it. Needless to say, the Democratic Party would remain the chief vehicle for social reform. The current process verifies realignment, but there is no second party with a purchase on power.

12. William Z. Foster, *The Twilight of World Capitalism* (New York: International Publishers, 1947).

13. Hannah Arendt subsumed fascism and communism under the single rubric of "totalitarianism." In the cold war era, this perspective was widely interpreted on the left as a sign that Arendt had provided anti-communism with its most sophisticated intellectual justification. In retrospect, one might want to radically revise this negative judgement. See Hannah Arendt, *The Origins of Totalitarianism* (New York: The Free Press, 1951).

14. The story of this debate (1956–1958) is a dramatically unusual episode in the party's history of otherwise militant intolerance to inner-party discussion and difference. Stunned by the Khrushchev revelations of Stalin's crimes, the CPUSA sponsored a wide ranging discussion of the implications for the party's future, for socialism, and for democracy. The documents reveal little intellectual engagement and much sterility, but also a surprising amount of openness and creativity. Having encouraged dissent, the party's summary closing of the forum prompted mass resignations on both the left and right of the leadership.

15. Eugene Genovese, "What We Should Have Known," *Dissent* (Summer 1994).

16. C. Wright Mills, "Letter to the New Left," in *Power, Politics, and People; the collected essays of C. Wright Mills,* ed. Irving Louis Horowitz (New York: Oxford University Press, 1963).

17. Joel Kovel, *Anti-Communism* (Boston: Beacon Press, 1994).

18. Jeff Lustig, *Corporate Liberalism* (New York: Macmillan Press, 1978); William Appleman Williams, *Contours of American History* (New York: Quadrangle Books, 1961); James Weinstein, *Corporate Ideal and the Liberal State* (New York: Vintage Books, 1970).

19. Tom Hayden and Carl Whitman, *Toward an Interracial Movement of the Poor,* SDS pamphlet, 1963.

20. SDS, *The Port Huron Statement,* 1962. The view of two Americas promulgated in this veritable manifesto was heavily influenced by Harrington's *The Other America: Poverty in the United States* (New York: Penuin, 1962).

21. Wini Breines, *Community and Organization in the New Left* (South Hadley, Mass.: Bergin and Garvey, 1981).

22. Judith Butler, *Gender Trouble* (New York: Routledge, 1990).

23. Of course, there are organizations of activists, but there are no movements, except at the local level.

24. In several large cities, notably New York, San Francisco, and Detroit, there are the beginnings of a vital movement in the high schools, and there is something of an undergraduate movement. Among graduate students, union organizing has occupied the energies of some, but the professionalization of the intellectuals is fairly complete.

25. Both the social issues and the social justice lefts are correct about each other.

7

REVIVING DEMOCRATIC ACTIVISM

THOUGHTS ABOUT STRATEGY IN A DARK TIME

RICHARD FLACKS

WHEN YOU ASK VETERAN AMERICAN LEFTISTS ABOUT the meaning of their political lives, you will rarely hear a despairing story of failure. Instead, you are likely to be regaled with tales of a certain glory. These tales are about their roles in the development of a grass-roots, popular struggle. Their lives as radicals are justified by the rights won, the closed spaces opened, and the empowerment gained by the social movements they helped build. They are likely to say the socialist vision, the revolutionary dream had to be put on hold—but we fought a good fight and made the world a better place.[1]

Personal stories sharply contrast with interpretations of left history provided by both Marxist and mainstream intellectuals that emphasize how compromised such victories were, how cooptative the results, how often movement-won concessions actually strengthened the 'system.'[2]

Are the veterans' stories merely exercises in self-delusion and denial? Or does the subjective sense of historical relevance felt by generations of left activists provide a clue to a deeper—and truer—sense of the American experience than do prevailing theoretical analyses?

THE NARRATIVE OF DEMOCRATIZATION

American radicals have always sensed that 'socialism' as a definition of their mission was more a burden than a resource. As long as socialism was said to be the true mission of conscious leftists, then their participation in popular struggles that led 'merely' to reform was discounted. From an orthodox socialist perspective, movements, in and of themselves, were preliminary to the real thing: a Party of socialism, which would provide a coherent ideological and programmatic framework and a coordinated and systematic strategy for realizing popular aspiration. The Party not only would make popular struggle more effective, it would be the vehicle of power, the means by which demands could be translated into policy and protest into command. The inability of American leftists to get to first base in the construction of such a party has always been regarded as a measure of their weakness. This failure is tied to the further painful fact that 'socialism' never had a broad popular base within the labor movement.

As long as the object of the left project is understood to be the replacement of capitalism by socialism, and the essence of its strategy the construction of an independent mass party having such an object, the project will be a failure.

Yet it is plausible, as Stanley Aronowitz suggests, to construct a broader conception of the left as a force in American history.[3] There were the efforts of ideologically grounded party-style organizations, whose strategies, however much they differed, shared the premise that the building up of the organization as a vehicle of power constituted a crucial measure of success for the Left. Aronowitz suggests that we need to include as an integral dimension of the left the social movements: the movements for economic justice (labor, civil rights, urban movements of various sorts) and the 'new' social movements (the women's movement, environmentalism, and others focused on social 'identity'). These movements are carriers of the left tradition and are at least as much the 'real thing' as any of the explicitly ideological parties.

These two wings of the left were intimately connected, but not in ways that Party socialists officially hoped. Historically, the ideological organizations of the left talked as if they could provide programmatic and strategic direction for the movements through the dissemination of their public positions in the party press and other literature, through agitation and education. At times, as in the early twentieth century, socialists even hoped to make an explicit alliance with the labor movement—akin to relations between party and unions in England. No doubt such organizational efforts, and the party lines of the ideological left, had some effect on movements over the decades, but the evidence is that their effects were often more damaging than helpful.

The real link between the two wings of the left was provided by generations of activists, many of whom were affiliated with one or another ideological group, but who worked within the movements in various levels and modes of leadership. Sometimes—as in the 30s— party-influenced activists formed cells or caucuses within movement scenes and organizations in order to try to influence their direction on the basis of a party line. More often, though, such people were guided by the imperatives of the movement in which they were imbedded, bringing to the movement not a party policy but a fervent dedication, instilled and reinforced by party affiliation, and a degree of experience and skill derived from the training afforded by the party. One of the dramatic tensions in the stories told by veteran activists has to do with their need to act against the party line, or even to break with the party if they were to be true to the popular struggle that they were trying to aid.

One key to the difference between the New Left and the Old was that New Left activists believed that their role was to foster popular struggle as an end in itself. The Student Nonviolent Coordinating Committee (SNCC) sang: "Freedom is a constant struggle." The Students for a Democratic Society ERAP projects had a slogan: "Let the people decide." Both groups resembled the old left parties in that they were centers for organizers, activists, and movement intellectuals, but both groups deliberately refused to become vehicles for power and refrained from trying to represent mass constituencies in arenas of public discourse. These sixties activists knew that they wanted to abandon the party form; unfortunately, they did not know what to substitute for it in terms of national organization. What was most 'new' about the New Left—and what was perhaps its primary contribution to the refashioning of left theory and practice—was its claim that the essence of the left project was not socialism but 'participatory' or radical democracy. [4]

Democratization is an endlessly unfolding process of societal, institutional, interpersonal transformation. Democracy is not realized by efforts to replace one 'system' with another—nor can it be implemented by expanding the power of a party-like organization (no matter how 'democratic' its ideological claims). These are fundamental insights the experience of the twentieth century has compelled us to internalize. The 'collapse' of communism and the discrediting of 'socialism' are expressions of these insights. But the end of the Left's ideological and organizational foundations does not mean that the Left as an historical tradition, as a framework of practice and belief, has come to an end. That tradition continues in the contemporary practices and identities of movement activists. For, despite their evidently 'reformist' and 'ameliorative' character, social movements are the vehicles of whatever chance for democratization we now have. What are the grounds for such an assertion?

First, movements are inherently the primary framework for direct democracy, providing the moments in which ordinary people directly and consciously participate in the exercise of voice rather than allowing others to speak for them. The fact that such moments actually happen is the empirical basis for validating a vision of radical democracy. It is in the movement moment that the people show, at least spasmodically, that they can decide, can take control of their history.

Second, democratic structural reform—the democratization of power relations—is the premise of all movement demands. The demand for such structural change takes two broad forms: on the one hand, there is the demand for individual rights—to freedoms or entitlements now denied. Winning such rights changes a power relation, ends a particular condition of subordination, of top-down control. Thus labor's struggle for 'bread-and-butter' gains is not only a demand for better wages but also a challenge to management's authority to set wages.

On the other hand, movements typically demand more than particular concessions and individual rights. Movements demand institutionalized voice—a permanent change in the way authority is structured so that the movement's constituencies will from now on be represented in the decisions that affect them. The Wagner Act—despite its profound limitation—was a structural reform of authority relations in the corporation, establishing collective bargaining as the means by which wages and working conditions are to be decided. The environmental quality legislation of the seventies promoted a structural reform in power relations at the community level by compelling open accountability with respect to the environmental impact of new development. The voting rights legislation of the sixties restructured power relations in the American south.

We can better grasp the transformative significance of such reforms when we see them as happening within a broad narrative of democratization. The story of the last hundred years can be told as an ongoing, if halting, unfolding of democratic possibility in which the popular movements separately won piece-meal reforms that cumulatively have constituted a dynamic of democratization.

From one angle, these reforms 'strengthened the going system.' In their aftermath, activists' energies flowed into previously blocked institutionalized channels while mass constituencies demobilized. Disruptive protest was replaced by bureaucratic organization and institutionalized politics. Indeed, democratic movement is always contradictory. In fact, whoever wants to chart the history of the Left anywhere in the world inevitably has to deal with wrenching moral contradictions. Every victory, whether "reformist" or "revolutionary," contains seeds of its undoing. Every gain in worker empowerment may set the stage for capitalism's flight; power corrupts the leaders of democratic struggle; movement gains for one oppressed group entail increased costs for another; communal solidarity breeds blind conformity; brave commitment turns into murderous dogmatism; beloved communities become self-righteous enclaves.

Nevertheless, in the face of these contradictions, we can discern the unfolding democratic narrative. The society we inhabit today is not the 'going system' of a hundred years ago. It has been reconstituted continuously by popular demands for rights and voice. Partial achievement of some of these sets the stage for further awareness of democratic possibility. Threats to past achievement energize new mobilization. The struggle continues.

SEARCHING FOR STRATEGY

There is today a pervasive belief among activists in all of the great popular movements that the "next stage" requires the overcoming of the particularism of the movements and the fragmentation of "progressive" politics. This understanding has been expressed for a number of years in calls for "coalition" based on the recognition that no single movement is powerful enough to fulfill its particular agenda alone, that a politics of identity (struggles for symbolic representation and cultural space for example) has to be coupled with a politics aimed at achieving economic security, and that certain battles between movements, such as labor versus environmentalism, were mutually suicidal.

Two sorts of coalition have been talked about and attempted over the last twenty years. On the one hand, there are the issue oriented efforts to unite diverse movement constituencies around a common threat. Examples include the anti-Bork alliance of several years ago, and the recent effort to defeat NAFTA. In addition to efforts to rally common action to defeat a shared threat, there have been occasional attempts to construct a coalition to win positive reform. For example, despite recent frustration and defeat, a considerable coalition may yet develop at both grass-roots and national levels in support of progressive health care reform. We can only hope that such ad hoc, immediate, practical coalition efforts lead to more permanent structures. But whether or not they do, there is now no hope for significant social reform without, at a minimum, ad hoc, issue-oriented mobilization.

More far-reaching—and less successful—has been the long-standing vision of constructing a progressive electoral coalition, uniting the labor movement, minority civil rights movements, the women's movement, environmentalists, and the peace movement in a common political agenda and shared platform. Michael Harrington advocated such an effort for years—with the goal being the development of a coherent strategy for the left wing of the Democratic Party aiming at the party's transformation. But the organization he founded, the Democratic Socialists of America (DSA) has, for various reasons, never seriously pursued the strategy he advocated. The Jesse Jackson campaigns embodied such a strategic idea, but these too were not sustained as a strategic framework for long term efforts to reshape the party. While the left wing of the Democratic Party refrained from a determined effort to seize power, more conservative elements were not similarly skittish. Accordingly, Bill Clinton, catering to his base in the Democratic Leadership Council, announced himself as a "New Democrat," claiming to be distancing himself from the social movement base of the party. Despite its lack of coordination and its fitful mobilization, that base could not, however, be jettisoned or ignored. Indeed, the fundamental problem for Democratic Party professionals is the near impossibility of building an electoral majority that can encompass both its "centrist" constituency (White males over 30) and its movement oriented constituencies.

Meanwhile, in a number of cities and states, electoral coalition building by movement activists was attempted during the eighties, spurred in part by the Jackson effort and the inspiration of the Harold Washington movement in Chicago that preceded it. These efforts succeeded in winning some significant elections, but rarely have such victories been able to translate into long-term progressive reform—

given the endemic fiscal crises besetting American cities, and the polarization and fragmentation of the electorate.

It is tempting to imagine that the electoral process is irrelevant for radical democratization. By definition, democratization must occur at the grass-roots level and can't be made dependent on government action. And, after all, doesn't history suggest that the fate of elected politicians, no matter how well-meaning, is to become enmeshed in the roles and rules of the going system? Still, despite the innumerable snares and delusions that electoral activity creates, movements inevitably need to engage in normal politics. For, despite the fact that movements are expressions of direct democracy, they are shaped by and dependent on the state. State action institutes the reforms movements demand. The rhetoric and symbolic gestures of politicians help legitimate—and delegitimate—movement actions and goals. Structural reforms that provide space for organizing and voice for movement constituencies must be enacted into law.

Furthermore, the electoral arena is the primary forum for developing, articulating, and inculcating the philosophical and programmatic grounds for structural transformation. The greatest failing of the western lefts in the last twenty years has been to let the Right take the initiative in public discourse. This shift in public rhetoric and agenda setting was accomplished in large measure because right wing politicians (namely Reagan and Thatcher) learned how to use the forums of electoral politics to preach ideas—while, at the same time, social democrats in Europe and liberal Democrats in the United States lost the will and competence to speak to popular majorities in moral and philosophical terms. Meanwhile, just when radical intellectuals had both the chance and the duty to provide fresh ideas, they were preoccupied with *academic* rather than *popular* discourse.

Despite the evidently debased character of political debate and the media coverage of it, electoral competition compels those who seriously take part in it to find a language and a program that can address the deep fears and perplexities of ordinary people. It isn't only Democratic Party politicians who have lost their tongues. The movements themselves need to find a common language and program that can appeal to large numbers of people who are alienated from them. All this requires a wide-ranging, fresh examination of the relationship between movements and electoral politics. The discussion needs to examine where, in the United States, such relations have gone in the past (taking seriously the degree to which the Democratic Party is—as well as is not—a party shaped by popular movement and grass-roots interests). But the past is not going to be a guide to where we are headed. It is clear that the mass electoral parties—all over the world—are now exhausted. These parties—the European social democratic parties (both traditional and former communist) and such formations as the PRI in Mexico, the Congress Party in India, and the Israeli Labor Party—based their popular appeal on the capacity to provide programs of economic growth that would fund a welfare state and provide some semblance of full employment. Such promises are now invalidated by the globalization of the economy.

The "crisis of national leadership" is not simply an American experience. It is a world-wide phenomenon, neither accidental nor temporary. Indeed, nationally based strategies of development may well be obsolete. National states no longer have the power to do the steering that Keynesian/welfare state programs required, nor do they have the power—which the logic of Keynesianism demands—to control capital flight or develop new mechanisms to substitute for private investment. Perhaps a *global* Keynesian perspective can be made real in the coming years—though the new international trade agreements seem to be moving in fundamentally different directions.

It is crucial that American liberals and progressives recognize that the political problems of the Clinton Administration and the Democratic Party are rooted in this global situation. In this situation, it becomes virtually impossible for stable electoral majorities to be constructed on the basis of promises of jobs or welfare state protections. The interests of relatively well-paid workers and those being left behind by economic dislocation increasingly appear incompatible. In theory, a bridge could be built among these constituencies if job-creating investments (of the type Clinton seemed to be promising) could be launched or stimulated by government action. But, unable either to direct private investment or to raise revenues—and no longer able to use the military budget to prime the pump—activist policies are frustrated. As the established policy framework for the social contract disintegrates, voter alienation grows—expressed in both electoral abstention and support for a government-bashing right-wing populism.

How can democratic activists make sense and use of the electoral process in this situation? Can we imagine the reinvention of government so that democratic practice might be sustained as the national state loses its efficacy?

In the short-run, the politically conscious cannot abstain from the governments they are stuck with. They feel morally compromised by the continuous necessity of supporting "lesser of two evil" politics in order to stave off the primitive destructiveness that right wing electoral victory ushers in. Such feelings are evidently shared with the millions of less-politicized Americans (and voters in every other country on earth) who feel disgusted with the choices they are compelled to make. For, in the current context, politicians who seek the support of the bottom half of their societies, even when they are well-intentioned, inevitably must promise much they cannot deliver or must drastically dilute their populist claims in efforts to try to build elite consensus on behalf of reform. Support for Clinton in his agony is to many on the Left the only way to keep at least some hope alive, while others are bitter in their retailing of Clinton's failures. Moralistic sniping at the president has contributed much to the prevailing political cynicism and demoralization—but uncomfortable support of the national Democratic administration has not inspired democratic activism in the Clinton years.

Despite the relative demobilization of such activism in recent years, there are, at this writing, some signs of electoral ferment on the left—signs that may portend creative initiatives. There is, for example, the "new party" effort, which is searching for a way to build an independent electoral formation that allows participants to both support acceptable mainstream political leadership while organizing to its left. Independent, 'third party' efforts on a community and state level are gaining votes (albeit they are still quite marginal in most cases). In the 1994 elections, despite the widespread political withdrawal of working class and minority voters, movement coalitions in several states succeeded in nominating their candidates, defeating centrist Democratic Party politicians. The passage of the Motor Voter Bill provides, according to some analysts, an opportunity to bring movement constituencies into the electoral process.

These fragments of electoral initiative are, however, uncoordinated and occur below the level of national visibility. There is an obvious organizational vacuum on the left side of the political spectrum, a glaring for a national structure that will coordinate efforts to mobilize grass-roots support for possible short-term reforms: health care, child-care, refunding of education, job creating public investment, and so on. Given the plethora of well-budgeted Washington-based lobby groups that promote progressive causes, the organizational/strategic vacuum is bewildering.

At the grass-roots level, and in a variety of movement sectors, there are thousands of people ready to be mobilized by a progressive electoral agenda—which is independent on the one hand and strategically rational on the other. The point of such an effort would not be to pretend that a left electoral force can produce a radical remaking of the country. Rather the goal of electoral action would be to defend the bottom fifty to eighty per cent against the ravages of the global economy by putting the president and the Democratic party leadership's feet to the fire. The more such a forum on national and local levels could be created, the more would social alternatives become imaginable and available for debate. The more strategically such a formation deployed itself, the more capable it would be of pressuring mainstream politicians to respond, and even succeeding in reconstructing the electoral majority to embrace the interests of the disadvantaged.

Such an electoral project—which, in principle, could be initiated by leaders in the labor, African-American, women's, and environmental movements and by liberal-left politicians—would signal the reemergence of 'class' politics, offering a chance of enabling people of diverse 'identities' to find a common ground politics relevant to their daily lives. If such a national formation gained real political weight, it might even have the salutary effect of slowing the degradation of living standards threatened now by global economic dynamics. Absent such an effort, it seems likely that the Clinton Administration will shift toward the right—thereby increasing the alienation of the bottom fifty percent and paving the way for intensifying social polarization and authoritarianism.

An organization that balances the Democratic Leadership Council and other forces pulling the Democratic Party to the right and that credibly represents the shared agenda of the main social movements is an absolute requisite for the survival of an egalitarian social agenda in American politics. But such a formation is not enough. Indeed, the very global dynamics I've alluded to may invalidate it even as a short-term strategy for protecting American workers from the ravages of globalization.

REVITALIZING DEMOCRATIC ACTIVISM

Electoral activity is only one dimension of movement strategy. The main power of grass-roots movements rests not on their capacity to mobilize votes but on their capacity to disrupt the routine institutional processes of society, to renegotiate the rules and terms by which people live, and to reorganize the cognitive structures that shape meanings and identities. Democratization depends on the revitalization of direct action and the revival of utopian dissent.

Democratic reawakenings (as in the 1930s and 1960s) seem to take everyone by surprise, arising in unexpected locales and social sectors, out of seemingly unplanned initiatives taken by previously unknown actors. It is possible that the great democratic awakening of the 1990s is already in the process of being born. But a careful reading of the 'origins' of the 30s and the 60s suggests that spontaneous outbursts had roots in systematic efforts by organizers and intellectuals to create space for new action and frameworks for new thought. Movement "halfway houses" (institutional frameworks for education, training, and experiment); years of frustrated agitating and organizing; the creation of small, seemingly marginal, activist organizations preceded the sit-downs of the thirties and the sit-ins of the sixties.[5]

Democratic activists continue to work in virtually every community in the United States. In the aftermath of the sixties, tens of thousands of young people graduated and moved into localities and institutions across the country. Many became full-time organizers in the social movements. Many became credentialed professionals—academics, lawyers, doctors, planners—and utilized their skills and positions for systematic projects of social change. Thousands of experiments in alternative journalism, broadcasting, film-making, and popular culture were conducted; thousands of social change enterprises and non-profit organizations were undertaken. "Acting locally, thinking globally," many of these projects deeply affected community cultures and politics and landscapes across the United States. Structures, networks, institutions, and individuals shaped in the last twenty years of localized activism remain in place.[6]

These activities are, no doubt, quite routine, compared with those earlier days. Today's progressive activist is likely to be spending her time tending a well-defined agenda that is specialized and tailored to the interests of a specific constituency of clients, funders, and supporters. Much energy is necessarily expended on maintaining the organization itself because it is always precariously budgeted. "Thinking globally" is something of a luxury the activist feels, and envisioning the ways in which daily work and organizational priorities fit into a scenario of democratic social change is not something the activist can easily find energy for.

In some towns, such activists may be linked together in formal or informal networks. Coalitions form and reform over the years, with varying degrees of political impact. In any event, there is likely to be some sense of community among activists across the movement boundaries—even as identity politics, ideological disputes, and turf wars also create rancor and division. Every so often, the routine work of local activists is for a moment put aside for crisis organizing and the mobilization of protest. At such moments, activists glimpse the fact that in their towns there are thousands ready to take action—under conditions of shared threat.

National movement organizations, headquartered in Washington or New York, have little capacity to energize or direct local activists, preferring to utilize their grass-roots base for direct mail fund appeals and letter-writing campaigns. Thus every movement has a kind of dual organizational structure—a set of national organizations with large centralized staffs, which function largely as lobbies for particular interests and occasionally venturing into ad hoc coalitions, and, distinct from those, a vast decentralized array of local groups, some of which may be locals or chapters of national organizations but many of which are not. Local activism is the key resource for democratization. This resource continues to be available—but it is in danger.

A national coalition of movement organizations directed at constructing an electoral strategy and advancing a common agenda would energize local activism and help channel it. But, alongside that, another kind of linkage among local activists is necessary—one aimed not at creating an electoral force but at remobilizing grass-roots direct action and protest.

In earlier eras of the Left, efforts to coordinate and inspire grass-roots activism would be undertaken by an ideologically oriented national party. As we've seen, this model of activist organization was always deeply problematic for its participants and for the social movements in which they swam. Today such a model would be impossible. The extraordinary decentering of the left in the last two decades is not going to be overcome by a new national organization—nor should it be. If the left tradition continues to have any vitality it will rest on the ways in which such decentralization releases creativity and prevents enclosure.

The kind of organization needed would have to be simpler and far more modest in aim than the party models of the past claimed to be. One might envision a framework for mutual discussion, criticism, and debate that brings together organizers and activist intellectuals across the boundaries of "identity" without requiring agreement on policy— a grass-roots, fluid, inclusive forum; a "virtual" seminar or think tank, which provides opportunities to systematically debate ideas and reflect on local experience in a critical but mutually supportive way.

RE-IMAGINING RADICAL DEMOCRACY

Such an organizational space would facilitate the recreation of democratic vision, ideology, and program. But the demoralization and demobilization now being experienced by democratic activists isn't primarily the result of organizational weakness. Nor is it just that the right is ascendant and capable of energizing popular support and grass-roots action; indeed, threats from the right always provide left-wing activists with opportunity for effective organizing and action. The fundamental problem is ideological—an inability to formulate and articulate meaningful *democratic alternatives* to the social options now taken for granted in mainstream discourse. Resistance to right-wing efforts to reverse the gains made by social movements continues to be mobilized. Efforts to protect the interests of disadvantaged groups continue to be organized. But the problem resides in going beyond resistance, to find again a framework for thought and action that would foster democratic initiative rather than just defense.

Can we find visionary goals that have logical relation to contemporary reality and at the same time enable people to see that what appears to be real is not necessarily so? Can we articulate such "utopian aims" in ways that would enable people to struggle for them—and see that the struggle itself is socially productive, even if ultimate realization is elusive? And is there any possibility of articulating a vision that can be embraced across the boundaries of identity that now fragment democratic movements?

The fundamental barrier to such ideological construction is not the collapse of communism nor the disarray of European social democracy. American radicals have always sensed that 'socialism' was a problematic ideological framework in the American context. The core problem is that economic globalization has profoundly weakened the political structures that, for the last hundred years, movements have assumed would be usable for securing rights and advancing interests. Democratization was a project aimed at the national state and at institutions (corporations, local governments, etc.) subject to the rule-making authority of the national state.

Ideological reconstruction—the re-envisioning of the meaning and relevance of democratization—must begin with the fact of globalization. It starts by letting go of the assumption that our goal is primarily to turn the national government into a tool for democratic reform. Indeed, a fundamental political goal for democratic activism is to use the remaining powers of the national state to promote its decentralization.

Our impulse is to defend "government" against the increasingly virulent attacks emanating from the right. Those attacks are aimed at freeing capital to the greatest possible extent from controls that historically enabled some degree of distributive justice, some protection of living standards and dignity for those who lacked capital, or who were losers in competitive struggles. The increasing popularity of the right stems in part at least from the fact that statist political leaders no longer are credible when they claim to be providing such support and protection for the relatively disadvantaged. The national state has lost much of its economic steering authority, while fiscal crisis reduces the resources available for entitlements, subsidies, and social investment.

When the "New Frontier" and the "Great Society" were ascendant, New Left activists and intellectuals glimpsed the limitations of statist liberalism and socialism. They saw the dangers of expanding state bureaucracies to community self-determination and individual dignity. The new left was more anarchist than socialist, more Jeffersonian than Marxist—at least in its early days.[7] Democratic intellectuals and activists need to pick up the ideological threads spun then and see how they can be rewoven in the new era of globalized economy, polity, and culture. Here is the question: How can radical democracy be re-envisioned and social movements be reconstructed in the era of global capitalism?

The future of democratic grass-roots organization is going to revolve around efforts by people to protect ways of life, living standards, and other interests from the intrusions of global corporations, the ravages of global market forces, and the penetration of the global cultural apparati. The reconstruction of democratic belief, the revival of inspiriting utopianism might rest on the premise that it is in the places where people's lives are centered that power ought to be available.

We can already see some signs of democratic social movement appropriate to the global age. The following lines of action and program contain seeds of the future of a resurgent democratic activism:

a. *A new internationalism.* Resistance in the global age begins with protectionist impulses. Protectionism resists economic changes that threaten the wages and well-being of relatively well-off sectors of the working class. Obviously, such resistance can turn nativist and exclusionist and form the basis of authoritarian rather than democratic populism. The alternative is to support improved living standards for workers in the poor countries. The most obvious way to do this would be for American unions and labor organizers to provide direct assistance to labor struggles in those countries to which industrial jobs and capital have been and are being exported. Concerted action by Americans in support of such struggles—sympathetic demonstrations, political action, and job action—is necessary. Environmental internationalism—already evident in growing international networks of environmental activists and global environmental conferences—provides a second, equally important, track for strategic internationalism.

Americans have not been averse to mass action that either directly or indirectly expresses cross-national solidarity. Such action was integral to the anti-war and anti-interventionist activity during the Vietnam war, and of course was manifested in strong grass-roots opposition to United States policy in Central America. The most effective and explicit solidarity movement was the anti-apartheid struggle, which made extensive use of economic leverage. The campaign against NAFTA, although labeled as protectionist, undoubtedly raised popular awareness about the plight of Mexican workers and peasants, and may well have stimulated movement networks that could be activated for longer-term internationalist projects.

Such projects are made more likely by a fundamentally new social reality—Americans increasingly are in the same boat as the rest of the world. If historically American living standards were enhanced by imperialism, today the American population is increasingly being colonized by the same supranational forces as the rest of the planet. American elites no longer can credibly promise Americans that they will be advantaged in the global economy. The increasing congruence of interests between the peoples of the northern and southern hemispheres provides a material basis for a new internationalist consciousness. The growing popularity of "world music" is a cultural manifestation of this potential.[8]

b. *Community empowerment.* As the nation state declines, the local community becomes the focus of hope for collective power to maintain everyday life. Whenever corporate decisions threaten economic loss and social dislocation, community based mobilization has been an increasingly frequent—and often surprisingly effective—response. Struggles to prevent or mitigate plant closings and relocations, against corporate pollution, against destructive development—or the mitigation of these—are integral to local scenes everywhere. Increasingly, communities have developed considerable expertise about the means of resistance; the need for "outside organizers" is less than in the past and indigenous leadership grows in sophistication and creativity.

In the United States, a growing body of law has provided some legal foundation for community empowerment. State and national environmental legislation adopted over the last twenty-five years incorporates rights previously unavailable for local movements to challenge proposed developments because of their environmental impacts. Efforts to win similar legal protection for communities that are threatened with economic disruption—as for example the effort to pass plant closing legislation—indicate how the concept of community regulation of economic decisions might be expanded. Instead of demanding increased federal regulation administered by top-down bureaucracy, the logic of the EIR is to press for community voice in corporate decisions through mechanisms of public accountability, open hearings, and corporate negotiation with the local government.

In addition to the need for legal support for community voice in corporate decisions, communities need access to capital for local investment—capital not available from conventional private sources of finance. Community economic development grounded in democratic planning may be a fundamental strategy for protecting living standards against the ravages of the global market. I refer here not to the commonplace and often disastrous efforts by communities to invite their own rape by corporations and developers, but to efforts to develop community investment and ownership of enterprises that might be job creating and locally beneficial. Moreover, the provision of life necessities—including food, housing, recreation, and child care—through community directed, non-market mechanisms can provide social wage substitutions for declining or insecure private wages.

A promising strategic direction for community-based movement activists, therefore, would be to formulate an agenda for national legislation to empower localities. Such an agenda would include establishing national rules for community voice in corporate decisions that affect localities and providing major national resources to support community planning, development, ownership, and control aimed at "sustainable" local and regional economies. As the nation state declines and the trans-national corporation burgeons, it is at the level of community that self-determination and security is likely to be protected.[9]

c. *Workplace democratization*. The global market and the decline of the state compel the restructuring of private and public institutions. Corporate and bureaucratic "downsizing" when carried out from above is designed to protect the incomes and perquisites of those at the top, while imposing the costs of economic realism on those with the least leverage. Within each institution, fear, demoralization, and resentment are the result. In the larger society, increasing economic insecurity and dislocation for previously comfortable middle layers accompanies further degradation of the poorest. In the name of efficiency, environmental protections are threatened, previously taken for granted fringe benefits are liquidated, all of the institutional "frills" that make up a reasonably varied daily life are abolished. Rearguard resistance to such changes often proves frustratingly ineffective.

The alternative is to enable, and indeed compel, all of the constituencies of a given institution—workplace, school, government bureaucracy—to participate in the planning of institutional change. This means, of course, open books, the diffusion of expert knowledge, the development of institutional mechanisms of representation, voice, and accountability.

Indeed, demands for participation are a typical response to the threat of retrenchment and downsizing. Cuts are often administered so quickly that the opportunity to mobilize a response from below is short-circuited. But where retrenchment warnings appeared in advance of implementation, the mobilization of energy and the capacity of affected groups to grasp technical issues, and to bargain about these, is evident.

A democratic strategy of response to downsizing and cutbacks focuses not simply on resistance, but on demands for the democratic restructuring of institutional life. Such demands are not for the self-interested or privileged protection of particular groups. They are, in fact, quite the opposite. For the aspiration to exercise institutional voice is integrally connected with the need to take institutional responsibility.

d. *Global mass unemployment requires a restructuring of work*. Freeing people from enslavement to alienating labor was once a cornerstone of radical action. It is striking to realize that the American labor movement has not focused on the issue of work time for decades. In recent years, some European labor unions have achieved some reduction in work time, seeing this as a part of a strategy for protecting jobs. Workers in advanced societies need to be able to fully examine and debate the shorter work week as a means to share work, while freeing time for citizenly participation and community service. How might reductions in work time be accomplished without destruction of living standards? Would the reallocation of work time actually create significant numbers of new jobs? Can the social wage and collective goods be substituted for job-related wages while sustaining adequate living standards? Can definitions of "paid work" be expanded to include the full range of caring and helping now required of families and volunteers? These questions are at the heart of an examination of the meaning of democracy for personal fulfillment and development—as well as potentially important in the struggle for a definition of full employment in the global era.

These then are some of the key elements for democratic activist strategy in the global era. I've suggested that such a strategy would be much facilitated if there were a national framework of discussion and support for radical activists and intellectuals. But the work of democratic reconstruction, embodying the sorts of themes sketched above, doesn't require such an organized framework. The material conditions for a new—global—stage of social movement development are at hand. The choices offered the majority by existing political leaderships promise little in the way of sustaining the basis for decent everyday lives. The current popularity of authoritarian populism suggests one possible future. The chances for a democratic option depend on the capacity of radical activists/intellectuals to think beyond their particular identities and their institutionalized niches to create a politics grounded in personal autonomy, community control, and collective decision-making.

NOTES

1. Some recent examples of such accounts include D. Healey, *Dorothy Healey Remembers a Life in the Communist Party* (New York: Oxford University Press, 1990); M. Andrews, *Lifetimes of Commitment* (New York: Cambridge University Press, 1991).

2. See, for example, A. Kraditor, *The Radical Persuasion* (Baton Rouge: Louisiana University Press, 1981); C. Lasch, *The Agony of the American Left* (New York: Vintage Books, 1969); J. Weinstein, *Ambiguous Legacy* (New York: New Viewpoints, 1975).

3. See Stanley Aronowitz, "Towards Radicalism: The Death and Rebirth of the American Left," in this volume.

4. For a detailed interpretation of the Left tradition in the United States, see R. Flacks, *Making History: The American Left and the American Mind* (New York: Columbia University Press, 1988).

5. There is a literature documenting processes that preceded such awakenings. See, for instance, A. Morris, *Origins of the Civil Rights Movement* (New York: Free Press, 1984); A. Jamison and Ron Eyerman, *Seeds of the Sixties* (Berkeley: University of California Press, 1993); M. Isserman, *If I Had a Hammer . . .* (New York: Basic Books, 1987); L. Rupp and V. Taylor, *Movement in the Doldrums* (New York: Oxford University Press, 1987).

6. See J. Whalen and R. Flacks, *Beyond the Barricades* (Philadelphia: Temple University Press, 1989).

7. See, for example, J. Miller, *Democracy is in the Streets* (New York: Simon and Schuster, 1987), for a discussion of early new left ideological perspectives, and also for the text of the Port Huron Statement, which provided the first political use of the concept of "participatory democracy" as an alternative to both socialism and capitalist democracy.

8. See J. B. Childs and J. Brecher, *Global Visions* (Boston: South End Press, 1993), for discussion of potentials for international social movement development.

9. See R. Fisher and J. Kling, *Mobilizing the Community* (Newbury Park: Sage Publications, 1993); A. Kirby, *Power/Resistance* (Bloomington: Indiana University Press, 1993). The Grassroots Policy Project promotes progressive state and local economic and environmental policy: 1875 Connecticut Ave. NW, Washington DC, 20006.

8

LET'S GET RADICAL

WHY SHOULD THE RIGHT
HAVE ALL THE FUN?

IT'S A DIRTY JOB, BUT SOMEBODY HAS TO DO IT—ASSERTS
the left in reaction to the 1994 electoral putsch. It is difficult, however, to identify the left as making this assertion.
Conventional notions of the political spectrum have been
shifting to the right with a speed reminiscent of German
hyperinflation in the twenties. It is equally difficult to identify,
with any certainty, what constitutes the ideological foundations
of the right. Go to bed assuming Bob Dole is a bona fide
member of the hard right, wake up, and he's become a moderate. Clinton, on the basis of his feeble lurch toward health care
reform, is branded as the next thing to a Marxist revolutionary,
while the modest social liberalism that was one of his selling
points in 1992 (and that he's been backing away from ever since)
is equated with the extreme in radical "femqueerthink." The
Democratic Leadership Council is hectoring him to "move to the
center" occupied, presumably, by Newt Gingrich. At this moment

a leftist appears to be defined as anyone who doesn't want to repeal the income tax, thinks public schools are a good idea, and doubts that putting poor kids in orphanages is the solution to welfare dependency.

This ideological bracket-creep lends a certain absurdity to the right's determination to interpret the election results as an omnibus revolt against New Deal liberalism and sixties cultural radicalism. So enthusiastically are conservatives pushing this line that both the *Wall Street Journal* and the *New York Post* quoted my comment that the Clintons are "inescapably sixties figures," when, in fact, I was making precisely the opposite point: that Clinton's frantic attempts to distance himself from his "countercultural McGovernik" past and socially liberal impulses had, if anything, increased his political enemies' contempt, while confirming most people's impression that there's nothing there. This election was not a repudiation of the left: you can't repudiate something that for all practical purposes doesn't exist. Rather, it demonstrated that the electorate abhors a vacuum.

The list of American frustrations is long and growing: economic insecurity, overwork or not enough work or stultifying, regimented work at insultingly low wages, no prospect of improvement, no margin for illness or retirement; recognition that the dream is over, that education and hard work guarantee no reward whatsoever; crime, lousy schools, disintegrating public services, lack of community, racial and ethnic tension, conflict between the sexes, familial instability, no time for personal life and child rearing, and so forth. All this exacerbates people's sense of government as an alien institution that takes their money for purposes decreed by arrogant bureaucrats and corrupt politicians, is impervious to their influence, and does nothing to address their problems.

The right puts these grievances in the context of its own vision; it offers and analyzes a set of principles, a program. While much has been made of the divisions among Republicans—economic libertarians versus religious rightists, internationalists versus isolationists—they have so far subordinated their disagreements to a coherent overall message. Politically, they identify the cause of our problems as a government that neglects its primary duty to maintain law and order, discourages the economy by taxing and regulating business, and confiscates the hard-earned money of productive citizens to support an out-of-control debt, a huge bureaucracy, and a parasitic, immoral, dangerous underclass. Culturally, they blame the sixties—shorthand for the decline of traditional religious and moral authority; the demand for individual freedom and social equality; the revolt of blacks, women, and gays; the sexual revolution; and the normalization of divorce and single parenthood.

The Democrats respond to the conservative challenge in two characteristic ways. They defend the status quo—mainstream social liberalism and the shrinking welfare state—or (more often) they agree but offer no clear answer. Since people desperately want their lives to change, and since they much prefer passionate ideological conviction to half-hearted, opportunistic pandering, both these Democratic strategies are losers.

Judging by the 1994 election post-mortems, the effective life of the left is gone. There is little leftist commentary that, references to current events and issues aside, couldn't have been written in 1980; and its prescriptions won't work any better now than they did then. The common theme is a call for economic populism, with or without an explicit invocation of New Deal liberalism (i.e., liberalism before 1968). On the counterculture McGovernik question, populism promoters are divided. Some, like Daniel Cantor and Juliet Schor in the *Times*, argue that social conservatism is a displacement: "In the absence of a convincing populist program, the economic anxieties of the day . . . leave people wide open for sucker shows on immigration, race, and crime." Others see cultural conservatism as an integral part of the populism the left should embrace: as Joe Klein put it in *Newsweek*, "there *was* a subtle alliance between 'left-wing elites' and the nascent black underclass in matters of personal morality in the 1960's."

In New York, the most conspicuous polemic in this vein was Jack Newfield's front-page-of-the-Post appeal to "my fellow Democrats" to Dump Bill Clinton: "Liberals ought to stand for traditional values like work, family, law, discipline, patriotism, and individual moral responsibility. . . . The Democratic Party must fight like hell for economic programs that benefit blue-collar workers at the same time they help the poor." (In a follow-up column, Newfield professes amazement that his views have been enthusiastically promoted by Rush Limbaugh and Jay Diamond, and wonders, "Are they using me, or am I using them?")

Meanwhile, at the *Voice*, our post-election cover was devoted to Michael Tomasky proclaiming, "Tuesday's returns were the final referendum on a left-liberal agenda that paid too much attention to its tiny narcissisms and too little attention to the needs of most Americans." For any feminist or gay liberationist who experienced the first wave of pro-family backlash in the seventies, "narcissism" is a fighting word. As popularized by Christopher Lasch's *Culture of Narcissism*, the term was regularly used against those of us who argued that real radicalism is about affirming the right to freedom and pleasure, and unmasking the repressive functions of institutions like Family and Work. But in the grim context of the nineties, this sort of narcissism, tiny or huge, is rarer than steak tartare.

That the left's problem is not an excess of self-love but a paucity of ideas is amply demonstrated by Tomasky's brand of belligerently anti-intellectual populism. "Most people," as he sees it, work, pay taxes, have children, want the trash picked up, and go to school so they can get a secure job, "own a home, and do the regular things Americans want to do." They "think Fish and Jameson stand for a dinner of carp and Irish whiskey (and [are] little the worse for thinking it, incidentally.)"[1] Whereas the "liberal elites," who presumably don't work, pay taxes, have kids, or believe in garbage collection, and are off doing perverted rather than regular things, "sit around debating the canon at a handful of elite universities."

Tomasky's portrait of Average Joe is as condescending as anything the "liberal elites" could dream up. (In fact, the apathy about class that pervades the academic left is the flip side of his know-nothingism.) Even more telling is his assumption that academic debates are inherently trivial. The right is winning in part because it doesn't make such mistakes. Conservatives know that it matters what goes on in universities, especially the elite kind. Decisions about what gets taught there—what counts as bona fide knowledge—resonate through the educational system and the culture as a whole. This is why the right—not the left—has made changes in the canon and other aspects of academic culture a major public issue.

Tomasky does make one statement with which I entirely agree: "There's no surer way to create new generations of conservatives . . . than to let the right take the lead on welfare, crime, immigration . . . the left isn't offering [people] an alternative way of doing things that makes any sense in their lives, and people can only select from what's on the menu." Exactly! And what might that alternative be?

In a subsequent piece that retracts the "over the top" (his phrase) rhetoric of the former article, Tomasky argues that the left should combine a progressive economic program with a rethinking of the "categories of left and right" on social issues. Regarding education, for instance, he asks: "Why is it wrong for the left to advocate higher learning standards, a longer school day, a longer school year . . . ?"[2] "Higher learning standards"—who can disagree with the need for them? But what that entails is not as self-evident as Tomasky seems to think. Conservatives have strong ideas about what should be taught, how, and to whom. They like old-fashioned authoritarian pedagogy, indoctrination in morals, official, inspirational versions of history, great books for the elite, and vocational training for the masses. There are radical alternatives to this agenda, but developing and presenting them entails the kind of discussion Tomasky would no doubt dismiss as elitist thumbsucking, on the grounds that Average Joe thinks John Dewey was governor of New York. As for a longer school day and year, why should the left uncritically embrace this nose-to-the-grindstonism, which also demands that adults work longer hours? My ten-year-old has school five hours a day plus homework time, ten months a year. Why isn't this enough? What's wrong with having the time to play, to relax in hot weather?

"The left resisted welfare reform for years," Tomasky continues. "Some on the left even argued, years ago, in favor of expanding welfare rights. . . . Well, these arguments were lost. The welfare laws are going to be rewritten. The point is to write them in a humane way." Not so fast. The sixties left criticized the welfare system as a means of pacifying and controlling the poor instead of attacking economic inequality. This is a genuine alternative view, but convincing people it makes sense involves challenging the notion that people are poor because of their laziness and immorality—the very assumption behind welfare reform. How do you "humanely" pretend there's a job out there for any welfare recipient who tries hard enough? How do you "humanely" punish women for having children outside marriage?

This is not to equate Tomasky with Newfield, who, like Klein, comes from a pre-feminist generation of New Leftists and never came to terms with sexual politics. Rather, Tomasky belongs to a post-backlash generation that has had little exposure to genuine cultural radicalism, as opposed to the platitudes of identity politics. (When he complains that campaigns to abolish Columbus Day turn the working class off, he's talking as much about himself as he is the working class.) Similarly, Cantor and Schor cannot be labeled with the left's long history of misusing the culture-as-displacement-of-economic-anxiety argument. Though it's true enough that economic anxiety feeds social conservativism—encouraging people to cling to whatever forms of power, status, or stability they can find—leftists have long seized on this point to argue against confronting cultural issues directly and to deny their own anxiety about cultural conflict. Today, however, left suggestions that cultural problems can be solved with economic remedies reflect less an active avoidance of cultural politics than fifteen years of systematic repression of cultural radical thought.

In the absence of a publicly visible cultural radical movement, populism looks attractive to many leftists in search of a non-statist, decentralized model of democracy. But like communitarianism, populism is inherently conservative. At a recent conference sponsored by the journal *Telos*, which brought together a group of leftists and conservatives to discuss the possibilities for a new American populism, Sam Francis of the right-wing *Washington Times* observed, "In most discussions of populism I have heard from the left, any celebration . . . is always hastily qualified by assurances that of course the 'dark side' of populism—what an early prospectus for this conference described as 'bigotry, xenophobia, racism, and provincialism' . . . functions as the protective guardian of local community and autonomous social institutions against the meddling of the left and (its) social engineering."

Populism does not aim to abolish class distinctions. Rather, it's a form of identity politics or cultural nationalism for so-called ordinary people—in Tomasky's formulation, self-assertive ignorance of pointy-headed debates, or, in another common left-populist metaphor, beer and chips instead of wine and cheese. Like other variants of nationalism, populism defines membership in a community through the exclusion of others and defends the received values of that community against outsiders. Uninterested in or actively hostile to individual freedom, populism equates collective values with dominant values, denying conflict within the community and punishing dissidence.

Nor can populism deliver on its promises of economic justice. In the short run, a class-oriented, New Deal politics might well win some elections; certainly such a movement would excite more enthusiasm than Clinton's abjectness. But the conditions that sustained the welfare state, or what New Left types used to call corporate liberalism, no longer exist. Those conditions included: the unquestioned preeminence of the United States in the world economy, which is to say a national capitalist class more or less invulnerable to global competition; the military and ideological threat of Communism; and computers still only a product of science fiction. American capital needed large numbers of industrial workers and managers; it had an investment in protecting the American standard of living to insure a prosperous market for its goods and stave off any threat of socialism, and it had enough surplus profits to devote to that investment.

Under these conditions, the social contract that business offered millions of American workers was assent to the corporate system in return for secure jobs at middle class wages and a safety net in the form of social security, private pensions, and medical insurance. The labor movement and most other potentially radical constituencies accepted this contract, making a mistake of historic proportions. The contract also promised social stability, to be bought with welfare and other social programs that defused potential revolt among the poor.

Today, with the globalization of the market and the spread of computer technologies that radically reduce the need for human labor, American workers *and* managers are increasingly expendable. Unions have no bargaining power; they work on the employer's terms or not at all. With the collapse of Communism, the absence of any serious left opposition in America or anywhere else, and the stranglehold of free-market ideology on all conversation about economics, capital no longer sees a need even to give lip-service to social responsibility: if the poor sleep in the streets, if laid-off workers lose their homes, so what?

The central irony of the post-Cold War era is that the end of totalitarianism, thrilling as it was, cleared the way for the triumphant and vengeful resurgence of nineteenth-century laissez-faire, on a grander scale than was ever possible before. The failure of socialism was evident long before 1989: its revolutionary version was tyrannical, its social democratic version indistinguishable from welfare-state liberalism. But it did serve to discipline capitalism. American mass prosperity was in a sense financed not only by the fruits of American empire, but by the subjugation of Russians, Czechs, and Poles.

It is tempting, but reinventing socialism is a dead end. Socialism has failed not simply because it put too much faith in the state but because it put too little value on freedom. As a political movement, socialism relentlessly marginalized its cultural radicals; it privileged the collective over the individual, survival and self-sacrifice over pleasure, economic equality over happiness in everyday life. Defining themselves as anti-capitalists rather than anti-authoritarian, socialists have typically regarded the liberatory aspects of capitalist society—the undermining of familial and religious authority, the ideology of individual rights and liberties, the social permissiveness of a consumer-oriented market—with great suspicion. For many, these fruits of capitalist individualism are as much the enemy as its economic tyranny.

Challenging this underlying anti-libertarian, anti-pleasure bias—which links the socialists to the populists—was the great contribution of the sixties cultural radical left and of the first powerful surge of the women's and gay liberation movements. The challenge has been muted by today's respectable social liberals, caricatured by mindless cultural pluralists, subverted by feminists who foment sexual hysteria, and obliterated by leftists determined to enlist the state in suppressing their opponents' speech. At present there is no politics that can link a defense of pleasure with an attack on the new capitalist world order. Ironically, it's the right that's perceived as the party of pleasure, giving permission to enjoy the sadistic release of bashing the government and the media, and venting tabooed, "incorrect" feelings about blacks, women, gays, or immigrants. This is a sadly limited release to be sure, but better than no release at all. As long as there is nothing better, the right will keep winning.

NOTES

1. Michael Tomasky, "Pointing the Finger at Progressives," *Village Voice*, 39, no. 47 (Nov. 11–16, 1994):47.
2. Ibid.

ELLEN WILLIS

9

A FOREIGN POLICY FOR RADICAL DEMOCRATS

BOGDAN DENITCH

THE CLINTON/GORE ADMINISTRATION CAME INTO OFFICE having made exceedingly few promises or commitments in foreign and defense policy. This is the area in which criticism of the outgoing Bush administration was least pronounced, and where the greatest degree of continuity was promised. The more the pity: the essentially bi-partisan defense and foreign policies of the past decade have left entire herds of sacred cows ready for slaughter. The famous foreign policy successes of power-projection by "the only remaining superpower" have been at best ambivalent.

The Gulf War, where Bush proclaimed victory and Congress passed a measure praising Bush's leadership, left Sadam Hussein firmly in power; the Shiite rebels, encouraged by the United States to rise up in South Iraq, mercilessly slaughtered; and the Kurds insecurely huddling behind a fragile and temporary United Nations shield. Meanwhile, in Kuwait, the same rapacious dynasty is back in power without a whiff of democratic reforms, keeping large numbers of inhabitants of the state without citizenship or a vote. In Panama, the bipartisan victory succeeded in killing thousands of Panamanians in order to save them from a CIA-allied drug-dealing thug and left in place the corrupt Panamanian army. Panama is not notably closer to democracy or popular rule than before the American operation. Adventures in Grenada and the Philippines have not been any more encouraging, at least as far as popular rule and stable democracy are concerned. All this should make for some wariness about the United States capacity for policing the world, particularly in cases where the United States has a major historical responsibility for the unpopular regime being targeted.

Seemingly determined to get in one last military adventure before he left office, George Bush committed troops to Somalia without any clearly stated goals. And, typical of the new status quo, Bush initiated military action without any proper debate in Congress, with little meaningful public discussion, and with no indication that the troops could accomplish their mission within the time frame Bush indicated. The situation in Somalia was developing for over a year; there was ample time for debate.

In a parliamentary democracy, the British remind us, the administration would have to propose a policy and a rationale. Experts would be heard from and the public would get involved. Nothing of this sort happens here. The decision to send over twenty-thousand Marines and light infantry was made by a lame duck President, with the presumed agreement of the incoming administration. Where is the Congress? Where are the Congressional committees? The problem is that we are still faced with an imperial presidency.

Whatever the issues around Somalia are, they are not for technocrats and experts alone to settle. Issues that desperately call for a vital public debate include: Should the United States act as a world police force (with United Nations approval) in areas where orderly government has so broken down as to jeopardize the lives of large numbers of people? If so, then how do we determine *where* the United States should go? After all, the slaughter, rapine, and disorder in equatorial Sudan, Kurdistan, Bosnia-Herzegovina, Myanmar, Armenia, and Georgia are no less brutal than in Somalia. Why, then, Somalia and not Sudan?

This is not to say that there are not reasons to intervene in one place and not in another, but they should be clearly stated and debated before our troops are sent. How risky is this in terms of lives? Who will have to take responsibility if it turns out to be a bloody error? All these are normal questions that should be asked publicly—before another military intervention, even a most humane one.

One caveat radical democrats should make to the Clinton administration is that we are tired of manipulative, neo-machiavellian "grand" politics of the type made popular by the "Wise Men" during the years of the high Cold War. We should propose a foreign policy arrived at through normal political debate, with issues made as transparent to the public as possible. Secrecy has served legitimate interests of the United States very poorly. Radical democrats must insist that foreign policy is part and parcel of the democratic political process—or rather that it should become so, since at this time it clearly is not.

We should be wary of Bill Clinton, who so far shows little desire to open up this area to genuine debate. A Democratic administration will not necessarily be notably better on this score than a Republican one. Many of the people with ties to the administration are the familiar, "respectable" figures closely linked to the tired assumptions of the military-industrial complex and the dead-but-not-forgotten Cold War. The very worst of the neo-conservative cold warriors previously allied with the hawkish wing of the AFL-CIO are among the "Reagan Democrats" who have returned to the fold, and they can be expected to wreak considerable damage behind the scenes.

One agency to look at in particular is the National Endowment for Democracy (NED)—an ongoing scandal through the Reagan and Bush years. Under Carl Gershman, the NED has backed right-wing student groups in France, raving nationalists in Eastern Europe (particularly in Ukraine), and reliable anti-communist thugs in the third world, especially in Central America. Progressives and radical democrats must mobilize to make sure the character of the NED changes dramatically in the Clinton administration.

For too long, progressives in the Democratic Party have generally tended to ignore defense issues. Or, to be fair, they have tended to be for smaller defense expenditures in principle without much attention to what was being bought and for what purpose. There have been exceptions—Admiral LaRoque, Congressman Dellums, and Gordon Adams, for instance, have critiqued not merely waste, but the assumptions behind our military budgets. We need to do this much more, and much more systematically. The question is not the size of the budget, but rather, what is sufficient for a sane defense policy in the post-Cold War world?

An analysis will reveal that a whole range of weapons systems is redundant and can be eliminated. Nuclear submarines, heavy battle tanks, stealth bombers and fighters, as well as half of the Aircraft Carrier Battle Groups could be cut out, for starters. To this, one can immediately add most of the troops in Europe and Korea, as well as about half of the navy and air force. If it is our fate to be a mainstay of United Nations-sponsored police actions—not a bad thing in itself— then what we will end up keeping are the marines, light infantry divisions, flexible air strength, and some naval transport and support units. This makes for a very much smaller budget than anything imagined by Clinton's advisers.

After trimming the military to a reasonable size for the post-Cold War world (which will still be a place with all kinds of nasty and dangerous situations that might require limited, multi-lateral applications of military power), we are left with an uncomfortable question: What is an appropriate kind of military force for a democracy? As a radical democrat, it is my belief that the answer cannot be a professional army, in particular not one separated from civil society. The only consistent position for people who take civic responsibility seriously is for a citizen army to be based on universal (not selective) service of all men and women at the age of 18. Alternatives to military service should be available—a Citizen Corps for service in developing countries, hospitals, schools, and national forests. Women and gays should be assured full equality at all levels and in all branches of the services. But the principle should be that every citizen must serve as an expression of the mutual responsibility and rights between a society and the individual. On this we base citizens' rights to education, health, and the other rights of citizenship in a developed modern democracy.

A second principle is that the army should be as much a part of civilian society as possible. In Holland and Sweden, non-commissioned officers are unionized as are civilians when not on active duty. In the French system, reserve officers and soldiers broke the back of a right-wing military revolt against DeGaulle when he ordered a withdrawal from Algiers. Professional armies are not a secure basis for security in a democratic society.

The greatest sin of the Bush administration will turn out to have been its mean-spirited inability to grasp the historical opening the end of the Cold War provided for democracy. We may not have a similar chance for very long to come. Eastern Europe and the former Soviet Union are going through a prolonged agony of attempting to transform their economies and societies during a phase of the world economy when funds are short and the largest industrial power in the world is locked into a mantra of "No More Taxes."

The Clinton administration must be pushed to provide sustained long-range help in rebuilding the economies in this part of the world. We spent billions for the military and for the Gulf War, yet we cry poverty when it comes to the post-communist countries and the former USSR. We are playing with fire. Economic misery has been the backdrop for tentative experiments in fragile new democracies, but economic misery is more suited to full-blooded nationalism or authoritarianism than to "cool" democratic pluralism. We should join in mobilizing a massive multi-national effort that includes the European Community and Japan as well as the United States. Not only will this aid the new democracies (and therefore support geopolitical stability), but it will also bolster the world economy. It would provide vast new investments analogous to those the Marshall Plan provided in Europe for a good decade after the Second World War. Make no mistake: the Marshall Plan greatly helped rebuild Europe, but it was also very good for the United States, economically and socially.

That kind of approach—blending humanitarianism with enlightened self-interest—has the best prospects of being broadly acceptable, thus providing what is more essential: a long-range commitment to helping stable democratic regimes and effective economies grow in former communist-ruled countries. This is more or less what the Brant, Manley, Palme Report proposed for a North-South relationship, and is the only road toward a secure world.

10

RADICAL DEMOCRACY AND CULTURAL POLITICS

WHAT ABOUT CLASS?
WHAT ABOUT POLITICAL POWER?

BARBARA EPSTEIN

O VER THE LAST DECADE OR SO, "RADICAL DEMOCRACY" has come to replace "socialism" as the point of reference for what used to be called left politics. This is true, at least, for many intellectuals, but most notably for those who address questions having to do with strategy or directions for what, for lack of a better term, might be called progressive politics in the United States. The depth of the crisis here is indicated by the immediate need to qualify or step back from every name for the political tendency being discussed. Every term is tainted in one way or another. "Socialist" and "left" are associated with discredited regimes and outmoded predictions of proletarian revolution; "progressive" has the unacceptable connotation of a teleology of progress. "Radical" remains acceptable, but largely because its meaning is entirely elastic—with the consequence that it can be claimed by the right as well as the left.

I continue to use the term "left" to mean a politics directed toward a society that would be more egalitarian on many levels (in economics as well as politics in relation to race, gender, and a range of other social categories, as well as class). I use the term "progressive" to indicate a similar orientation but more modest aims—probably excluding explicit consideration of a transition to socialism.

Many intellectuals who might be described, in these terms, as "on the left" are now talking about "radical democracy," though giving it a variety of meanings. In 1984 Ernesto Laclau and Chantal Mouffe, in *Hegemony and Socialist Strategy,*[1] argued that the Marxist association of socialism with the working class encumbered it with a crippling essentialism. They argued for a conception of radical democracy, associated with the new social movements, that would rest on a conception of politics in which every position was constructed and negotiated anew, in which no connection between class location and political position was assumed. Since then, increasing numbers of left or progressive intellectuals have renounced socialism for radical democracy. Anthony Giddens has argued that socialism, as much as capitalism, is a creature of the Fordist era of massive, hierarchical structures and organizations, and that in the new era of the "risk society" we must put socialism behind us and make radical democracy our goal.[2] Stanley Aronowitz, in the lead article in *Socialist Review*, writes that it is time to give socialism a decent burial and replace it with a demand for radical or participatory democracy.[3] In *October,* Cornel West associates himself with the call for radical democracy.[4]

It is not hard to understand why so many people are replacing "socialism" with "radical democracy." The unappealing example of actual socialist or communist societies, especially in relation to democracy and human rights; the apparent global victory of capitalism; the collapse of hope for any alternative to it—all make it difficult to continue to talk about socialism. The term "radical democracy" has a set of positive connotations: it is associated with the social movements of the seventies and eighties, in particular feminism, gay and lesbian rights, environmentalism, and multiculturalism; it suggests a politics oriented more toward cultural than toward political or economic struggles; and it is associated with decentralization and has vaguely anarchist, or at least anti-bureaucratic, overtones. It suggests grassroots politics, diversity, a playful political practice that is not bound by rigid structures but is continually in the process of transformation. All of these aspects of the politics suggested by "radical democracy" are genuinely appealing.

However, there are also serious problems associated with the adoption of this term, and I believe that the problems outweigh the advantages. To state the problems briefly before exploring them in more detail: the term radical democracy is anchored in the "new social movements," a category that did not entirely fit the map of social change activism even at the moment when it was most useful—roughly the mid-seventies to the mid-eighties—and which is considerably less relevant to social movements of the mid-nineties than it was to those a decade or so ago. The "new social movements" are a thin basis for a left perspective for the nineties. If one regards radical democracy as rooted not in the particular kinds of movements described by new social movement theory but associated simply with the range of existing movements, then this is an even thinner basis for a radical perspective. If the left has nothing more to contribute than to refer to the current map of social activism, it has little reason to exist. Furthermore, current activism includes as much on the right as on the left; in fact, the term "radical" is easily appropriated by the right.

The turn toward radical democracy involves a turn away from class as a key category of left politics, and also a loss of interest in politics or the question of who controls states (and other governing institutions) and what policies they produce. The shift away from class and state power is understandable, given the disappointing record of left politics in both arenas, but it is a big mistake, especially at a moment when class polarization is proceeding rapidly both in the United States and internationally, and when economic globalization is raising the question of who will hold power and what those who hold it will do with it. For the last ten years or so, much of the intellectual left has celebrated cultural and political marginality. The left, especially the intellectual left, is in danger of becoming entirely irrelevant to the major shifts that are taking place nationally and internationally. This essay will trace at least some of the political and intellectual currents that have led to the current rejection of class (and of the issue of state power), argue that these currents should be seen critically rather than being made the basis for left politics, and try to suggest more promising directions.

New social movement theory is an intellectual tendency that presents an analysis of contemporary social movements while at the same time identifying with those social movements, and in effect prescribing particular directions for radical politics. First developed by continental social analysts such as Alain Touraine, Alberto Melucci, and others in the seventies and early eighties, new social movement theory sharply distinguished between "old" and "new" social movements.[5] The "old" social movements were those organized around class, especially the working class; they were concerned with political power and with economic structures, or issues of economic redistribution. The concept of "old" social movements carried a flavor of communism or of social democracy; it referred to the movements that set the tone for radical politics, in Europe at least, from the mid-nineteenth century through the thirties. The "new" social movements, according to the theoretical model, were organized not around class but around other kinds of identities; these movements were not interested in political power or in economic restructuring, but rather in cultural change, in the transformation of values and of everyday life. "New" social movements were anti-hierarchical as opposed to bureaucratic. Internally highly democratic, they were concerned with the defense and construction of community, and of particular identities. These were presented both as descriptions of emerging forms of social movement practice, and as prescriptions for a form of radicalism appropriate to Western society, at least, in the late twentieth century.

Particularly in its claim to describe a form of radicalism appropriate to late twentieth-century Western society, new social movement theory interacted with two other strands of theory, both of which were taking hold in Europe, especially France and Germany, at roughly the same time: Fordist/post-Fordist theory, and poststructuralism. Fordist analysis suggested that the form of capitalism that was based on the compromise between capital and labor, a welfare state, and massive assembly-line production of commodities had gone into crisis, and that more decentralized or fragmented forms were emerging not only in the realm of production but in politics and the organization of social life. This analysis could be seen to have implications for the arena of culture. An economy driven by consumption and a social order held together by a capital-labor compromise required a high level of consent, making culture a crucial arena of struggle. The stable structures and bureaucratic organizations of Fordist society had helped to inculcate discipline; as these broke down, culture became an increasingly important arena both of the inculcation of ideologies of social control, and of protest. Though Fordist theory was developed by people who in many cases remained close to Marxism, and new social movement theory was generally associated with an anti-Marxist stance, the two came together in suggesting that the era of class politics based on struggles at the point of production was over, and that new movements were likely to be locally based, decentralized, and focused on issues of culture and daily life. [6]

New social movement theory, enhanced by Fordist theory, also intersected in some respects with poststructuralism, which though based in France was gaining wide influence elsewhere by the late seventies and eighties. On the whole, the circles in which new social movement theory was being developed were quite distinct from poststructuralist or postmodernist circles. Despite the fact that leading poststructuralist theorists looked back on May '68 as a key moment in their lives, poststructuralism was considerably more remote from actual social movements than new social movement theory, which required interaction with actual movements. Poststructuralism did, however, reinforce certain aspects of new social movement theory. poststructuralism's emphasis on language overlapped with the new social movement emphasis on culture. Its emphasis on the unstable, fragmentary, and fleeting, its rejection of unity and coherence either as reality or as goal reinforced the emphasis on decentralization and spontaneity as qualities of social movements. Poststructuralism's rejection of universal values as "totalizing" was absorbed into the discussion of new social movements. In fact, the leading theorists of new social movements had never claimed that new social movements rejected universal values; for Touraine, for instance, the leading characteristic of such movements was that they presented a new set of values as those that should govern society. But as poststructuralism and new social movement theory have been absorbed into left intellectual discourse, the distinctions between them have tended to be forgotten. [7]

The problem is not that new social movement theory has become overlaid with poststructuralist aesthetic preferences but that even from the mid-seventies to the mid-eighties—the high point of actual "new social movements"—the fit between the theory and the social movement reality was never very close, and that in the nineties there are few social movements that fit the "new social movement" model. New social movement theory was inspired by the amalgam of oppositional youth movements that gained strength in Western Europe, especially West Germany, in the late seventies. The anti-nuclear movement—opposition to US-imposed nuclear weapons, and also to nuclear power plants—was at the center of this movement culture; it was infused as well with feminism, pacifism, anarchism, a network of alternative institutions, and efforts to construct a viable counter-culture. This movement culture impressed students of social movements and other left-leaning intellectuals because of its size (at least in some areas), its attractive style (the efforts to build community, the renunciation of machismo and authoritarianism), and its fit with the new theories of capitalism that were being advanced at the time.

Even when the new social movements were flourishing in Western Europe, many movements and organizations did not fit this model. One respect in which the theory was broadly borne out was that the organized working class had ceased to be the main basis of movements for social change. But this did not mean that all or even most collective efforts for social change fit the anti-bureaucratic, anarchist-oriented model described by the theory. Through the seventies and eighties more conventionally organized movements, oriented toward elections and policy reform rather than broad cultural change, continued to exist; as the counter-culture began to decline (or at least to become detached from social protest) in the mid- to late eighties, it was these more conventional organizations that were able to retain popular support around concerns such as peace and the environment.[8]

In the United States there has been even less cohesion between new social movement theory and the actual shape of movements for social change. Over the same time period when new social movements were flourishing in Western Europe, there were a few movements in the United States that more or less fit the same model: for instance, the nonviolent direct action movement, which addressed, in turn, nuclear power, nuclear arms, and United States intervention in Central America. Each phase of the movement, after a series of dramatic mass mobilizations, went into decline; in the mid-eighties the movement as a whole came to an end. Ecofeminism, which shared the same approach to politics, had a brief life as an activist social movement and then retreated into the academy and became a branch of theory. Radical Christian activism (expressed, for instance, in the Sanctuary movement), which fit much of the "new social movement" model, also flourished in the early eighties and attracted many activists not associated with the churches; it continues to exist but has to a large degree lost its former mass character.[9]

Some gay and lesbian organizations of the seventies and eighties fit the description of new social movements; this is perhaps the arena in which the "new social movement" impulse has best survived into the nineties, especially in the form of ACT UP and Queer Nation. But much of the gay and lesbian movement has become strongly, and quite effectively, oriented toward the electoral arena. Through the seventies and the eighties there were many movements and organizations organized around issues of identity—race, gender, sexuality—and by virtue of addressing these issues contributed to a transformation of culture. But they did not necessarily participate in the more specific cultural radicalism that new social movement theory described, and that the concept of radical democracy presumes.

In the nineties there is still an arena of countercultural activism, oriented toward cultural transformation and infused with an anarchist or anti-state sensibility (Earth First!, for instance). But it is no longer possible to describe "new social movements" as a growing tendency. As in Europe, in many arenas—such as the women's movement, the environmental movement, and movements of groups of color—more conventional organizations continued to function through the seventies and eighties, and remain strong today. Meanwhile, different (that is, new but not "new") forms of grassroots social activism are emerging. Perhaps the most promising grassroots movement is the toxics/environmental justice movement, the overlapping networks of local groups opposed to chemical contamination and protesting the particular exposure of communities of color to such hazards. These groups exhibit some of the characteristics associated with new social movements: they are locally based and democratic. The movement as a whole is not organized around class (though it is composed mostly of people at the lower ends of the economic ladder, since these are the people most exposed to toxics). Race and gender are major issues for this movement, due to its focus on environmental racism, the large and growing numbers of people of color within its ranks, and the fact that it is overwhelmingly a movement of women. But it is not a movement that is about identity. Groups within the movement often find themselves opposing the state, or more precisely, agencies of the state.[10]

Toxics/environmental justice groups are not culturally radical, except in the broad sense that the demand for a livable environment is a critique of prevailing values. They are also not anarchist. They do not want less state power, but do want more effective regulation on behalf of the public. The toxics/environmental justice movement is not primarily concerned with issues of production, but it has not entirely left these issues aside: experienced activists argue that ultimately it will be necessary to go beyond struggles against particular local toxic dumps and facilities and demand that production be transformed to eliminate toxic hazards at their point of origin.

The above thumbnail description of the toxics/environmental justice movement is not intended to suggest that this is the new model of social movements for the nineties and beyond. It is more likely that this will be one among many forms that social movements will take. But this description does highlight certain differences. The new social movements of the seventies and eighties (and beyond, to the extent that they still exist) have been made up overwhelmingly of young people, and in most cases of young people of middle class status or at least origin. The age range within toxics/environmental justice groups is much broader, with older people playing a much larger role; it is skewed toward people for whom economic constraints are a bigger issue. Its constituencies, though diverse, are much more distant from university and related intellectual cultures. This is not to argue that there is some necessary connection between these constituencies and a grassroots politics that regards both the state and issues of production as important terrains of struggle. Broad popular constituencies can be associated with any number of political positions—including, for instance, the Christian right, or anti-abortion. But it does suggest that the ascendancy of the "new social movements" have been more tied to a particular moment, in particular national contexts, and to a constituency of a particular age, class, and cultural orientation than theorists of the movements believed at the time.

Radical democracy has been associated not only with the new social movements, via new social movement theory, but also with poststructuralism, especially as it has been expressed in the realm of social analysis. It is important to stress though that radical democracy has not been *equated* with poststructuralism; some of those who invoke it, such as Cornel West, have explicitly dissociated themselves from aspects of the poststructuralist perspective[11]; occasionally it is used by people whose concerns are quite different from those of poststructuralism (for Bogdan Denitch, for instance, "radical democracy" is imbued with something like a social democratic perspective).[12] Nevertheless, on the whole what might be called "the discourse of radical democracy" is strongly influenced by a poststructuralist mindset. One of the consequences of this is the absence of class from that discourse.

Ernesto Laclau and Chantal Mouffe's book, *Hegemony and Socialist Strategy*, has done more than any other single piece of work to set the terms for the discussion of cultural politics, or radical democracy.[13] This may be particularly the case in the United States, where their book was widely read and taken by many as the authoritative statement of the implications of poststructuralism (or postmodernism, the term that was then more widely in use) for radical politics. The book was also received with a certain amount of relief among those who wanted to engage in poststructuralist analysis and at the same time lay claim to radical politics. The appearance of a poststructuralist tour de force with "socialist strategy" in its title seemed to establish the connection between the two.

The book presents a thoughtful critique of Marxism, including an appreciation of some aspects of the Marxist tradition. Laclau and Mouffe argue that the fundamental flaw in Marxism, its essentialist element, is its equation between the working class and socialist politics, the claim that there is an innate or automatic relationship between the working class and socialism. Laclau and Mouffe want to argue instead for a contingent concept of politics, one in which there is no given relationship between a particular class position and a particular political stance: every political position, in their view, is constructed, negotiated on the terrain of shifting alliances and changing struggles, among many social actors.

Laclau and Mouffe do not entirely castigate Marxism. They argue that both Lenin and Gramsci introduced concepts of class coalition, and also more complex conceptions of political consciousness, according to which no one political path is predetermined. They note that Gramsci's concept of hegemony introduced an indeterminacy to the relation between class and political position: in Gramsci's view, creating a progressive or socialist bloc required ideological struggle and the construction of alliances among various classes and sections of classes. Emphasizing Gramsci's view of politics as a terrain of ideological struggle, they portray him as a forerunner of a poststructuralist perspective in which politics becomes entirely contingent, entirely detached from class position. What Laclau and Mouffe leave out is that for Gramsci there remained a profound connection between class and politics. The working class, in Gramsci's view, might not attain a socialist politics easily. For long periods most workers might hold other political views; the working class would not be able to win socialism alone. But for Gramsci socialism remained the most authentic expression of the interests of the working class. In his view socialism could not be achieved unless the majority of the working class, especially its most politically active members, came to support it.

In *Hegemony and Socialist Strategy* Laclau and Mouffe give their readers a choice between a reductionist version of Marxism, in which class position determines politics, and a poststructuralist or "constructionist" position according to which there is no relation between class and politics at all. This leaves out a middle option (held by most Marxist theorists): that working class people may be conservative, and people of wealthier classes—even capitalists—may be politically radical, but economic and social position remains a kind of baseline for politics. Working class people may vote against social services if they become convinced that it is supported out of their taxes and going to people other than themselves. But the fact remains that people on the lower economic rungs need social services more than those above them. Societies in which the working class is highly organized, and in which there are labor parties, tend to have much more extensive welfare states than societies in which these are weak or absent—a prime example of the latter being the United States. Another way of making the same point: it is hard to imagine a situation in which a socialist program, proposed by the capitalist class, is defeated by working class opposition.

Radical democracy suggests a politics that is detached from issues of the state as well as from class. This is partly a heritage of the new social movements, which tended to avoid the arena of electoral politics, especially on the national level. The avoidance of the state also reflects the influence of Michel Foucault, and a particular reading of his approach to power. In the arena of cultural radicalism, Foucault's critique of the repression hypothesis, his argument that power is productive (of social relations, identities, resistance, and so forth) has been taken very seriously; meanwhile his recognition that power is also repressive tends to be forgotten.[14] Foucault, used in this way, has become the point of reference for a large and influential theoretical literature, especially in queer and feminist theory, that equates radical politics with play, parody, and the subversion or reversal of existing cultural forms, that is not concerned with social repression and finds efforts to either understand it or confront it uninteresting.[15] This reading of Foucault is of a piece with the current tendency to oppose the cultural to the political and economic realms, and to claim a superior place for cultural politics, not on grounds of efficacy but of aesthetic sophistication.

Foucault's influence has reinforced the turn away from the state as an arena of struggle in another way as well, at least among those who take his work to be the new foundation of radical analysis. In *Discipline and Punish* Foucault describes the repressive effects of state power and traces its changing character over the centuries, arguing that while the state at one time employed spectacular displays of force and violence to ensure its will, it has evolved into a much more sophisticated instrument, resting on surveillance, discipline-instilling habits of subordination, and the creation of subjects who participate in the state's project of social control.[16] This portrait captures the increasingly sophisticated, and insidious, forms of social control that we find ourselves subject to. But it leaves out the possibility of positive social intervention on the part of the state. Capitalism means class polarization and immiseration at the lower levels of society: if the state fails to intervene, suffering increases. There is a long history of popular, and left, struggles to reorient state power, to incorporate popular forces into the state and transform it to whatever degree possible into an instrument of social welfare. Foucault's view of the state as consisting of technologies of intrusive control leaves no room for the fact that in industrial societies people, especially poor people, need social services. In his view of the state as a concentrated location of disciplinary power, there is no room for struggles on the terrain of state power.

Though the term radical democracy can be used in many ways, on the whole the discourse of radical democracy has been framed by the assumptions of cultural politics, by the view that the object of radical politics is to take control of discourse. This is to some extent a sign of cynicism, or resignation, after repeated defeats on other terrains. Dick Flacks has argued that the United States left has failed where it set out to succeed—on the terrain of political power—while it has succeeded where it did not intend to, on the terrain of culture. He points out that in the United States the left has never managed to organize a party with any hope of taking power, but that it has created many enclaves of alternative culture and has had some influence on mainstream culture as well.[17] It is as if cultural politics (and, on the whole, radical democracy) takes this description of history as a proscription for action.

Though class struggle has never come anywhere near bringing socialism, and the left has never approached the point of taking power, there have been real accomplishments. Principles of workers' rights, civil rights (in relation not only to race but also to gender, sexual orientation, and other social categories), and the responsibilities of the state in relation to social welfare have all been won through struggle and have had lasting implications for the quality of most people's lives. A retreat into the arena of discourse does nothing to address the erosion of these rights. The orientation of cultural radicalism toward the deconstruction of the concept of "rights" is politically extremely dangerous. It is true that rights are not given but constructed through struggle. The implication of this, for the left at least, should be to defend and extend them.

In a recent article, Arif Dirlik addresses the relation between cultural radicalism, specifically postcolonialism, and global shifts in the organization of capital. Dirlik argues that "postcolonialism" is the moment when intellectuals from nations of what would until recently have been called the Third World arrive in the universities of the First World and begin to speak in the vocabulary of poststructuralism, celebrating cultural diversity and rejecting categories of capitalism and class. Dirlik situates this in the shift between two forms of international capitalism. The old form, now on the way out, was firmly tied to national states, grounded first of all in the United States and secondly in Western Europe. This (Fordist) capitalist order, he points out, was culturally conservative: it was dominated by white male elites who regarded challenges from others as threats to their power. The emerging, multinational form of international capitalism is oriented toward the United States and the West as a whole, but never quite puts its feet down anywhere. The new elites recognize their need to make room for a range of cultures and therefore the value of a multiplicity of voices, especially elite voices from the parts of what used to be the Third World in which multinational capital operates or hopes to operate. As long as such elites do not point to the global capitalist order that has created their privileged status, their voices are welcome.[18]

The nineties is a very poor time for the left to turn aside from issues of class and state power—of who has it and what they do with it. This is a period of accelerating class polarization, in the US and also globally. In the United States it is impossible to take our understanding of race, gender, or questions of social division and disintegration further without acknowledging the fact of class polarization. The majority, including the overwhelming majority of people of color and large numbers of women, are being pushed down the economic ladder, and many are losing the few protections or benefits they once were able to claim from the state. On a global scale, a different version of the same points holds: some nations in the category once referred to as the Third World are being drawn into the circuits of multinational capital and subjected to the same pressures toward internal class polarization while others are being left aside, to starve. The realm of politics, nationally and internationally, is where decisions are being made about how globalization will be shaped and what restrictions will be placed on it. Standing aside from this arena means leaving it to the right.

The contest between two forms of international capitalism (and the fact that multinational capital is winning, and that the globalization of capital is proceeding rapidly) poses an awkward situation for the left, and for social movements generally. What positions should the left, or progressive social movements, take on the issue of free trade? On international conventions that reduce the scope of national sovereignty? Should national boundaries be strengthened, or allowed to become more permeable? There is a certain pull toward strengthening the boundaries of the nation: how else is it possible to exert any control over capital? How are progressive social policies possible if capital is free to move at will? But reinforcing national boundaries means ignoring the impact of globalizing capital, placing obstacles in the way of the waves of migration forced by the reorganization of economies and environmental degradation. There is also a pull from the side of multinational capitalism: it is much more sophisticated; it invites cultural diversity; and it makes room for (and even gives financial support to) many discourses, including the discourse of cultural radicalism. It is more fun.

The danger for the left is allowing itself to be caught up in the contest between declining and ascendant forms of capitalism; for culturally oriented intellectuals, the danger is confusing the ascendant form of capitalism with radicalism. Following Dirlik I would argue that we have to focus our attention on the transformation of international capital and on the question of class. We have to develop political principles and initiatives that point toward a progressive alternative to the existing choices. In the United States, the two-party system is on the verge of collapse; entering a Democratic Party that is in the process of disintegrating is not a good idea, except possibly as part of a larger strategy. It is likely that third parties will begin to be formed; it would make sense for the left to be part of this process. But the prior question is not whether people on the left should turn their efforts toward a third party, but what its politics would be.

I am suggesting a politics involving, on the national level, demands for an improved welfare system and a state more accountable to the needs of the people, especially those on the lower economic levels of society. I think we should revive our commitment to democratic socialism, not as a goal for the foreseeable future but as a vision, a moral reference point for a more modest program for the present. We need international movements around questions of labor, the environment, and human rights. There is a need for coordinated national and international structures enforcing international standards on these issues. It is unrealistic to think of world government (and also frightening to speculate on who would run it, given the weakness of movements of the left and the strength of multinational capital). It is more realistic to think of international agreements based on conceptions of human rights and environmental protection.

Rejecting the idea that culture is the main arena of struggle and that subversion lies at the margins of society does not have to mean going back to the authoritarian structures of the Communist movement or the domination of social movements by white men. An updated social democratic politics would have to be internally democratic. It would have to address questions of whose agendas are to be included, who will shape the coalitions and frame the demands. It would have to find forms that would enable full expression for all of the overlapping groups that form the potential basis for a progressive politics: working class people, groups of color, women, sexual and other cultural minorities. It would have to find ways of incorporating the recognition that none of these groups speak with one voice. Such a movement—perhaps involving one or more parties, and networks of groups and organizations of various kinds—would also have to be majoritarian: whites, men as well as women, would have to have a legitimate place.

Perhaps the term radical democracy can be stretched to incorporate something like the above politics. Some people use the term to suggest that we need to go beyond a narrow identity politics; this is certainly compatible with the approach that I am outlining. So is the aim of constructing a movement based on a wide range of democratic grass-roots groups. But if we want to pose a credible challenge to the right, I think we need to also put forward a program that addresses questions of inequality and power, of how resources are used and who decides.

NOTES

1. Ernesto Laclau and Chantal Mouffe, *Hegemony and Socialist Strategy: Toward a Radical Democratic Politics* (London: Verso, 1984).

2. Anthony Giddens, lecture at panel on Social Movements and Social Classes, Bielefeld, Germany, July 14 (1994).

3. Stanley Aronowitz, "The Situation of the Left in the United States," *Socialist Review* 93/3, vol. 23, no. 3 (1994).

4. Cornel West, "A Matter of Life and Death," *October* 61 (Summer 1992): 20–23.

5. See Alain Touraine, *The Post-Industrial Society: Tomorrow's Social History: Conflict and Culture in the Programmed Society* (New York: Random House, 1971); Alberto Melucci, *Nomads of the Present: Social Movements and Individual Needs in Contemporary Society* (Philadelphia: Temple University Press, 1989), "The New Social Movements: A Theoretical Approach," *Social Science Information* 19, no. 12 (1980), "The Symbolic Challenge of Contemporary Movements," *Social Research* 52, no. 4 (Winter 1985): 789–816; Claus Offe, "New Social Movements: Challenging the Boundaries of Institutional Movements," *Social Research* (Winter 1985); Jean Cohen, "Rethinking Social Movements," *Berkeley Journal of Sociology* (1983): 97–98.

6. See Joachim Hirsch, "The Fordist Security State and the New Social Movements," *Kapitalstate* 10–11 (1983): 75–87; Michel Aglietta, *Capitalist Regulation: the US Experience* (London: Verso, 1979); and "Phases of US Capitalist Expansion," *New Left Review* 110 (1978).

7. Alain Touraine, "An Introduction to the Study of Social Movements," *Social Research*, 52 (1985): 749–787.

8. On the peace movement in Western Europe, and the inadequacy of new social movement theory in relation to it, see Thomas R. Rochon, "The West European Peace Movement and the Theory of New Social Movements," in Russell J. Dalton and Manfred Kuechler, *Challenging the Political Order: New Social and Political Movements in Western Democracies* (New York: Oxford University Press, 1990). On the institutionalization of the new social movements in Germany and elsewhere, see Margit Mayer and Roland Roth, "New Social Movements and the Transformation to Post-Fordist Society," in *Social Movements and Cultural Politics*, Marcy Darnovsky, Barbara Epstein and Richard Flacks, eds. (Temple University Press, forthcoming).

9. On social movements in the United States in relation to new social movement theory, see Carl Boggs, *Social Movements and Political Power: Emerging Forms of Radicalism in the West* (Philadelphia: Temple University Press, 1986), and Margit Mayer, "Social Movement Research and Social Movement Practice: the U.S. Pattern," in *Research on Social Movements*, ed. Dieter Rucht (Boulder and San Francisco: Westview, 1991).

10. For accounts of the toxics/environmental justice movements, see Andrew Szasz, *Ecopopulism: Toxic Waste and the Movement for Environmental Justice* (Minnesota: University of Minnesota Press, 1994); Robert Gottlieb, *Forcing the Spring: the Transformation of the American Environmental Movement* (Washington, DC: Island Press, 1994); *Confronting Environmental Racism: Voices from the Grassroots*, ed. Robert D. Bullard (Boston: South End Press, 1993); and *Toxic Struggles: The Theory and Practice of Environmental Justice*, ed. Richard Hofrichter (Philadelphia: New Society Publishers, 1993).

11. Cornel West, "Race and Social Theory," in *Keeping Faith: Philosophy and Race in America* (New York: Routledge, 1993).

12. Bogdan Denitch, "A Foreign Policy for Radical Democrats," in this volume.

13. Laclau and Mouffe, *Hegemony and Socialist Strategy*. On related questions, see the following exchange: Norman Geras, "Post-Marxism?" *New Left*

Review 163 (1987): 40–82, and Laclau and Mouffe, "Post-Marxism without Apologies," *New Left Review* 160 (1987): 79–106.

14. Michel Foucault, *The History of Sexuality*, volume one (New York: Pantheon, 1986).

15. For examples of this approach, see Judith Butler, *Gender Trouble* (New York: Routledge, 1990); Eve Kosofsky Sedgwick, *Epistemology of the Closet* (Berkeley: University of California Press, 1990).

16. Michel Foucault, *Discipline and Punish: The Birth of the Prison* (New York: Pantheon, 1977).

17. Richard Flacks, *Making History: The American Left and the American Mind* (New York: Columbia University Press, 1988).

18. Arif Dirlik, "The Postcolonial Aura in the Age of Global Capitalism," *Critical Inquiry* vol. 20, no. 2 (Winter 1994): 328–56.

RADICAL DEMOCRACY AND CULTURAL POLITICS

11

IDENTITY AND DEMOCRACY

A CRITICAL PERSPECTIVE

ELI ZARETSKY

Is IT REALLY SO IMPORTANT FOR THE LEFT TO STOP talking about socialism as a universalizing ideology? I don't think so. Should we substitute for socialism a call for radical democracy—"direct, popular participation"—in all spheres, including the economy? No, I don't think that will take us very far.

Let's start with who the left is and what it should be. Many contemporary assumptions concerning "gatekeeper" Marxists and the like apply to minor sectarian currents. Even in the twenties and thirties, for example, when the Soviet Union was going strong, any reasonable definition of the Western left would have included social feminists, Weimar culture critics, Bloomsbury experiments in personal life, psychoanalytical radicals, Trotskyites, surrealists, pacifists, and a million other tendencies of which Marxist-Leninism was one. If Marxist-Leninism did not then define the left, why should we assign so much importance to the far more marginal sects of our own time. Yet they are the only ones who have been talking about socialism as a universalizing ideology in the sense that Stanley Aronowitz argues against.

What is a left then, and what can it do? No one has yet improved on Marx's 1843 definition: "the self-clarification of the wishes and struggles of the age." Marxism, for better or worse, was an attempt at self-clarification in an epoch characterized by the expansion of industrial capitalism—hence its familiar emphasis on the industrial working class, the factory, the economy, and so forth. The sectarian is one who carried this understanding over from spheres of life and periods of history for which it had relevance to ones for which it did not. No one can plausibly place industrialization at the center of our age. How then are we to understand today's wishes and struggles?

I believe the starting point for a contemporary left has to be a critical—historical and dialectical—understanding of the impulse behind today's identity politics. In relation to those issues I want to raise three points: (1) how we are to understand the identity impulse, especially its relation to the radicalism of the 1960s from which it was born; (2) why "radical democracy" is not a sufficient "self-clarification" to bring to bear on these movements; and (3) why we still need an understanding of capitalism, especially in its most recent socio-cultural and political as well as economic transformations, if we are to understand the identity impulse critically.

It has become popular in some circles to refer to the New Left and the 1960s as sexist, authoritarian, homophobic, and so on. We are all familiar with this view, which has become almost obligatory for those who write on the sixties. In fact, it distorts an exceedingly complex reality. I would like to consider the break between feminism (which, of course, is far more than an identity movement but included identity elements) and the New Left and offer my book, *Capitalism, the Family, and Personal Life* as an example.[1]

The main influences on this text were E.P. Thomson, Herbert Marcuse, Raymond Williams, C. Wright Mills, Antonio Gramsci, and the school of mostly American historians associated with the University of Wisconsin and *Studies on the Left* (and that included Stanley Aronowitz). It originated as a review of Shulamith Firestone's *Dialectic of Sex* and derived much of its punch from that encounter.[2] Written from within neo-Marxist New Left currents, it was not anti-feminist, nor did it attempt to offer socialism as a cure-all for sexism. On the contrary, in explaining how capitalism in its development had created a particular division between men and women (two spheres), it sought to explain why a separate ("autonomous") women's movement has developed.

I tell this story to make two points. First, the New Left was a far more diverse phenomenon than is often acknowledged, and there were many tendencies within it that welcomed feminism and gay liberation as these movements emerged. (The New University Politics in the early seventies is another instance.) There are many reasons to be clear about this, but one must be stressed: the roots of the identity politics that emerged in the seventies and that continues to characterize our age are in the New Left, in a much stronger and dramatic way, than the mere truism that the roots of anything are to be found in the past. Illustrating this often obscured continuity are such phenomena as the enormous performative dimension of the New Left movements, the close relation at a deep level between the New Left and the counterculture, and the significance of the media that appeared in that decade. *Capitalism, the Family, and Personal Life* is another example: its ideas concerning the centrality of the categories public and private in their modern, capitalist, and gendered form are described endlessly in feminist theory and women's history writings in expressions like "as feminist writers have shown" or "as the women's movement of the seventies argued." In fact, these ideas appeared, fully worked out, under the inspiration of contemporaneous neo-Marxism, at a time when Kate Millet and Shulamith Firestone were the most important feminist thinkers, in a wholly New Left journal then called *Socialist Revolution*.

The first point to be made then, is that the roots of the social movements of our time are in the New Left. The tendency to succumb to a set of simplistic dichotomies—sexist New Left versus feminism, homophobic New Left versus gay liberation—greatly limits one's ability to contribute to the self-clarification of the movements that characterize our day. The second point is that by minimizing the diversity of the New Left, one fails to comprehend how profound the nature of the break that took place in the years after 1968 actually was.

I well remember my shock when, around 1971 or 1972, a large number of women who were married or living with men went to New York for a women's studies conference. We were all New Leftists, all heterosexual (at least as far as I knew), and all living in the already tolerant environments of San Francisco and Berkeley. We had all been familiar with the new idea of women's liberation for several years, and had not only been in consciousness raising groups but had been organizing them. At the New York conference we were confronted with the then-new argument that we should not sleep with men, since men were the enemy, and that it was incumbent upon women to become lesbians. This surprised me, but it did not shock me. I thought at the time, as I do now, that it was an obvious attempt at political intimidation—although the attempt was obviously based in real and painful experience. What shocked me was the extraordinary effect these demands had on pretty much *all* the women in my circle.

Worth noting here is the profundity and the intensity of the identity impulse among women that emerged in the early seventies. The majority of these women found the argument at least reasonable. The new loyalty they felt to other women came into conflict with the loyalty they had previously felt to their male partners. In some cases they switched their sexual orientation, a fact that struck me at the time as amazing. Although preceded by the history of racial and nationalist movements and "imagined communities," the emergence of a politics based upon group identities of gender and sexual orientation in the seventies was a dramatically new development.

It is this development that requires self-clarification. We have to ask such questions as: What is the identity dimension within feminism, and what should our stand toward it be? What place do demands for recognition have in movements such as trade unionism? How do the fundamental structural forms of oppression such as those related to race and gender differ from demands for cultural representation, the "politics of difference?" Finally, we must ask whether or not "democracy" is the term within which we can describe and understand the struggles of our age.

Probably our greatest theorist of democracy is Alexis de Tocqueville. Basing himself on his master, Charles Luis Montesquieu, de Tocqueville argued that like any political form, democracy has to be understood in terms of passions—what we would call today the mass psychology of the people living within its regime. Democracy was newly invented, at least in its massive, modern form, when de Tocqueville encountered it in Jacksonian America, and he sought to delineate the passion motivating it. He called this passion "equality." By equality, de Tocqueville did not mean what the leftist means—namely, hatred at seeing others disadvantaged. Rather, he meant that this new breed, Americans, could not stand to see anyone set above them.

If we read de Tocqueville, we will understand one of the recurring conundrums in much progressive thinking today: the link between political democracy and market capitalism. Both satisfy the narcissistic needs of modern men and women. It is not greed that led people to welcome the market system (and in the United States, white people did welcome laissez-faire capitalism in the early nineteenth century); nor was it rationalization, the desire for control, as Max Weber believed. It was narcissism: the desire to see themselves, their products, their achievements, in the world outside the self. The same impulse led them to prefer to keep their politicians ordinary, their political sentiments lofty and vacuous, and their statues of politicians short and unimposing.

It is clear that what is needed is a *critical* approach to democracy. Democracy is itself too close to the identity impulse to clarify the nature and direction of that impulse. The nationalist movements of the Baltic states—of Georgia, Serbia, and Rumania—are all, in part, expressions of mass democracy, of what de Tocqueville called the tyranny of the majority. The talk show phenomenon of our country, which allows people to bypass the representative aspect of democracy entirely, is also often seen as an example of direct democracy. We have yet to explain its spiteful, right-wing, and ignorant equality; its hatred of elites and intellectuals. We need a left that holds *liberal* principles—individual freedom, checks on the majority, constitutionalism—as sacred. I would not like to overemphasize democracy or separate it from an Enlightenment-based emphasis on freedom, which we need to uphold.

There is another reason to question the growing emphasis on democracy. A society in which everything is up for discussion, even decisions about what technology to use, could ironically, be a nightmare. The classical idea of a society where one's political commitments are minimized—where one is honestly and accurately represented—still has merit. The old Greek notion of the *polis*, brought into the left by republicanism and bought hook, line, and sinker by a lot of Marxists and by the New Left leaves me cold; I value the private sphere. Regardless of the argument for more political involvement, the sphere of politics itself may be shrinking, or at least changing its character in ways that are still too obscure to specify; and this raises the need to think about capitalism historically.

Although class is sometimes mentioned in discussions of radical democracy, it generally functions to designate identity—as in the slogan "class, race, and gender." This approach is important, but it has little to do with availing ourselves of Marx and of the Marxist tradition. The reason we need this tradition is that it is the only body of modern thought that conceptualized capitalism (as opposed to simply taking it for granted and discussing it). And if we don't understand that the society that we live in is a capitalist society in a way that is different from—but not more important than—male-dominated or racist or classist society, then we'll never get outside of our own assumptions. To understand our society as capitalist situates it historically in a way that characterizations of its identity formations do not. It is difficult to see how we can even make the distinction between markets, which have many positive functions, and the buying and selling of labor power without drawing on Marxism. Yet without this distinction, how can the left really reform itself. We don't necessarily need Marx to think historically; we could rely on Hegel—but how many of us want Hegel without at least some Marx? Historical thinking is the great contribution the left can make to the profoundly anti-historical "postmodern" thinking that surrounds us.

Above all, we need Marx's analysis of capitalism as it appears in Volume I of *Capital*. The subject of that book is how a surface appearance of equality (that is, exchange) maintains and is itself maintained by subtle, complex, and impersonal relations of domination: the extraction of surplus value and its transformation into capital. Although being a worker in Marx's sense of the term is not an identity, an understanding of capitalism is not irrelevant to understanding the identity struggles of our age; for capitalism worked *through* racially organized plantations and colonies, and *through* male-dominated families, and *through* hierarchies of exclusion and rituals of degradation.

We need to understand the changes of our own time as changes in the structure of capitalism. The transformation of the public sphere into a great universal mirror for identities; the collapse of the distinction between the intrapsychic and the external with its profound consequences for psychoanalysis; the decline of what Foucault called monarchical, centralized forms of power and the rise of capillary power, of "disciplines" that work through the constitution of knowledge; the struggle for control over the line distinguishing the public and the private; the growing irrelevance of Marxism itself: all these reflect global, structural changes in capitalism itself. We have to reject a certain dogmatic privileging of Marxism, and we need to situate Marx in a critical tradition descending from the Enlightenment, as Habermas sought to do in his *Philosophical Discourse of Modernity*.[3] Such a tradition would certainly include such figures as Nietzsche, Foucault, Derrida, and

Freud, whose contribution to the history of the twentieth century left seems larger and larger as time goes on.

It is imperative that we acknowledge the psychological aspects influencing society when we try to understand how society functions. Human beings do not exist on one level only. We have affective relations based on immediate identity, on feelings of being similar or different. We also live in a world of consciousness and of structural and historical understandings, a world in which we can see ourselves as objects. In order to function as critical agents within the latter sphere, we need the abstract, mediated, and systematic relations discussed by Marx. Long familiar in social theory are terms such as primary and secondary relations, *Gemeinschaft* and *Gesellschaft*, and spontaneity and consciousness; two different ways of feeling and thinking likewise appear in psychology: the id and the ego.

Above all, though, we have to understand our immediate history, especially the history of the New Left. The movements of the period had no monopoly on demagoguery, posturing, or empty rhetoric. The need to continually apologize for having lived through a utopian moment paralyzes much more than the contemporary left. The Clinton presidency is itself continually on the defensive because Clinton, no less than proponents of radical democracy, cannot simply affirm the achievements of those years.

NOTES

1. Eli Zaretsky, *Capitalism, the Family, and Personal Life* (New York: Harper and Row, 1976). This book was originally published in this journal in issues dated January–June, 1973.

2. Shulamith Firestone, *The Dialectic of Sex: The Case for Feminist Revolution* (New York: Morrow, 1970).

3. Jürgen Habermas, *Philosophical Discourse of Modernity: Twelve Lectures*, trans. Frederick Lawrence (Cambridge: MIT Press, 1990).

145

IDENTITY AND DEMOCRACY

12

A NEW AMERICAN SOCIALISM

MANNING MARABLE

AMERICANS WHO IDENTIFY THEMSELVES AS "THE LEFT" —independent progressives, radical feminists, democratic socialists, Marxists, and others—have never lived in a more depressing, challenging, and potentially liberating moment. With the collapse of the Cold War and the demise of the Soviet Union, the immediate reaction was "capitalist triumphalism" all over the world, but especially in Europe and the United States. Many social democrats repudiated their commitment to the liberal welfare state and adopted the rhetoric of the free market, the *laissez faire* entrepreneur. Communist parties in the West fragmented or disintegrated as many Marxists renounced any identification with historical materialism.

The surprising defeat of the Labour Party in last spring's general election in Great Britain, combined with growing mass movements inspired by racism and anti-Semitism, from Germany to Louisiana, reinforced the general perception that the world's center of political gravity had suddenly shifted fundamentally to the right. Western liberals weighed the mounting evidence and announced their latest version of the Lesser Evils Thesis—that even traditional liberal goals were unrealizable in the immediate future, that anything just barely to the left of Reaganism or Thatcherism was preferable to being held hostage by the militant right.

But before we deliver a solemn eulogy to socialism, let us re-examine the corpse. Internationally in recent months, the Left has won several important electoral victories without sacrificing its principles. In New Zealand and Guyana, socialists have won. In Mexico, the Democratic Party of the Revolution of Mexico has won millions of adherents and is now poised to challenge the government's pro-corporate policies. The Workers Party of Brazil is the largest democratic popular force in Latin America's largest nation. In Haiti, it required the brutality of a military coup to overthrow the popular electoral Lavalas movement of Jean-Baptiste-Aristide. Even in Nicaragua, the Sandinistas stand an excellent chance of being returned to power in the next national elections. In Europe, the situation is less optimistic for the left, but not entirely bleak. Last November, ex-communists were swept into power in Lithuania. And inside the United States, that same spirit of political unrest, which has erupted into socialist and labor movements elsewhere, simmers just below the surface of our political culture.

Part of the reason for the new worldwide activism of the left is the radically different international environment in the aftermath of the Cold War. In reality, both the United States and the Soviet Union "lost" the Cold War. The decayed factories of the Rust Belt, the doubling of the number of homeless Americans within a decade, the thirty-seven million-plus who have no health insurance, the 1,500 Latino and black teenagers who drop out of school every day—these stand as graphic illustrations of the failure of rampant militarism and Cold War economics. If the USSR's disintegration symbolizes the bankruptcy of Stalinist communism, that is no reason to believe that American capitalism has solved its problems.

What is the left to do? What's required is not a blanket rejection of Marxism as a critical method of social analysis but a fundamental rethinking and revision of "socialist politics." The Leninist vanguard-party model of social change, evolving in the context of a highly authoritarian, underdeveloped society devoid of any tradition of civil liberties and human rights, has finally been thoroughly discredited. The idea of seizing state power by violence in a computerized, technologically advanced society is simply a recipe for disaster.

But if socialist politics are defined specifically and solely as radical projects for democratic change, what set of political perspectives and concepts can still guide the renaissance of the American left? What is still worthwhile and valuable in the concept of "socialism" for a new generation heading into the twenty-first century?

For starters, we should examine the practical problems confronting American working people and racial minorities and respond with a series of political interventions that actually empower the oppressed. We should advance our political agenda in concert with larger, stronger currents for social change in America—feminists, people of color, trade unionists, lesbians and gays, environmentalists, neighborhood and community organizers, and many others—recognizing that, at best, we socialists will play a secondary role in the struggles immediately ahead.

This vision of a new American socialism will certainly not be the same as that of others on the left. The objective here is not to present a theoretical blueprint, but to build a framework for dialogue among democratic socialists across organizational and ideological boundaries. All too frequently, the disorganized, fractious Left has made its sectarianism a red badge of courage, refusing to speak to others who share 90 percent of its own politics because they differ on the remaining 10 percent. But we can no longer afford to dwell in the political ghettoes of ideological purity.

We must champion a renewed commitment to internationalism—espousing global solutions to global problems. We must link the question of the environment with labor issues, recognizing that the export of United States industrial and manufacturing jobs to Third World nations is not just a capitalist search for lower wages but also a desire to avoid pollution controls and health-and-safety standards. With a new vision of socialism, we must rethink the character of capitalism and the means by which the corporate-dominated economy can become more egalitarian and democratic. Our economic system is based on private greed and public pain, but it is also much more flexible, dynamic, and creative than earlier generations of Marxists, including Marx himself, ever imagined.

The immediate task for American socialists is to support and build strong workers' movements and to defend the rights of trade unions. Also, transitional economic structures must be created—ones that address working-class needs and build solidarity across the boundaries of race, ethnicity, and income, giving people a concrete understanding of what economic alternatives are needed.

We should establish a clearer public identity for "socialism," outlining in a common sense manner our theoretical and political boundaries. A new American socialism must make a clear and unambiguous distinction between our politics, values, and vision, and those of American liberalism. Irving Howe has defined "democratic socialists" as "the allies of American liberalism," pressuring "liberals to hold fast to their own ideas and values, without equivocation or retreat." Howe argues that liberals and socialists alike share "an unshakable premise of our politics that freedom is the indispensable prerequisite for social and economic progress." By "freedom," what Howe means is "liberty," in the context of classical Western European political philosophy. Howe described his commitment to the struggle for human equality as secondary to his faith in liberty. Within his scenario, there is a logical continuity and cordial ideological kinship between socialism and liberalism.

The problem is that there are too many historical examples in which both liberals and social democrats have sacrificed their high ideals of liberty and equal justice upon the altar of expediency. During the Cold War, thousands of workers were expelled from unions, lost their jobs, or were imprisoned at the urging of most liberals and not a few liberal-socialists. The Communist Control Act of 1954 made membership in the Communist Party a crime and stripped the Party of "all rights, privileges, and immunities attendant upon legal bodies." Even Howe wrote that the "Congressional Stampede" to outlaw Communists and Marxist ideas illustrated that Democrats and Republicans alike were prepared "to trample the concept of liberty in the name of destroying its enemy." Other prominent instances in recent history in which liberals repressed radicals include the Kennedy Administration's surveillance and lack of support for the desegregation movement and, more recently, the capitulation by many Congressional liberals to key elements of Reaganomics.

The single, defining characteristic of socialism, the prerequisite from which all else flows, is the commitment to human equality. An individual's personal liberty to speak freely is insignificant if one doesn't own or have genuine access to the press. An individual's freedom to vote means little if one is unemployed, homeless, hungry, or poor. The unequal distribution of wealth under capitalism—in which the top one per cent of all households have a greater net wealth than the bottom ninety per cent—makes liberty a function of power, privilege, and control.

In a typical American election, more than eighty percent of the citizens who earn more than $50,000 annually vote; only forty-four percent of all African-Americans, thirty-five percent of all Latinos, and thirty-eight percent of the unemployed voted in the 1988 Presidential election. The affluent and comfortable classes logically recognize that they have a stake in the outcome, and they exercise their franchise. Without material and social equality, the political consequences are always unequal, unfair, and discriminatory, despite the existence of legalistic freedoms.

The essential socialist project is about equality—efforts promoting the empowerment of working people and other oppressed sectors of society, and the redistribution of power from the few to the many. If "equality" and "empowerment" are what socialists seek—not the "equal opportunities" under capitalism and "greater social fairness" sought by liberals—then socialism's relationship with the Democratic Party and the character of its interventions within the electoral arena must be rethought.

For several decades, many democratic socialists have supported the liberal wing of the Democratic Party, attempting to shift its political center of gravity to the left. Michael Harrington's "Democratic Agenda" efforts more than a decade ago developed some productive relationships between socialists and key liberals in Congress and within organized labor. Unfortunately, the emergence of Bill Clinton and the neoconservative Democratic Leadership Council clearly shows that the Democratic Party will never become a social-democratic or labor-oriented party. Ideologically and programmatically, the current Democratic leadership occupies the space once reserved for "moderate Republicans"—Wendell Willkie, Jacob Javits, or Charles Percy, for example.

Harrington never really understood that the natural political behavior of liberals is cautious, timid oscillation: When strong social-protest movements are in the streets, liberals will drift to the left;

with the rise of Reaganism in the 1980s, they scurried to the right. As Stanley Aronowitz observed in *The Progressive* in 1986, "The Democrats are not an alternative to the Republican conservatives. At best, they slow down the most retrograde aspects of the GOP program; at worst, they bestow legitimacy on conservative goals, leaving their constituents bothered and bewildered."

Harrington's well-meaning mistake was modest, compared to the profoundly flawed electoral strategy of the American Communist Party. For more than four decades, Erwin Marquit recently observed, the Communist agenda "never went beyond progressive politics." The "implementation of the Party's program was reformist in content and sectarian in form." It extended nearly uncritical support to liberals and progressives in the Democratic Party but viciously attacked Marxists outside its own ranks as the "phony Left." Finally, some Trotskyist-oriented parties and formations have denounced for a half a century any relationship with progressives inside the Democratic Party, elevating sectarianism to the level of a political principle.

A number of independent Marxists and progressives have been critical of all these approaches to electoral politics. Arthur Kinoy's characterization of the two-party system as being "controlled by the powerful corporate, industrial, political, military establishment" is essentially correct. Kinoy argues that the task of the left is to work "inside" and "outside" of that system.

My own inside-outside approach to electoral activism rests on four key political activities:

- We must work for and support progressive and liberal Democrats, strengthening the party's liberal wing but making clear distinctions between their politics and ours.

- We must support the development of nonsectarian, popular third-party efforts, such as the pending formation of the Vermont Progressive Party led by that state's member of Congress, Bernie Sanders.

- We must aggressively work toward structural reforms within the electoral system. These would include fair ballot access for third parties and independent candidates; permitting candidates to have "cross endorsements" or "fusion" between small third parties and the major capitalist parties, as advocated by the New Party; proportional representation in local races and ultimately in Federal elections; and, most importantly, public financing of elections, to take the corporations' and capitalists' special interests out of the public's decision-making process.

- We must do much more to expand the potential electoral base of the Left by engaging in voter education and registration campaigns. Part of the success of the Rainbow Coalition in 1984 and 1988 came from registering hundreds of thousands of new voters, most of whom were African-Americans, Latinos, students, working people, and the poor.

These four approaches must be integrated to promote a more radical, multicultural definition of democracy, giving the left a more clear-cut identity in electoral politics.

Socialists must also link progressive electoral endeavors to ongoing social protests and democratic movements of the oppressed within American society. It is imperative to work in collaboration with progressive and left-wing leaders and activists, and groupings within the trade-union movement.

There is a direct, inescapable connection between working-class organizing, antiracist activism, and the empowerment of people of color. The vast majority of African-Americans, Puerto Ricans, Chicanos, and other people of color are, after all, working-class women and men. And the emphasis in labor organizing should be in the workplaces with the highest concentration of workers of color.

Extreme conservatives on the Republican right are searching for a new political and ideological framework for their assault on American working people, racial minorities, and the poor. The collapse of Soviet communism has meant that sterile anticommunism and red-baiting are much less effective in attacking their political opponents. That is why the Right has moved aggressively to connect a number of cultural and social issues: opposition to "political correctness" and multicultural education on campuses; advocacy of vouchers and use of school funds for private schools; homophobic state referenda such as the recently passed constitutional amendment in Colorado banning local ordinances that protect lesbian and gay rights; legislative initiatives to void women's freedom of choice on abortion; and attacks on affirmative action as "quotas."

The role of socialists is to get into the thick of the debates on all of these issues. By joining broad, mass organizations fighting for women's rights, against homophobia, for academic pluralism and multicultural education, we increase the capacity of oppressed people to resist, and we strengthen democratic currents throughout society.

The struggle to define the left and to build movements for radical democracy will fail, though, unless progressives squarely confront the issue of race. Marx recognized the importance of the race question to the politics of socialist transformation: "Labor cannot emancipate itself in the white skin where in the black it is branded."

Historically, racism has been the most decisive weapon in the arsenal of America's ruling elites to divide democratic resistance movements, turning fearful and frustrated whites against nonwhite working people. Today, we live in a nation in which nearly thirty per cent of our population is Latino, American Indian, Arab-American, Asian/Pacific-American, and African-American. By the middle of the twenty-first century, the majority of the working class will consist of people of non-European descent.

The Left must ask itself why most socialist organizations, with the exception of the American Communist Party, have consistently failed to attract black, Latino, and Asian-American supporters. It must honestly and critically confront the fact that most radical whites have little or no contact with grass-roots organizing efforts among inner-city working people, the poor, or the homeless. The left should be challenged to explain why the majority of the most militant and progressive students of color in the hip-hop contemporary culture of the 1990s have few connections with erstwhile white radicals and usually perceive Marxism as just another discredited "white ideology."

Part of the left's problem is the rupture between the theory and practice of social change. A good number of white socialists have the luxury to contemplate "class struggle" in the abstract. People of color and working people generally don't.

I didn't become a socialist because I was seduced by the persuasive materialist logic of Karl Marx. Nor did I equate the "freedom" of liberal socialists like Irving Howe with the gritty struggles for "freedom" that were the political objective of W.E.B. Du Bois, Martin Luther King, Jr., and Malcolm X. Socialism is only meaningful to African-Americans and other oppressed people of color when it explains how capitalism perpetuates our unequal conditions and when it gives us some tools to empower ourselves against an unfair, unjust system.

That is not a metaphysical enterprise but a practical, concrete analysis of actual, daily conditions. A social theory is useful only to the degree that it helps to explain reality, to the degree that it actually empowers those who employ it. And the day-to-day reality lived by millions of African-Americans, Latinos, and others along the jagged race/class fault line beneath American democracy is the continuing upheaval of social inequality and racial prejudice. Socialists must find a way to speak directly to that reality holistically, not as an afterthought or an appendage to their chief political concerns.

A concrete example of the efforts and failures of current socialist practice will serve to illustrate the state of the movement and how it can be improved. As Vice Chairperson of the Democratic Socialists of America from 1979 to 1984, I helped to create DSA's National and Racial Minorities Commission and raised funds to sponsor DSA's first gathering of socialists of color, which was held at Fisk University in Nashville in 1983. I also edited and largely financed a short-lived DSA publication, *Third World Socialists*. Much of DSA's leadership remained unenthusiastic about the publication, and the national organization committed relatively few resources to working with Asian-American, Latino, or African-American activists. The growing student groups linked to DSA on college campuses had serious difficulties recruiting students of color.

To their credit, DSA members were prominent in support of the Presidential campaigns of Jesse Jackson in 1984 and 1988. DSA's Antiracism Commission is active, and DSA honorary chairperson Cornel West is one of the most influential intellectuals within the black community today. Nevertheless, unfairly or not, DSA retains basically a "white identity" which it has never been able to overcome. The reason for this is simple.

No American socialist organization has ever been able to attract substantial numbers of African-Americans and other people of color unless, from the very beginning, they were well represented inside the leadership and planning of that body. When that does not occur, individual radical intellectuals, such as West, can be affiliated with a socialist group, but that affinity remains marginal and secondary to their primary political endeavors. When forced to make a hard choice of priorities between the "socialist project" and "black liberation," the vast majority of black activists throughout the twentieth century have chosen the latter.

Fortunately, some leftists are trying to learn from the errors of the past. A majority of the national executive of the Committees of

Correspondence consists of people of color. The New Party, which has initiated organizing efforts in nearly twenty states, has a rule that forty per cent of all leadership groups be people of color. A precursor chapter of the New Party also elected African-American activist Jackie Kirby to the Pine Bluff, Arkansas, city council in 1991. Activists of color were prominent in the leadership of the People's Progressive Convention held at Eastern Michigan University in Ypsilanti last August.

A new socialist vision must be identified with peace and the resolution of social problems without resort to force or violence, unless absolutely necessary. This is not to argue for pacifism. The work of W.E.B. Du Bois is crucial for understanding the essential connection between peace and social justice. "Peace" in the context of race relations means the empowerment of people of color, the reduction of racist language and behavior, and ultimately the obliteration of the very idea of racial categories. Peace is not the absence of social tensions and class conflict but the achievement of social justice and equality of conditions for all members of society.

This is a period of political thinking and organizational realignment within the left. The former League of Revolutionary Struggle, which was notable on the Left for its predominantly Asian-American, Latino, and African-American composition, has split in two political directions: the majority tendency, which has moved sharply away from Marxism-Leninism and produces the Unity newspaper, and the minority grouping, the Socialist Organizing Network. The Network is now engaging in collaborative discussions with the Freedom Road socialist organization, which in turn publishes the very impressive publication *Forward Motion*. The former Line of March organization developed into the nucleus of the journal *Crossroads*, which has played a central role in the theoretical and organizational reconstruction of a wide section of the left. Taking advantage of the wide exposure print affords, a new theoretical journal, *Rethinking Marxism*, has become an important forum for many radical scholars.

A number of national conferences on the left in the 1980s and early 1990s have also brought activists and socialist intellectuals together into productive dialogue. These have included the annual Socialist Scholars Conference in New York City, closely associated with DSA; the Midwest Radical Scholars Conference in Chicago, initiated by veteran leftist Carl Davidson; the Activists of Color conference in Berkeley in April 1991. In addition, the National Committee for Independent Political Action, based in New York, has brought together a number of well-respected community organizers, progressives, and socialists such as radical law professor Arthur Kinoy and Alabama's Gwen Patton, a former leader of the Rainbow Coalition.

Perhaps the most important step toward a new type of nonsectarian left unity has been the creation of the Committees of Correspondence, the merger of those Marxists who recently left the United States Communist Party with a number of independent socialists and activists. The leadership of the Committees embraces an unprecedented range of women and men who have struggled, in various formations and socialist parties, for a democratic society: former Communist Party leaders Angela Y. Davis, Charlene Mitchell, and

Kendra Alexander; former Socialist Workers Party Presidential candidate Peter Camejo; lesbian activist Leslie Cagan; Chicana activist Elizabeth Martinez; as well as Arthur Kinoy and Carl Davidson.

In recent months, some have suggested that the next stage of left unity should be the development of a "socialist united front" among various American socialist groups. The election of Bill Clinton and the Democratic Party's repudiation of key tenets of its traditional liberalism certainly help this process by pushing the Democratic Party's public-policy boundaries to the right, leaving a growing political vacuum on the left.

Such a front is premature. Certainly there needs to be greater dialogue and practical cooperation among socialist organizations and progressive, independent political movements. This process should begin with joint projects, local conferences, and collaborative activities among a wide range of groups that share a commitment to socialism and democracy.

Nothing is more urgent than establishing practical joint activities and discussions between the two largest entities on the left, the Democratic Socialists of America and the Committees of Correspondence. Such unity should be based on the democratic right "to agree to disagree" on certain questions, to respect the organizational autonomy and integrity of the various formations, but should seek areas of cooperative relations and joint action, striving for greater consensus about the character of our socialist vision for American society. Unity which rests on such practical accomplishments today may culminate in a unified, but pluralistic and democratic, socialist organization in the future.

The central questions confronting the left are not, however, located within the left itself but in the broader, deeper currents of social protest and struggle among nonsocialist, democratic constituencies—in the activities of trade unionists, gays and lesbians, feminists, environmentalists, people of color, and the poor. We must accept and acknowledge the reality that, for the foreseeable future, the essential debate will not be about "capitalism versus socialism" but about the character and content of the capitalist social order and whether we as progressives can strengthen movements for empowerment and equality within the context of capitalism.

This means advancing a politics of radical, multicultural democracy, not socialism. It means, in the short run, that tactical electoral alliances with centrists like Clinton, within the Democratic Party, are absolutely necessary if we are to push back the aggressive, reactionary agenda of the Far Right. Bush's defeat last November was critical for the left; it allows us to raise a series of issues, from the adoption of a single-payer national health system like Canada's to the enforcement of civil-rights initiatives. As the focus of national-policy debates shifts from right to center, progressive and democratic forces have a better chance to influence the outcome. And as we move national policy toward radical democratic alternatives, we establish the preconditions necessary for building a democratic socialist America in the next century.

Finally, our new vision of socialism must approach the question of social transformation not as a project that is essentially oppositional, but as a collective, protracted task filled with hope, affirmation, and

MANNING MARABLE

human aspirations. The theoretical history of the Left is basically a rich, if often contradictory, legacy of criticism. Marx's *Kapital* was not a blueprint for the construction of a socialist, democratic society; it was a trenchant, brilliant critique of the inequalities and class contradictions of capitalism as an economic system.

But there was also something mechanistic in this projection of a socialist future—the idea that impersonal, amoral social forces and economic factors will determine the outcome of history. Marx explained that the working class had "no ideals to realize." Many communists interpreted this to mean that undemocratic measures that grossly violate human rights and morality could be justified in constructing a future society that was perfectible in principle.

In a different way, white social democrats generally shared this contempt for the ideals and human aspirations of working people, focusing instead on the utilitarian mechanics of winning elections and running governments. A century ago, Edward Bernstein, the very first "socialist revisionist," proclaimed, "To me that which is generally called the ultimate aim of socialism is nothing, but the movement is everything."

It is here that the insights of the Black Freedom Movement most sharply contradict the theoretical and political legacy of white socialism. As Martin Luther King, Jr. observed, every truly profound movement for human liberation is driven by a "revolution in values." Much of the world's continuing social unrest and class struggle exist because the means of power are radically severed from the ends—by both the right and the left.

"We will never have peace in the world," King insisted, "until men everywhere recognize that ends are not cut off from means, because the means represent the ideal in the making, and the end in process."

To achieve a truly just, egalitarian society, we must actualize our ideals in our daily political endeavors and activism with the oppressed. And we must do so with a sense of urgency, because there is nothing preordained about our ultimate victory. In the words of Albert Einstein, "The existence and validity of human rights are not written in the stars."

As socialists, we must be critical of the Government and its policies, opposing such American adventures as the invasion of Iraq, protesting cutbacks in education, health care, and other areas of human need. But the politics of criticism is an act of negation. We cannot construct a political culture of radical democracy simply by rejecting the system. We cannot win by saying what we are against. We must affirm what we are for.

"It was as a Socialist, and because I was a Socialist," Michael Harrington observed years ago, "that I fell in love with America. If the Left wants to change this country because it hates it, the people will never listen to the left and the people will embrace the right. To be a Socialist—to be a Marxist—is to make an act of faith, of love even, toward this land. It is to sense the seed beneath the snow; to see, beneath the veneer of corruption and meanness and the commercialization of human relationships, men and women capable of controlling their own destinies."

Harrington was right. America has an incredibly rich history of radical democratic protest. The socialist critique can only succeed as an extension, not as a departure, from that heritage of Frederick Douglass, Fannie Lou Hamer, Vito Marcantonio, and César Chavez. We have a political responsibility to speak to that tradition, to identify with the working people of this land, to express their dreams and hopes.

American democracy is an unfinished project, and its central creative power is found in the talent and energies of its working people. Yet millions of Americans find themselves divorced from the reality of equality and empowerment, and the promise of a better life. They stand in isolation from the comfort, the power, and the privileges of an upper class which is determinedly dedicated to the preservation of the economic status quo.

It is the task of American socialists to call for a new social contract for this country, a common understanding about the principles of power and human development, cutting across the rainbow of cultural and social class, of ethnic diversity. What if we challenged the idea that virtually all corporate, political, educational, and cultural leadership must be selected from a narrow band of white, upper-class males? What if we employed the full power of government to provide the basic human needs—universal health care, decent shelter, quality education for our children, improved public-transportation facilities, and the right to a job or guaranteed income—for every citizen? How much would all of our lives be enriched, how much more productive?

To revitalize our cities, to put people back to work, to create a social environment without the discrimination of race, gender, and sexual orientation, to improve the quality of public schools, to address the growing crisis of our deteriorating environment, we Americans desperately need a new vision of what democracy could be. To be a socialist is to pursue this radical democratic project: taking back the power from the upper class which dominates the state and the corporations, empowering the people to fight for full human equality in all aspects of daily life.

I have no doubt that the current glorification of triumphalism of capitalism will continue, at least in the short run. But, as the South African expression goes, "Time is longer than rope." The fundamental reasons for class struggle still exist. Our challenge is to grasp the new problems and concerns of oppressed people and to transform their awareness of the issues into a political culture and consciousness favoring radical democratic alternatives, aimed at fighting corporate capitalism.

So long as corporate greed continues to destroy the environment, so long as several million Americans are homeless, so long as anti-Semitism, racism, sexism, and homophobia are manipulated to divide neighborhoods and communities, so long as factories shut down overnight and corporations hold cities as economic hostages in their demands for concessions, the vision of socialism will continue to be relevant and essential to the construction of a truly egalitarian, democratic America.

13

IMAGINE THERE'S NO HEAVEN

RADICAL POLITICS IN AN AGE OF REACTION

MICHAEL OMI AND HOWARD WINANT

DE MORTUIS NIL NISI BONUM: OF THE DEAD, SAY ONLY
what was good. Well, after the sweeping Republican victory in the 1994 mid-term elections, it's hard to say much
good about the Democratic Party. If it is not altogether
dead, it is at least among the undead, staggering about
corpselike, afraid of the bright lights of television, looking for
"moderate" Republicans from whose veins it can drink.
Listening to the Democrats' election post-mortems was more
than a little scary; from the President, to the defeated Speaker
of the House, to the resolutely centrist incumbent senators
(such as Wofford and Sasser) and governors (like Cuomo) who
had been rejected as big-spending, big-taxing welfare statists,
there was little offered but puzzlement and demoralization. No
alternative vision, no memory of the New Deal coalition, no hint
of the legacy of the 1960s.

In this menacing atmosphere, to discuss even the possibility of a radical democratic politics seems futile: empty political posturing from a movement which doesn't exist. Yet today a radical view is more desperately needed than ever. Already, right-wing Democrats are taking advantage of the "opportunity" provided by the disastrous 1994 elections to move even further in the direction of "me-too" Republicanism. As Dave McCurdy, the leader of the Democratic Leadership Council, the very Democratic organization that helped propel Clinton to power, put it:

> While Bill Clinton has the mind of a New Democrat, he retains the heart of an old Democrat. The result is an Administration that has pursued elements of a moderate and liberal agenda at the same time, to the great confusion of the American people.[1]

McCurdy assumes that the erosion of the Party's power occurred because Clinton, presumably following his heart rather than his head, leaned too far to the left. We, by contrast, suggest that the Party has abandoned its traditional constituencies on the moderate left to adopt a weaker version of its opponents' politics. Thus it has condemned itself to irrelevance, to the politics of waffling, to the indifference if not the contempt of the voters. Yet the problems of the Democrats go deeper than that. The Party lacks ideas. It lacks ways to galvanize its previous constituents and reach out to new ones. What existing movements or sources of inspiration can potentially revitalize a radical democratic vision? We cannot fully answer that question here. But we can take some preliminary steps to begin the process of answering it, and that is significant in itself.

DEAD MARXISTS SOCIETY

The dilemmas faced by the moderate Democrats have their origins in the weaknesses of the radical democrats. Historically in the United States, progressive politics have travelled from their origins on the radical left, to their eventual home in the political mainstream. This is the history of labor legislation and social security, of civil rights and abortion rights, as well as a host of other policies. But today, there is a notable crisis of vision on the left, an exhaustion which is more than temporary.

This crisis of vision has come about, not by some mere lull in left movement activity, but as a result of the death of Marxist ideals. Until quite recently and despite all its betrayals and vulgarizations, Marxism continued to inspire left movements in the United States, as well as around the world. Marxist theory and socialist politics constituted the horizon that the 1960s movements contemplated. There were many problems associated with Marxist thought: its nineteenth-century view of nature as inexhaustible, its naive equation of statism with socialization, its limited commitment to popular sovereignty and meaningful democracy, its faith in planning as an alternative to markets, and its practical commitment to repression, to name but a few. But in one respect Marxism remained untarnished, and therefore vital to the left:

it provided a vision of a world free of exploitation, of a society from which the "logic of the lash" had been expunged. However much "actually existing socialism" failed to live up to that ideal, the ideal itself—of a society based on cooperation instead of competition—was not lost to us until the destruction of the socialist regimes at the end of the 1980s. The pain of this loss cannot be overstated: at present a new ideal of comparable moral and political power cannot even be imagined. Thus the bitterness of defeat is compounded by the distinct possibility of a philosophical anthropology based on oppression; as a result the idea that it is immutable "human nature" to form social orders based on inequality and hierarchy has now escaped from the laboratories of the right and become intellectually pandemic. These galling *sequelae* of the death of Marxism complete the disillusionment experienced by earlier generations of socialists; the deformed and betrayed revolution that had eaten its own young in the 1930s has now truly succumbed.

More prosaically, when we look at the two issues on which the left has traditionally staged its most important battles with the powers of state and capital in the United States—that of socioeconomic inequality and that of imperialism—we can see the wreckage of Marxism everywhere. Domestically, the resistance to "big government"—a sort of anarchism in the service of big business—resounds across the land. Few voices are raised today even in defense of mainstream social democratic initiatives. Probably the last best effort of this type was the attempt to put a single-payer health plan on the reform agenda in 1993–94; it never received a serious hearing in Congress and as a ballot initiative in California went down to ignominious defeat. And the United States anti-imperialist tradition, which stretched from turn of the century opposition to the seizure of the Philippines to the anti-Vietnam war movement, is also in a terminal state. We probably saw the last of it in the resistance to the Gulf War. Today, from Bosnia to Haiti, there is no articulate left policy alternative to interventionism.

IDENTITY BITES

So when we contemplate the crackup of the United States left, what surviving elements do we glimpse? Not surprisingly, what has been called (often deprecatingly) "identity politics." This is what remains after the fall of Marxism: race, gender, and sexuality.[2] In these three general areas, there is still political conflict, there are still movements. Nor is this unexpected: in the United States, class politics has always been underdeveloped, even at its high water marks at the turn of the century and in the 1930s. Race, most particularly, has provided the primary axis of political conflict; out of abolitionism came feminism; out of civil rights came gay liberation.

It is less possible to be hopeful about "identity politics" after November, 1994. To be sure, there are still fairly high levels of conflict over race, gender, and sexuality out there. In 1994, anti-gay rights initiatives generally went down to defeat. The Christian Coalition (haven't these people read the Sermon on the Mount?), though phenomenally successful in its strategy of grass-roots burrowing into school boards and local Republican party organizations, has found it necessary to downplay its repressive social agenda. But we can take little comfort from this: it is now possible for respected public figures to advocate forced removal of illegitimate (read black) babies to state-run orphanages, and indeed to advocate the death penalty for homosexuality. Such proto-fascism is not very far from the main currents of the hard right; although the Republican Party retains some "moderates" on social issues (such as Weld, Jeffords, and Specter), these politicians are not rushing to challenge the metastasizing intolerance in their own ranks. Indeed, the racist Proposition 187 was the centerpiece of the reelection campaign of supposedly "moderate" California governor Pete Wilson. This resort to the time-honored scapegoating techniques of nativism and hysterical pandering to fears of crime (read black again) suggests that the consolidation of the Republicans as the straight white male party proceeds apace.

So racially-defined minorities, women, and gays continue to be targets of the right. Their demands, their intrusion into the political arena beginning in the 1960s, have not yet been contained or normalized. As Stanley Aronowitz recently noted, these groups and the movements they generated "have effected nothing less than a revolution in the moral economy of the United States, changing social and cultural practices in incalculable ways."[3]

Much of the right-wing resurgence can be understood as an unholy (or should that be holy?) alliance between the traditional business class politics of mainstream Republicanism and the reactionary social agenda of the Christian right. There are many tensions in this alliance: there are libertarian and repressive tendencies, social engineers and small government advocates, racists and antiracists, pro-choice and anti-abortion advocates, even a few "out" gays. But the overall thrust of the right is clearly a reactionary one, opposing with equal force the welfare state and the movements which have redefined social and cultural life in the United States since the 1960s.

The fuss is about blacks in the city and migrants crossing the border; women resisting the "traditional morality" of patriarchal rule; gays demanding an uncloseted, unstigmatized place; and supporters of the aforementioned in universities, foundations, and social agencies. We continue to mirror the right: we too are an alliance, a "power bloc," which contains deep divisions. We too have a class politics, which in our case links us to a recalcitrant and defensive working class.

Though we have been forced onto the defensive by the rightward drift in United States politics, in the absence of a coherent left, this alliance, based to a significant degree in the movements of "identity," remains the repository of our hopes. It is virtually the only thing left standing in the aftermath of the reactionary storm that has blown across the United States landscape.

This is an important recognition, particularly at a moment when not only the right but also some survivors of the new left are longing to overcome these supposedly "separatist" tendencies and dreaming of a new "universalism" of the left. Todd Gitlin, for example, has recently bemoaned the absence of the "commonality politics" that the left, he asserts, has historically upheld. For him, "identity politics" has fractured the fundamental commitment to a universalistic vision that the new left supposedly bequeathed us.

> The proliferation of identity politics leads to a turning inward, a grim and hermetic bravado which takes the ideological form of paranoid, jargon-clotted, post-modernist groupthink, cult celebrations of victimization, and stylized marginality.[4]

Our experiences of the New Left were considerably less universalizing, but apart from that, Gitlin's dream of restoration—of the Marxist project in particular—is hopelessly outdated. The problem with this is not a desire for unity, which the left desperately needs. The difficulty lies deeper: at whose expense, and in whose image, is unity to be forged? Lacking a vision of social justice that takes "identity" into account in as fundamental a way as it does "inequality," Gitlin is reduced to railing against the very movements which shaped his politics in the 1960s.

We should not fall into this trap. We should recognize the degree to which such nostalgia colludes with the neoconservative celebration of a largely mythical "common culture" of progress and integration. We ought to find the courage to support the critique that racial radicals, feminists, and queer theorists have made of hegemonic norms and values.

CULTURE AND STRUCTURE

Affirming this critical stance is not enough. We should recognize that our self-understandings as movements have been far too limited. We have seen "identity politics" too exclusively in terms of *cultural* movements, counterposing our politics to a rather economistic view of class. The very label "identity politics," with its slightly disparaging connotation of navel-gazing, reinforces this impression.

What if we broke decisively with that implication? What if we stressed instead the way these forms of political opposition necessarily link culture to social structure, identity to inequality? After all, movements develop not only, not even primarily, in order to identify their adherents through some collective representation, some shared experience, some unified subjectivity; they also obviously seek to transform the social structure, and these two "moments" are ineluctably connected. Looking at race, for example, we see that to interpret what race means is to propose or oppose definite social policies based on that interpretation. Conversely as well, to make political demands based on issues of race is to "signify" race culturally, to interpret its meaning in practical, political terms.[5] Race, as well as gender, sexuality, and even class, are indicators of inequality and stratification, and of identity.

The standard objection, raised from various points on the political spectrum, is that "identity politics" fails to address issues of economic hardship, that it neglects those (trade unionists, hard-pressed members of the middle class, Reagan democrats, and so forth) who "play by the rules," "pay their taxes," "believe in the system," and wind up getting taken advantage of. Such claims revive the reactionary populism of a century ago, which scapegoated blacks when the economy had turned downward and the radical movements of the day had been defeated. Although the activities of civil rights and feminist organizations in defense of working families and middle-class standards of living would probably stand up quite well in comparison to trade union efforts (not to mention Christian right) efforts on behalf of, for example, the homeless, this critique still has some bite. It suggests that, first, the fragmentation of the left is a luxury we can no longer afford; and second, without a vision of social justice broad enough to accommodate both the cultural and the social sources of its oppositional energies, that fragmentation will continue.

STRAIGHT OUT OF SUBURBIA

The crackup of the traditional left, particularly the defeat of its trade unionist and social democratic variants, has left those whose interests and identities it formerly articulated in a vulnerable position. The growing vacuum affects millions of white, working- and middle-class Americans, preponderantly suburbanites, who now find themselves bereft of a vision of progress and a better life. They constitute a vast potential base for reaction, for they have been failed not only by the left, but are experiencing the secular decline of the United States in both material and cultural terms. The problematic nature of whiteness, maleness, and heterosexuality in the contemporary United States is going to shape their political adventures for at least another generation.

These folks are now experiencing an "identity deficit": formerly whiteness and maleness (not to mention heterosexuality) constituted the cultural norms, and they were thus invisible, transparent. Now, this unquestioned identity is being replaced by a kind of "double consciousness."[6] Whites, males, and straights must now manage their racial, gender, and sexual identities to some degree, just as nonwhites, women, and gays have always done. Does this mean that they must necessarily identify with reactionary racial, gender, or sexual politics?[7] Not necessarily. If we look at whites, for example, we see that there are all sorts of people out there, some who have bought into the politics of resentment and division being propagated from the right, and some who have not. While residential integration has not even been approached—a tremendous failure of the last quarter-century of racial politics—integration has advanced in many other social spheres.[8] Various feminist demands and at least tolerance of gays (admittedly incomplete but nevertheless real accomplishments) have also been achieved. In addition there are synergistic connections here: millions of white women and gays understand something about the ongoing realities of racial discrimination, for example. White identities remain uneven and contested: white workers, even white ethnics, are not uniformly "Reagan democrats"; even conservative whites may be anti-racist; class and gender play important parts in determining racial attitudes; and other factors such as age, work experience, and neighborhood are also involved. The volatility of contemporary white identities, not their consolidation, is what must be emphasized.

But without an alternative vision emphasizing social justice, and without a far more developed ability to build organizations based upon that vision, the new right may well turn out to be the closest thing to a movement these people ever experience.

WHERE TO, BUDDY?

The vision of socialism, and the left that it sustained, has collapsed. In a period of political instability, the threat of reaction looms menacingly on the horizon. What stands in opposition to the consolidation of reaction is no longer the theory and practice of socialism; it is the "identity politics" of racial radicalism, feminism, and gay/lesbian liberation, together with the submerged but still powerful (class) demand for economic equality.

This assertion comes with an important qualification. These currents are hardly a strong and coherent force. Within each there is a multiplicity of political perspectives, orientations, and practices. All have had difficulties in overcoming the many divisions among themselves, particularly the tendency to demand an unattainable ideological purity and an "authentic" oppositional identity. All have tended to neglect matters of class, and all have been unable to articulate a vision of emancipation larger than the critique of their particular oppressions. But despite their embattled and confused condition, these currents have withstood—thus far—the post-1960s tide of reaction far better than the socialist tradition has. In this sense, "identity politics" remains an indispensable component of any left opposition.

Any radical democratic opposition that does manage to emerge will face a daunting challenge from the ascendant right. In contrast with the demoralized left, the right *does* have ideas, although it too is far from unified. But having gained control of the Congress for the first time in four decades, the Republicans will now push their "Contract With America," with its assault on what little remains of the welfare state and progressive taxation, not to mention the "peace dividend."

The "Contract" also involves specific cultural projects. In accepting the Republican nomination to be Speaker of the House, Newt Gingrich said:

> . . . [W]e have to recognize our commitment to renewing American civilization by reestablishing the reality that this is a multiethnic society, but it's one civilization. People come here to be Americans, and they want to be Americans, and that implies a civilization with a set of habits and patterns.[9]

While giving lip service to diversity, the main message of Gingrich and his Republican myrmidons is the (re)assertion of a core culture and the erasure of difference. Having won in 1994 by running against racial minorities and the poor, against welfare mothers and undocumented immigrants, against women and gays, and against unions, they are not about to tend to these constituencies' needs while in office. Alarmed by the "disuniting of America" and tired of a "culture of complaint," the right wants "victims" to "get over it."

Today, as ever, the country cannot be united on the backs of the subordinated. Inequality, intolerance, and exploitation are not going away; in fact they are intensified as society becomes more polarized along the various axes of oppression: race, class, gender, and sexuality. A compelling political project of opposition to this rightward drift does not yet exist, but this does not mean resistance will cease, nor does it suggest that the left's defeat is permanent. As we work to redefine our ideas in the post-socialist era now dawning, we will draw upon the radical democratic movements, upon the much-maligned "politics of identity." Our first step should be to recognize that there is no single "authentic" identity, whether based in race, gender, class, or sexuality, but instead a vast array of oppositional stances, potentially embracing many millions of political actors. We need each other's strength to fight the right.

Our second step should be to extend this recognition into a broader political discourse that emphasizes social justice, economic equality, and cultural tolerance. Such a politics would not submerge economically defined class interests, but would emphasize the ways in which culture and social structure are mutually defined and shaped. This connection will be crucial to the development of a radical democratic perspective that seeks to challenge the undemocratic and authoritarian character of the right, and to counterpose a different vision.

NOTES

1. Quoted in Douglas Jehl, "Group's Head Says Clinton Broke Faith," *The New York Times*, 7 December 1994, A12.
2. We neglect here the important subject of environmentalism, a key social movement of our time. Although the impulses of environmentalism are substantially different than those of "identity politics," the issues that environmentalism raises also suggest the eclipse of class politics in the United States context.
3. Stanley Aronowitz, "The Situation of the Left in the United States," *Socialist Review* 93/3 (1994): 15.
4. Todd Gitlin, "From Universality to Difference: Notes on the Fragmentation of the Idea of the Left," *Contention* vol. 2, no. 2 (Winter 1993): 21.
5. This analysis is developed in depth in Racial Formation in the United States: From the 1960s to the 1980s, 2nd ed. (New York: Routledge, 1994), and in Howard Winant, *Racial Conditions: Politics, Theory, Comparisons* (Minneapolis: University of Minnesota Press, 1994).
6. We draw this phrase from W. E. B. Du Bois, who used it to characterize the peculiarities of black identity in the United States. See W. E. B. Du Bois, *The Souls of Black Folk* ([1903]; New York: Penguin, 1989).
7. Paul M. Sniderman and Thomas Piazza, *The Scar of Race* (Cambridge: Harvard University Press, 1993); Anne Phillips, *Democracy and Difference* (University Park, PA: Pennsylvania State University Press, 1993).
8. See Douglas S. Massey and Nancy A. Denton, *American Apartheid: Segregation and the Making of the Underclass* (Cambridge, MA: Harvard University Press, 1993).
9. "Excerpts of Gingrich Comments After Nomination," *The New York Times*, 6 December 1994, A10.

14

CULTURE WARS AND IDENTITY POLITICS

THE RELIGIOUS RIGHT AND THE CULTURAL POLITICS OF HOMOSEXUALITY

SINCE THE 1970S AMERICAN POLITICS AND CULTURAL LIFE have become increasingly polarized between secular liberalism—increasingly identified with multiculturalism, pluralism, and the politics of diversity—and religious conservatisms.[1] The religious right is engaged in a campaign to achieve political and cultural hegemony in American life—built on the revival of traditional "family values." In the current period, homosexuality is a major target of its hegemonic project. Gay and lesbian politics has long been committed to achieving acceptance within a liberal framework of tolerance and equal treatment—following in the footsteps of the black civil rights movement and the assimilation of ethnic minorities. The framework of this "ethnic model" (increasingly characterized as "identity politics") is too limited to mobilize the cultural and political resources necessary to defeat the religious right's agenda. Existing

JEFFREY ESCOFFIER

alternatives modeled on AIDS activism and queer politics can only supplement but not replace identity politics. The only strategy that can offer a reasonable hope is a radical democratic politics that appeals to the disorganized bloc of Americans who remain opposed to conservative orthodoxy.

The culture wars of the last decade have their origins in the battles of the sixties and seventies: the black civil rights and Black Power movements, the movement against the war in Vietnam, the counterculture, the sexual revolution, the rise of feminism, and the emergence of the gay and lesbian movements. Each of these movements encountered resistance from a broad body of Americans. The spread of black civil rights activity made a growing number of whites aware of their own racism. The anti-war movement flew in the face of those Americans who believed that communism was a threat to the American way of life. The counterculture disseminated its powerful brew of drugs, sex, and rock music to young people across the country.[2]

By the mid-seventies, the energies that fed these movements had begun to wane. Black political movements, such as the civil rights movement, Black Muslims, and the Black Panthers were increasingly the targets of violent responses—in particular, the assassinations of Martin Luther King, Jr. and Malcolm X. Black communities rioted in response to long-standing injustices and anti-black violence. The left that emerged reinvigorated from the social struggles of the sixties reached its peak in the early seventies before the United States withdrawal from the war in Vietnam in 1976 removed one of the main provocations to progressive mobilizations.

Among the movements that emerged from the political struggles of the sixties, three continued to grow throughout the seventies and into the eighties. The environmental movement has had an enormous impact. Both the women's movement and the gay/lesbian movement also continued to grow throughout the seventies, putting issues like ERA, abortion, and gay rights before a wider and wider public. The impact of the AIDS epidemic on gay men aroused new political energies in the gay and lesbian community.[3]

The conservative opposition to the movements of the sixties and seventies was originally an amorphous group; they had no coherent identity. Political leaders and intellectuals sought to organize this conservative opposition, and they called it, among other things, "the silent majority." The religious right began to participate in American politics during the seventies.[4] The New Right that emerged victorious with Reagan's election in 1980 was an alliance that brought together traditional conservatives primarily preoccupied with communism and economic issues with religious fundamentalists such as Jerry Falwell.[5]

For many on the right, multiculturalism is replacing communism as the evil force threatening "the American Way of Life." Recently, Irving Kristol, the so-called "Godfather" of American conservatism wrote, "There is no 'after the Cold War' for me. So far from having ended, my cold war has increased in intensity, as sector after sector of American life has been ruthlessly corrupted by the liberal ethos. . . . Now that the other 'Cold War' is over, the real cold war has begun. We are far less prepared for this cold war, far more vulnerable to our enemy, than was the case with our victorious war against a global Communist threat."[6] This "cold war" is political-cultural struggle over the shape of American democracy.

In the seventies conservative opposition to this peculiar conflation of "liberalism" and the descendants of the counterculture increasingly found common ground on the "family values" agenda. Anything that seemed to challenge the traditional nuclear family was targeted by the conservative agenda. The "family values" agenda appeals to the many Americans whose family lives are threatened by the strains of maintaining conjugal commitments and the potential loss of authority over their children—drugs and violence in the schools, the social dominance of television and, in particular, the risks of teenage sexuality (e.g., pregnancy and AIDS). Family values is promoted both as the basis for religious proselytizing and as the basis of political mobilization, including PACs, lobbying, and electoral politics. It is the cultural core of the right's hegemonic project. It is supplemented with other planks of conservative ideology, such as dismantling of the welfare state, the privatization of public services, reviving prayer in the schools, a balanced budget amendment to the Constitution, and reinstituting the death penalty.

THE RELIGIOUS RIGHT'S GAY AGENDA

Abortion has been one of the most divisive social issues in American politics. As the linchpin of women's reproductive rights it is intimately connected with a whole range of other issues like sex education, teenage pregnancy, and the distribution of condoms to teenagers, which assume the individual's freedom of sexual choice. Abortion as an issue has united fundamentalists across the entire spectrum, from Roman Catholicism and Protestant fundamentalism to Orthodox Judaism. The conservative anti-abortion movement has waged an extremely confrontational and even violent war against abortion clinics and doctors who perform abortions. While a large percentage of the American population still opposes abortion, most Americans reject government interference in women's reproductive rights. The fundamentalists' momentum in the battle against abortion is now faltering. Thus the religious right has turned to the other key plank in their crusade to shore up "family values"—the defeat of gay and lesbian rights.

The growing visibility of the lesbian and gay community throughout the seventies forced conservative fundamentalists to take homosexuality to task. In part, this required fundamentalist churches to address homosexuality as it is interpreted by the Judeo-Christian tradition—with its history of hostility to homosexuals as "sodomites" engaging in "unnatural practices." But homosexuality was also seen as one of a number of threats to the traditional nuclear family. The first electoral campaign by Christian fundamentalists against gay rights was launched in 1977—Anita Bryant's Save Our Children campaign to repeal gay rights legislation in Dade County.[7]

The religious right's project to reconstitute American culture around traditional Christian values is increasingly dominant—it has had an enormous effect on the mass media, it has captured the Republican party, and it has won huge gains in the 1994 elections. By the mid-1990s gay issues have become the social issue—even more than abortion—that most effectively polarizes the American electorate. Homosexuals are now the primary target of much fundamentalist organizing activities. There are between eighteen to thirty-seven local and state initiatives on gay rights' issues scheduled to take place over the next two years.

Can gay and lesbian political organizations meet that challenge? Do lesbians and gay men have the cultural and symbolic resources to organize an effective political strategy? Identity politics cannot mobilize the cultural and political resources necessary to defeat the religious right's agenda—nor can politics modeled on AIDS activism or queer nationalism replace identity politics. Lesbians and gay men need a new and far reaching political strategy to combat the religious right's hegemonic project.

CIVIL RIGHTS, IDENTITY POLITICS, AND COMMUNITY ECONOMIC DEVELOPMENT

In the fifty years since the end of World War II, homosexuality has emerged as a significant cultural phenomenon. In a practical way it emerged as an issue during the war within the military. For military authorities it posed a problem of screening and control of sexuality within a same-sex environment.[8] In 1954 Alfred Kinsey's findings on the widespread experience of homosexuality caused a furor. Under the stimulus of military discharges, dismissals as security risks from federal government jobs, and growing public awareness, homosexuals began to experience a sense of group identity. Homosexual civil rights organizations began to form in the early fifties.[9]

At the end of the sixties gay political activity exploded in the wake of the Stonewall riots.[10] The act of publicly declaring one's homosexuality was the decisive innovation of the post-Stonewall gay and lesbian liberation movement. Through the process of coming out, homosexuals adopted a public social identity—thus homosexual activity was transformed into an identity. Before the coming out strategy, homosexuals were entrapped by the enforced secrecy of their sexual preferences. Secrets can have enormous power in defining a personal identity, but the power of shame that secrecy instills also reinforces socially repressive and stigmatizing norms.[11] Thus the coming out strategy made visible the huge population of people primarily engaged in homosexual behavior. Gay and lesbian political organizing gained an identifiable population, one could almost say a "quantifiable" goal, which provided the basis for residential and economic community-building, and political mobilization in the form of demonstrations, marches, and voting. "Coming out of the closet" became the essential pre-condition for gay and lesbian organizing and community-building—ideally all homosexuals were urged to come out and publicly declare themselves.[12]

Early homophile (the term adopted by the pre-Stonewall homosexual civil rights movement) activists had never even conceived of a coming out strategy. Many homosexuals in the period before Stonewall tended to think of their homosexuality as only one component of their personal identities. In that spirit Gore Vidal has always insisted that 'homosexual' is an adjective, not a noun.[13] But coming out, in effect, reifies one's identity as a homosexual. It initiates a public discursive process of identification.[14] The reification of homosexual identity brought about by publicly coming out continues to be reinforced by the active pressures of stigmatization and repression. The gay and lesbian movement's emphasis on coming out, nevertheless, did not totally dismantle the closet, nor did it lead spontaneously to the disappearance of the stigma or repressive laws.

The publicness of the new homosexual identity encouraged new forms of community-building and organizing. Openly lesbian and gay activists demonstrated in public places for increased tolerance and civil rights, particularly in housing and employment. While the number of gay and lesbian political organizations proliferated, lesbian and gay-owned businesses opened up in order to supply their communities with news and literature (newspapers, publishers, and bookstores), consumer goods (clothing, jewelry, sexual commodities, coffee houses and restaurants), and social services (psychological counseling centers, bathhouses). Gay neighborhoods formed around the old pre-Stonewall sexual zones, bars, and community-owned businesses. The economic development would have been impossible without the discursive reconstruction of homosexual identity based on coming out. Of course, the coming out strategy did not totally dismantle the closet. Ironically, the coming out strategy enabled many members of the lesbian and gay communities to come out in limited ways. They were able to remain in the closet at work or among their families, but they could be "out" in the protected environment of urban gay enclaves. One result of the strategy was the heightened visibility of the community itself. It was not necessary for everyone who engaged in homosexual behavior to come out unequivocally. The visibility of the lesbian and gay communities in conjunction with the economic development of those communities provided a framework for homosexuals to identify themselves as lesbian or gay without paying the price of full public disclosure.

Gay and lesbian political activity increasingly reflected the forms of community development compatible with the growth of lesbian and gay-owned small businesses. The formation of Gay Democratic Clubs and their success in local elections reinforced the process of community development—a process that was jointly discursive and economic. Harvey Milk's 1976 election to the San Francisco Board of Supervisors represented, in part, the consolidation of the Castro district as a gay neighborhood—and it was financed by many small business owners in the community.[15]

Once the coming out strategy unleashed the potentialities of gay and lesbian economic development, the economic stratification of American society along lines of class, race, and gender circumscribed the political and cultural possibilities of those homosexuals who did not or were not able to participate in the predominantly white and middle-class and male enclaves.

The economic development that had taken place by the late 1970s had never been equitably balanced between lesbians and gay men. As women, lesbians had many fewer economic resources at their disposal than gay men did. Lesbians and gay men had also specialized in different kinds of businesses and often lived in different neighborhoods. Lesbian political developments underwrote different economic priorities. Lesbian community-building and economic development reflected different needs and agendas—in the mid- to late seventies lesbians entered a separatist phase, partly in their efforts to build women's communities and businesses, and partly because gay men were no less chauvinist than straight men.[16] The development of a shared (between women and men) political and economic community occurred in response to a series of outside threats—the succession of the rightwing initiatives starting in 1977 to erase gay rights legislation where it already existed, and then in response to the AIDS crisis in the early eighties.

Gay men and lesbians of color were not fully included in these developments of the gay or lesbian communities. The political, cultural, and economic developments of the homosexual community reinscribed the economic and cultural stratification of white America.

The development of gay and lesbian identity politics is the result of the combined effects of discursive identification and economic development. Discursive identification is built on the process of coming out and on its cultural reinforcements, such as "the coming out novel" as a genre, the use of lesbian or gay consumer goods, residence in a lesbian or gay neighborhood, participation in lesbian softball teams or gay choirs, and so on, while the community's small businesses supply them with commodities. These are inseparable elements in the history of the post-Stonewall homosexual community. The joint play of these elements has encouraged some political leaders to think of the gay and lesbian community as an "ethnic group"—an analogy that enables those leaders to insert gay and lesbian identity politics into the continuity of American political history. Through the construction of communities, political machines, and eventual "assimilation," lesbians and gay men follow in the footsteps of the Irish, Italians, Jews, Polish, and Scandinavians. Yet this perspective is challenged by men and women of color, kindred sexual minorities such as the leather community, bisexuals and other sexual aberrants, and by those resisting the norms of gender conformity, such as drag queens, transgendered people, and transsexuals. The irony is that identity politics both resists assimilation, insisting that its identity is different, and strives for assimilation, claiming its identity is continuous with other American identities.

The gay and lesbian community's identity politics built on economic-cultural foundations resembling the classic American ethnic model cannot offer an effective political response to the religious right's hegemonic project of reconstituting family values as an official American ideology. If homosexuals are characterized as morally corrupt and irresponsible, as wealthier and better educated than the average American, adopting a fortress mentality to protect our existing economic and cultural enclaves could potentially isolate us.

THE AIDS CRISIS: THE BREAKDOWN OF IDENTITY POLITICS

Gay and lesbian identity politics, fostered by the economic/cultural "ethnic model" of community development, was unable to cope with the mounting realization, throughout the eighties, of the devastating impact of AIDS among gay men.

The complex of diseases that goes by the name AIDS was first discovered among gay men in 1981. From the first moment that the gay male community became aware of AIDS (it was first called GRID—gay-related immune deficiency) it triggered political responses. Already by the end of the summer of 1981 a group of gay men had met at author Larry Kramer's apartment in New York City and established the Gay Men's Health Crisis (GMHC), which is today the largest AIDS organization in the country.[17]

In the late seventies homosexuals were under attack from the religious right and other conservatives. Lesbian and gay communities had just barely fought off a series of conservative attacks in Dade County; in St. Paul, Minnesota; in Eugene, Oregon; and statewide in California with Proposition 6. Harvey Milk was assassinated in the midst of these campaigns by a disgruntled conservative "family values" politician. Milk's murderer was convicted of manslaughter and received a light sentence. In response San Francisco's gay community erupted in a riot outside of City Hall.[18]

Gay activists realized that an epidemic of a fatal, sexually-transmitted disease originating in the gay male community was a political time bomb. It could provide the occasion for drastic political action against the gay community. Homophobic conservatives would demonize homosexuals and promulgate anti-sexual morality. Doctors initially advised gay men to stop having sex. In addition, it soon became apparent that the public health authorities were less than responsive to the epidemic than had been the case in previous fatal outbreaks such as Legionnaire's disease in Philadelphia in 1975.

As the number of deaths in the gay community exploded, the inadequate response of Federal and local authorities provoked increasing despair and anger.[19] Soon gay men banded together to try to deal with the problems of the epidemic more effectively. Even before HIV itself was discovered, the epidemiological evidence suggested that the disease was probably transmitted through blood and sperm. Groups of activists in New York and San Francisco focused on education as a way to limit the growth of the epidemic. Safe sex guidelines were developed, and organizations were set up to disseminate information about the epidemic and counsel worried people who feared exposure.[20]

The dimensions of the epidemic expanded enormously; other communities were affected—Haitians, African-Americans, hemophiliacs, recipients of blood transfusions, and intravenous drug users; the incubation period seemed to be growing longer. The gay community's own organizing efforts, important and valuable though they were, were far short of the effort required to deal with an epidemic of such huge proportions.

It became increasingly clear that a more forceful political response was needed. In the fall of 1987 ACT UP (AIDS Coalition to Unleash Power) was formed in New York, and soon after similar groups were organized in cities across the country. ACT UP revitalized a style of radical political activity that had flourished in the early days of the gay liberation movement—it was grassroots, confrontational, and possessed a flair for imaginative tactics that captured media attention.[21] It targeted the FDA to speed up the approval of drugs to combat the opportunistic infections, pharmaceutical firms to lower the prices of drugs, the National Institute of Health (NIH) to increase its research on AIDS, and public indifference that hindered AIDS education and encouraged discrimination against people with AIDS by employers, landlords, and insurance companies.

The growing impact of AIDS throughout the American population forced activists to broaden the definition of their constituency. While ACT UP groups around the country primarily consisted of gay white men, the need to reflect the epidemiology of the epidemic and to build alliances with other communities affected by AIDS led to a politics that strived to be more inclusive and more open to coalition-building. It was never a smooth process. Various groups and communities affected by AIDS sometimes had little else in common, or were also socially stigmatized groups with even fewer resources than the gay community, or consisted of vocal segments which were uneasy with or disapproving of homosexuality. Strategically, AIDS activism increasingly experienced tensions with identity-based gay and lesbian political elites and their political agendas.

The politics of AIDS activism forced gay and lesbian activists into coalitions with activists from other communities and increased interaction with the federal, state, and local governments. AIDS activism transformed the relation between the lesbian and gay community and the state. Lesbian and gay community organizations dealing with AIDS received government funding and participated in policy-making to a much greater extent than had ever occurred before. The AIDS movement has had a significant impact on AIDS research, public health policies, and the funding of treatment, care, and education. In addition, AIDS funding created large-scale institutions with jobs and career possibilities that had not existed in the lesbian and gay communities before the AIDS crisis.

These economic and institutional developments had two major effects on the gay and lesbian communities. First, it encouraged lesbian and gay political institutions to engage to a greater extent than ever before with other communities, with governmental agencies, and with mainstream institutions. Secondly, it transformed the class structure of gay and lesbian leadership. The new jobs and career possibilities attracted a new generation of leaders who were upwardly mobile and educated at elite universities and colleges. This new leadership often developed from among those directly affected by AIDS, who in the past might have pursued careers along more conventional lines, but took up AIDS activism to fight for their lives. The older generation of gay leaders had also chosen gay political life as an alternative to mainstream career possibilities. But very early on in the epidemic they were both physically and emotionally devastated by AIDS and were soon displaced by the new generation.

AIDS seriously decimated the gay male community but also forced the community to reach out to other overlapping communities and social groups. It also seriously undermined the self-sufficiency of the community's cultural and economic developments. The countervailing pressures of gay and lesbian identity politics and of AIDS activism produced a political situation that required a new political perspective—one that recognized a stable conception of identity as well as the incredible diversity and kinship of all sexual minorities, the range of possible gender roles, and ethnic and racial identities. It was at this moment in history that Queer Nation was born.

QUEER POLITICS AND CULTURAL RADICALISM

The agenda of lesbian and gay identity politics was grounded on the appeal to "liberal" beliefs in equal treatment and tolerance. But civil rights for lesbians and gay men has always been under attack from the right—whether in the series of anti-gay initiatives in 1976–77 or in the current wave that started in 1991 and will clearly take us, at least, to 1996. But neither the growth of visible gay and lesbian communities in most major American cities, nor the increase in size of a measurable lesbian and gay electorate, nor the opening up of a lucrative gay market for major brand-name consumer products seemed to contribute to the political acceptance of homosexuals in American life.

In the face of the frustration by many activists that lesbian and gay identity politics was not able to achieve even the liberal benefits of tolerance and equal treatment, and that AIDS activism was leading to the dilution of gay and lesbian concerns, a new movement called Queer Nation was formed in spring of 1990.[22] The formation of Queer Nation was initially sparked by a wave of homophobic violence in New York City; it grew specifically out of a demonstration against the violence aroused by a broadside, announcing I HATE STRAIGHTS. The demonstration brought together many people who had been active in ACT UP/NY, and like ACT UP, Queer Nation groups soon appeared across the United States.

The foundation of Queer Nation was also marked by a revival of the politics of visibility. AIDS activist and journalist Michelangelo Signorile, in his column in the New York-based magazine *Outweek*, introduced a new tactic, "outing," to extend the coming out strategy of the early gay movement. Where coming out had been a voluntary "personal/political" act that contributed to lesbian and gay visibility, outing was a political commandment to expose famous and/or politically conservative closeted homosexuals. Outing was a punishment for remaining in the closet—and it was viewed by many activists as particularly appropriate to expose those gay men or lesbians who were on the right.[23]

Queer Nation was an openly militant challenge to the identity politics of the lesbian and gay communities; under the rubric of "assimilation" it rejected the traditional liberal goals of equal treatment and tolerance. "We're here, we're queer, get used to it," was one of its slogans. The name "Queer Nation" generated an extremely complicated notion of identity. By adopting the term "queer" it also expanded the definition of the community that it sought to represent and constitute—anyone who differed from the white heterosexual norm: lesbians, gay men, bisexuals, transsexuals, transgendered people, and sexual aberrants of all sorts, with hybrid identities of class, race, and ethnicity. By signifying the organization a "nation," queer activists called for a sort of nationalism, almost some kind of separatism, that was exclusive. Thus queer activists sought to combine seemingly contradictory notions of difference and identity into "an oxymoronic community of difference."[24]

Most of the Queer Nation groups have since ceased to exist. They foundered on the contradictory demands of the community of difference. Yet queer politics remains as a normative ideal, and in academia queer theory has emerged as a broad body of theorizing focused on the social role of heteronormativity in the discursive constitution of power and knowledge.[25]

Potentially, queer politics will help keep gay and lesbian identity politics honest about the diversity of racial and sexual differences and their significance. Queer politics can also help forge links between lesbian and gay politics and the broad political agenda of multiculturalism. But queer politics can not serve as a basis for waging cultural wars with the religious right—over such issues as AIDS education and funding, the development of gay-positive school curricula, or the protection of civil rights. Queer politics and queer theory are instruments of cultural politics, but they do not advance an engagement with the state or provide the institutional and economic resources necessary to fight the religious right.[26] Lesbian and gay identity politics and AIDS activism have contributed to those developments. The lesbian and gay communities must engage with a broad spectrum of the American population whom the religious right will ask to overturn already existing laws or to limit social tolerance. None of the existing political models that lesbians and gay men have developed are adequate, either separately or together. A new strategy must be developed.

THE RELIGIOUS RIGHT, GAY RIGHTS, AND RADICAL DEMOCRACY

The religious right's ambitious project to make the ideology of "family values" hegemonic is a violation of longstanding American political beliefs. The campaign both violates the separation of church and state and seeks to mobilize class resentments against a discriminated minority that does not differ significantly from the class structure of American society as a whole. Such a project can only be successfully opposed by expanding the lesbian and gay strategy from the narrow focus of identity politics or the predominantly cultural emphasis of queer politics to one of participation in a radical democratic project with other communities and groups.[27]

The religious right's campaign against homosexuality began with the anti-homosexual interpretation of Biblical texts, but it also sees homosexuality as one of the social causes of the breakdown of the family. Open homosexuality is disapproved of, not only because it implies a non-reproductive sexuality, but because young women and men coming out as lesbians, gay men, or bisexuals threatens the family's control over youthful sexuality. Homosexuality is interpreted in "moral" terms—as a moral choice on the part of men and woman who fail to see the moral responsibility of keeping religious laws. In addition, homosexuality as a moral (or immoral) choice necessarily implies that the reproductive sexuality that fundamentalists see as the basis of the family is rejected.

On one level religious fundamentalists have a right to think whatever they want, but where lesbians and gay men differ from the religious right is that, despite interpretations of Biblical and religious texts, homosexuality is not usually experienced as a choice. The religious injunctions cause enormous (and unnecessary) pain to those growing up in families that believe homosexuality is a sin and evil. Homosexuals are not necessarily unethical or evil people. Therefore homosexuality should not be the basis for stigmatization, discrimination, or abuse against a significant minority in our multi-cultural and multi-religious society.

These intellectual and ethical differences would not have any political significance if the religious right was not using widely-felt homophobia as the basis for making their beliefs about homosexuality into law and public policy. There are two basic approaches that the religious right has adopted to achieve their goals. Lesbian activist and lawyer Nan Hunter has identified the two different types of campaigns as either "No Promo Homo" or "No Special Rights."[28] Many of the most bitterly fought campaigns against lesbians and gay men are examples of the No Promo Homo strategy which strives to make sure that it is illegal to promote the tolerance or acceptance of homosexuality. For religious fundamentalists this translates into "the promotion of homosexuality." The other strategy is to argue that homosexuals need no "special" legal protections, that society does not discriminate against homosexuals. Usually a populist or class element supplements this argument that suggests that gay men and lesbians are wealthier and better educated than most Americans and therefore do not need "special" protections. Both of these political strategies appeal to the prevalence of homophobia among Americans.

Ironically both strategies appeal to populist sentiments, to longstanding American beliefs, beyond the obvious homophobia, that exist among even liberal and non-religious Americans: the distrust of "proselytizing," which was the basis for the separation of church and state in the United States Constitution's Bill of Rights, and the resentment against underground or "invisible" minorities that possess economic power. The appeal is ironic precisely because the religious right's tactics actually violate each of these beliefs. No Promo Homo campaigns are violations of the separation of church and state. The religious right is attempting to turn the religious beliefs of certain denominations into law. The No Special Rights campaigns, of course, obscures the fact that openly gay men and women usually earn less than their comparable (by age, occupation, and race) counterparts, and that the religious right with their conservative allies have dramatically shifted the distribution and wealth so that less than ten per cent of the population controls almost fifty per cent of the wealth.[29] This implies that gay and lesbian political strategies should focus more on the separation of church and state and on economic equality. These issues are related to the more narrow political interests of the lesbian and gay communities in the same way that AIDS activism has related, in general, to national health insurance. "Americans will have to recognize their gay family, friends, and neighbors as fellow citizens," Michael Nava and Robert Dawidoff have argued in their eloquent and forceful broadside, just to "protect their own individual freedom, not to mention traditional American democratic pluralism."[30]

There are two broad political strategies that can be adopted by the lesbian and gay movement to combat the religious right's hegemonic project. One strategy, proposed by Bruce Bawer, Marshall Kirk, Hunter Madsen and other gay conservatives (or "moderates" as they wished to be called) would require a major reconstruction of gay/lesbian politics, in particular a rejection of the "ethnic model" or identity politics. This "moderate" strategy focuses on "the ignorance that makes straight people fear homosexuality and consider it a threat to American society."[31] Bawer and his associates wish to embark on an educational and public relations campaign—partly to undo the negative effects of the gay subculture's radicalism and flamboyance, but mostly because they fail to understand how the religious right's hegemonic political project deliberately employs false and misleading representations and violates basic political guarantees like the separation of church and state.

A more realistic political strategy, but one that is incredibly difficult nonetheless, is to follow in the footsteps of the Rainbow Coalition—in which the gay and lesbian movement would join with political groups from other communities—racial and minority ethnic communities, working class and the poor, the declining lower middle class—to create a radical democratic politics.

Currently the Rainbow Coalition is moribund—many of its constitutient movements have fragmented, tensions between groups were never resolved, or perhaps it was tied too closely to Jesse Jackson's candidacy. But such a radical democratic coalition must be revived in order to counter the religious right. Lesbian and gay political leaders must not wait for others to take the initiative—they must reach out to other communities and build coalitions. No coalition politics will ever succeed unless there is a real process of learning going on throughout the coalition. This means that the lesbian and gay communities must be willing to learn about the issues important to other coalition members and incorporate that knowledge into our political common sense (and vice versa). The lesbian and gay movement as well as other currents on the left must also reach out to and work with churches and religious groups in the progressive religious tradition.[32] It is also important to recognize that the religious right, while it is interested in keeping homosexuality at bay, is also interested in using gay and lesbian rights as an issue to destroy "liberalism" which in the eyes of many conservatives is identified with "mulitculturalism." The protection of liberal gains such as civil rights legislation or medicare is an important component of the radical democratic project. The lesbian/gay movement will only defeat the religious right in its hegemonic ambitions if it can join with its allies to provide a counter-hegemonic project—a radical democracy which is open, pluralistic, and practical.

NOTES

This essay emerged from my despair after the right's victory in the November 1994 elections, but it was also politicallly and intellectually aroused by the political savvy and theoretical originality of Lisa Duggan and Nan Hunter, jointly and individually, in several of their essays. I want to thank Chris Bull,

Amber Hollibaugh, Loring McAlpin, Esther Newton, and Michael Rothberg for their comments on earlier versions of this paper. I owe special thanks to Matthew Lore, my companion in so many conversations about so many things, for his comments, encouragement and company throughout my writing of this essay. I'm afraid that I would never have written this essay without the encouragement (and persistent but gentle nagging) of David Trend.

1. See James Davison Hunter, *Culture Wars: The Struggle to Define America* (New York: Basic Books, 1991); for a view of these issues from the left in the U.K. see the essays in Jeffrey Weeks, ed., *The Lesser Evil and the Greater Good: The Theory and the Politics of Social Diversity* (London: Rivers Oram Press, 1994).

2. Todd Gitlin, *The Sixties: Years of Hope, Days of Rage* (New York: Bantam, 1987).

3. See Josh Gamson, "Silence, Death and the Invisible Enemy: AIDS Activism and Social Movement 'Newness,'" *Social Problems*, vol. 34, no. 6 (October 1989).

4. For a history of the religious right see, Sara Diamond, *Spiritual Warfare: The Politics of the Christian Right* (Boston: South End Press, 1989) and Dallas A. Blanchard, *The Anti-Abortion Movement and the Rise of the Religious Right: From Polite to Fiery Protest* (New Tork: Twayne Publishers, 1994).

5. E.J. Dione, *Why Americans Hate Politics* (New York: Simon and Schuster, 1991).

6. Irving Kristol, *The National Interest* (New York, 1993), 86.

7. On the Anita Bryant Campaign, see Randy Shilts, *The Mayor of Castro Street: The Life and Times of Harvey Milk* (New York: St. Martins Press, 1982).

8. Allan Berube, *Coming Out Under Fire: Gay Men and Women During World War II* (New York: Free Press, 1990).

9. John D'Emilio, *Sexual Politics, Sexual Communities: The Making of a Homosexual Minority in the United States, 1940–1970* (Chicago: University of Chicago Press, 1983).

10. Martin Duberman, *Stonewall* (New York: Dutton, 1993).

11. The social structural implications of secrets are explored in Georg Simmel's classic essay, "The Secret and the Secret Society," in *The Sociology of Georg Simmel* (New York: The Free Press, 1950), 307–75; and also in Erving Goffman's two books, *Stigma: Notes on the Management of Spoiled Identity* (Englewood Cliffs, NJ: Prentice-Hall, 1963) and *The Presentation of Self in Everyday Life* (New York: Double Anchor Books, 1959).

12. Jeffrey Escoffier, "Sexual Revolution and the Politics of Gay Identity," *Socialist Review*, no. 82, 83 (July-October 1985): 119–153.

13. Jeffrey Escoffier, "Homosexuality and the Sociological Imagination: Hegemonic Discourses, the Circulation of Ideas, the Process of Reading in the Fifties and Sixties," unpublished paper presented at the Center of Lesbian and Gay Studies, CUNY, October 1993.

14. Arlene Stein, "Three Models of Sexuality: Drives, Identities and Practices," *Sociological Theory*, vol. 7 no. 1 (1989).

15. Randy Shilts, *The Mayor of Castro Street*.

16. Alice Echols, *Daring To Be Bad: Radical Feminism in America, 1967–1975* (Minneapolis: University of Minnesota, 1989).

17. For the political, medical, and cultural context see the essays by Douglas Crimp, Paula Treichler in Douglas Crimp, ed., *AIDS: Cultural Analysis/Cultural Activism* (Cambridge, MA: MIT Press, 1988). For some historical and political background on GMHC, see Philip Kayal, *Bearing Witness: Gay Men's Health Crisis and the Politics of AIDS* (Boulder, CO: Westview Press, 1993).

18. Shilts.

19. Larry Kramer, *Reports From the Holocaust*, revised edition (New York: St. Martin's Press, 1995).

20. Douglas Crimp, "How to Have Promiscuity in an Epidemic" in Crimp, *AIDS: Cultural Analysis/Cultural Activism*.

21. See Douglas Crimp with Adam Rolston, *AIDS Demo/Graphics* (Seattle: Bay Press, 1990).

22. See the special section on Queer Nation, with articles by Allan Berube and Jeffrey Escoffier, Alexander Chee, Steve Cossen, and Maria Maggenti, in *OUT/LOOK: National Lesbian and Gay Quarterly*, no. 11 (Winter 1991): 12–23; Lisa Duggan, "Making It Perfectly Queer," *Socialist Review*, vol. 22, no. 1 (January–March 1992): 11–31; see also the introduction by Michael Warner, vii–xxxi, and "Queer Nationality" by Lauren Berlandt and Elizabeth Freeman, 193–229, in Michael Warner, ed., *Fear of A Queer Planet* (Minneapolis: University of Minnesota Press, 1993).

23. For an extensive exploration of this issue, see Larry Gross, *Contested Closets: The Politics and Ethics of Outing* (Minneapolis: University of Minnesota Press, 1993).

24. Louise Sloan, "Beyond Dialogue," *San Francisco Bay Guardian*, Literary Supplement, March 1991, 3.

25. See Michael Warner, "Introduction," in *Fear of A Queer Planet*. See also Jeffrey Escoffier, "Under the Sign of the Queer," in *Found Object* (Fall 1984).

26. Lisa Duggan, "Queering the State," *Social Text*, no. 39: 1–14.

27. For a comparable discussion of racial politics, see Howard Winant, "Postmodern Racial Politics in the United States: Difference and Inequality," *Socialist Review*, vol. 20, no. 1 (January–March 1990): 121–47.

28. Hunter's analysis is discussed in Lisa Duggan, "Queering the State," *Social Text*; see also Nan D. Hunter, "Identity, Speech, and Equality," *Virginia Law Review*, vol. 79, no. 7 (October 1993).

29. M.V. Lee Badgett, "The Wage Effects of Sexual Orientation Discrimination," *Industrial and Labor Relations Review* (forthcoming). For a general survey of economic issues see Jeffrey Escoffier, "Homo/Economics: A Survey of the Issues," in L. Witt, E. Marcus and S. Thomas, eds., *Out in All Directions: An Almanac of Gay and Lesbian Life* (New York : Warner Books, 1995).

30. Michael Nava and Robert Dawidoff, *Created Equal: Why Gay Rights Matter to America* (New York: St. Martin's Press, 1994), 122.

31. Bruce Bawer, "The Road to Utopia," *The Advocate*, September 20, 1994, 80; a detailed critique of the lesbian and gay movement and a detailed working out of the "moderate" strategy can be found in Marshall Kirk and Hunter Madsen, *After the Ball: How America Will Conquer Its Fear and Hatred of Gays in the 90s* (New York: Doubleday, 1989); see also Bawer's book, *A Place at the Table: The Gay Individual in American Society* (New York: Poseidon Press, 1993).

32. I owe this important realization to Matthew Lore who is working on a book about the progressive religious tradition.

15

PEDAGOGY AND RADICAL DEMOCRACY IN THE AGE OF "POLITICAL CORRECTNESS"

THE CALL FOR CONSTITUTING HIGHER EDUCATION according to principles that prefigure a radical democracy[1] has vitalized a generation of academics who came of age in the 1960s. Appropriating the principles of freedom, equality, and justice, progressives have increasingly struggled to reclaim higher education as a public sphere in which education provides the basis for an expanded notion of insurgent citizenship marked by real debate, the decentralization of authority, and the extension of democratic rights to the widest possible number of individuals and social groups.

Within a contentious climate that the popular press has labeled as the culture wars, the issue of how authority is constituted and secured in the university has been called into question by feminists, gays and lesbians, multiculturalists, and other dissident groups. These groups have challenged the exclusionary politics of the canon and the invocation of higher education as a privileged cultural site with its resident intellectuals as "free floating" guardians of high culture. Consequently, higher education, and in a lesser sense public education, have experienced a crisis over the relationship between authority and knowledge on the one hand, and the purpose of schooling and the responsibility of intellectuals on the other.

In response to those intellectuals and critics who have redefined public and higher education as an embattled public sphere, conservatives have mobilized under the ideological banner of "political correctness" and launched a counteroffensive designed to remove schooling from the relations of power and ideology that connect them with the institutions and problems of modern society.[2] Of course, public criticisms of education at all levels are not new and have a long historical legacy. In the past, schools have been repeatedly criticized for failing to educate skilled workers, develop adequate academic standards, or adequately prepare students to enable the United States to compete internationally in the global marketplace. What is new is that schools are currently criticized for failing to transmit the universal values of Western culture, shore up traditional family values, and reproduce the assimilative imperatives of a "common national culture."[3] Within the last few years, there has been a growing concern on the part of the popular press, politicians, and conservative and liberal groups over public and higher education increasingly "opening their doors to minority students, expanding curricula, questioning canons, breaking down monolithic disciplinary structures and searching for new teaching methodologies."[4]

For many conservatives public schooling and higher education have fallen prey to an adversarial culture that is touted as being at odds with traditional conceptions of citizenship, national identity, and history. Invoking the language of patriotism, conservatives argue that schools are increasingly undermining the very foundation of what it means to be American. Taken up under what has been criticized as the "tyranny of the politically correct," the terms of the debate about educational reform have been largely defined by a deep seated conservatism initiated during the Reagan and Bush administrations.

The debate over "political correctness" might appear to some as simply faddish or an invention of media hype with little relevance to serious educational issues.[5] In opposition to this view, I believe that the political correctness debate betrays a racist discourse and rising fundamentalism in American society that impairs the possibility for schools to address the democratic imperatives for civic courage, social responsibility, and critical citizenship in the name of educating students to live in and struggle for a radical democracy. Issues of equity, access, economic justice, the pluralization of cultural identities, and the positing of a common moral language and a set of shared values that defends democracy against inequality, racism, and oppressive social relationships have come under attack by "PC" bashers. Moreover, the increasing right-wing terms in which this debate is being structured have dire consequences for defining the purpose and content of teaching.

The debate over "political correctness" has been largely waged through the media and the popular press, and students and teachers rarely have access to the full range of issues associated with the debate.

If educators and students are to make sense of the "political correctness" debate in terms of the implications it has for analyzing the relationship between knowledge and authority, teaching and student learning, it will be necessary to analyze what is often left out of the discussion. This means having access to arguments that inform this debate from a critical, progressive perspective. More specifically, it means providing educators and students with at least two critical modes of inquiry. First, educators and students need a critical perspective on the anti-political correctness view of teaching, knowledge, and standards. Second, they need access to elements of a critical pedagogy that challenges and poses alternatives to the ideological and pedagogical assumptions that inform the attack on academics whose classroom practices are often summarily dismissed as merely a species of political correctness.

THE TYRANNY OF THE POLITICALLY CORRECT?

On May 4, 1990 President Bush, while delivering a commencement address at the University of Michigan at Ann Arbor, spoke to the issue of political correctness. He argued that while political correctness arises "from the laudable desire to sweep away the debris of racism and sexism and hatred," it has led to intolerance and has declared "certain topics off-limits." Provided with a presidential imprimatur, "political correctness" erupted in cover stories in major popular magazines such as *Newsweek*, *The Atlantic Monthly*, and *New York*. Sustained accounts of this new movement were given full scale editorial and journalistic treatment in *Time*, *The New York Times*, and *The Wall Street Journal*. At the heart of this coverage and popular fanfare is the general argument that:

> the academy is under siege by leftists, multiculturalists, deconstructionists, and other radicals who are politicizing the university and threatening to undermine the very foundations of the Western intellectual traditions. . . . Armed with affirmative action admissions and hiring, as well as new French literary theories, the politically correct hope to transform the university into a den of multiculturalism—silencing everyone who would dare to dissent by calling them "sexist," "racist," or anti-deconstructionist.[6]

For many conservatives such as Patrick Buchanan, Irving Kristol, and more recently Rush Limbaugh, the assault on "political correctness" indicates an important political transition necessitated by the break up of the Soviet Union and the "winning" of the Cold War by the United States. No longer unified in their fight against the external threat of communism, conservatives now point to the tyranny of the politically correct as an ideological rallying cry to ward off the cultural peril posed by the "enemy within." Patrick Buchanan puts it well with the exhortation that:

> Political leaders in Washington believe that the battle against communism is being fought in the jungles of Asia and Central America, while failing to realize the war is also raging on the

battlefield of [the humanities curriculum in schools and universities] and in the arts within our own borders. . . . The hour is late; America needs a cultural revolution in the '90s as sweeping as its political revolution in the '80s.[7]

As the battle lines of higher and public education are redrawn around American culture and national identity, conservatives have pointed to the political danger posed by the civil rights community and the adoption of multicultural curricula in many public schools. In its more alarmist forms, the right labels the struggles of subordinated ethnic groups as the most dangerous threat to American society. For example, national syndicated columnist Charles Krauthammer claims that such groups are "wards of the left" who are launching "an all-out assault . . . on America's cultural past" and on "common citizenship." He goes on to claim that "America will survive both Saddam and the snail darter. But the setting of one ethnic group against another, the fracturing not just of American society but of the American idea, poses a threat that no outside agent in this post-Soviet world can match."[8]

In this perspective, the communist danger is replaced by the domestic danger of the Rainbow Coalition in the political sphere and what Dinesh D'Souza calls the surge of the "victim's revolution on campus."[9] Behind this discourse of racial and political panic is the additional claim by the right that a generation of young "radical" academics have emerged who challenge the racial and gender admissions policies of the universities while simultaneously highlighting exclusions and biases built into the academic canon taught through the disciplines in higher education. Rather than being greeted as an insight into the workings of higher education, neo-conservatives view such criticism as both a species of anti-Americanism and a threat to Western civilization itself. UCLA public policy professor James Q. Wilson captures this sentiment by arguing that, "The university has always had leftists, but never before like the ones we have now. . . . These new leftists rebel against reason, not just against institutions."[10]

For progressives such a claim exemplifies less the perils of political correctness than a right-wing version of academic correctness. For example, *The Chronicle of Higher Education* reports yearly that left wing academics make up about four percent of college faculties and that most faculty define themselves as either liberals or conservatives. Similarly, Rosa Ehrenreich refutes the charge that radicals have taken over higher education with the comment:

> A national survey of college administrators released last summer found that "political correctness" is not the campus issue it has been portrayed to be by pundits and politicians of the political right. During the 1990–91 academic year, according to the survey's findings, faculty members complained of pressure from students and fellow professors to alter the political and cultural content of their courses at only 5 percent of all colleges. So much for the influence of radicals, tenured or otherwise.[11]

But neither the empirical evidence nor the charges of gross exaggeration lodged by many progressives have deterred many conservatives and liberals from strongly arguing that "political correctness" poses a serious threat to Western culture and its educational institutions. I want to take up this charge by focusing on a number of specific issues, and the implications they have for teaching.

THE POLITICS OF STANDARDS

Speaking at a recent symposium on "political correctness," Stephen Balch, President of the National Association of Scholars, argued that "the debate about political correctness . . . is actually a debate not about politics but about appropriate intellectual standards and appropriate academic ethics. . . . What is at issue here is to convey a sufficient knowledge base because without knowledge we can't think."[12] For Balch, as for many other conservatives waging a battle against political correctness, the issue of standards has become one of the key concerns facing public and higher education in the 1990s. Three major considerations frame this issue.

First, a resolute defense of the traditional curriculum serves to guard against the contamination that threatens the canon by "other" knowledge. In this perspective, the knowledge that shapes the canon of higher education and the curriculum of the public school is defended largely through rhetorical and poetic appeals to the timeless values of reason, truth, and beauty. Second, an insistence on "excellence" removed from the issues of equity and power points to the purity and alleged objectivity of academic pursuits. Here excellence is legitimated on the assumption that knowledge accumulated through the selective process of a tradition represents the best that can be offered through the evolution of Western culture within the intellectual grasp of an elite few. Third, the defining principle of traditional pedagogical practice is the transmission of bodies of knowledge from one generation to the next. The emphasis, crucially, is on processing received knowledge rather than transforming it in the interest of social growth or change.

According to conservatives such as Balch, the integrity of the university and public schooling is at risk because academic standards have been compromised through such programs as affirmative action, open admissions policies, and the inclusion of writers and cultural texts into the curriculum that undermine the tradition of the "great books" as well as standards of discipline and rigor. The call to standards as a rallying cry for conservatives gained enormous popularity in Allan Bloom's immensely popular book, *The Closing of the American Mind*.[13] Serving as both a manifesto and a call to action, Bloom's text boldly displayed his contempt for curricula reform that challenged his own version of classical education. As Aronowitz and I have written elsewhere:

> He bitterly castigates the handful of "first-class" private universities for pandering to women, people of color, and radicals who want to study Marx, Nietzsche, and Heidegger rather than Plato and Hegel; or Richard Wright and Zora Neale Hurston rather

than Charles Dickens; and whose critical sensibility is formed by their own time rather than by the Greek city-state. . . . Bloom goes so far as to claim that, however democratic, the recent efforts to open the doors of the universities to many who were formerly excluded through affirmative action and open admissions, are futile gestures because blacks and other people of color are so overwhelmed by economic and social problems that they could not possibly master a rigorous curriculum.[14]

Standards in this discourse are pitted against the threat posed by subordinate groups such as Afro-Americans, feminists, latinos, gays and lesbians, and others who take issue with the content and form of the traditional curriculum. Conservatives such as Dinesh D'Souza, Roger Kimball, and John Searle scorn the attempts of such groups to contest the claims to historical certainty and authority made on behalf of the traditional curriculum. Believing that the traditional curriculum should only change "in response to advances in knowledge and intellectual skills, and not at the behest of political imperatives or in response to every shift of intellectual fashion,"[15] conservatives routinely dismiss as political cant critical inquiries regarding the relationship between institutional interests and power and what counts as "literature," "history," and "knowledge" in the curriculum.[16] For example, the claim by subordinate groups that the act of knowing is integrally related to the power of self-definition and, in part, legitimates the call for schools to include knowledge rooted in the narratives of the oppressed and the popular in the classroom is seen by conservatives not only as a call to politicize the curriculum but as a corrosive social force that promotes national disunity and cultural decay.

But there is more at stake for conservatives than protecting the content of traditional education. There is also the threat of standards being "lowered" by admitting students formerly excluded from higher education. For instance, Jeffrey Hart, a major spokesperson against political correctness has argued that "a broadening of the student body has led to a corruption of the curriculum."[17] In this view, ideological differences are not the only threat posed by political correctness. Cultural, racial, gender, and class differences are also marked, by virtue of their very presence, as forms of subversion and a threat to the middle class, white cultural capital that largely characterize those who wield the power to secure the authority of the canon and enforce its claims to history, teaching, and learning. Christopher Newfield expands on this sentiment by arguing that challenges to the canon in the form of new courses are dismissed by conservatives

> not because of their particular content or methodology but because they presume the importance of the lives of their students. The predetermined truth the Right wishes to associate with political correctness is . . . a routine component of its own definition of legitimate classroom topics, since they seek to exclude the supplements or challenges to the truth that arise from students' active participation.[18]

Adopting a generally defensive posture, conservatives respond to critiques of the canon with a crusade to safeguard the traditional curriculum from what they view as a hostile appropriation. In an effort to protect the canon from being watered down, conservatives often cite attempts at various colleges to replace Shakespeare and Rabelais with contemporary novelists such as James Baldwin and Toni Morrison.[19] Standards in this case, at least for the Right, appear at odds with the democratization of power relations in either universities or public schools and the call by progressives that groups formally excluded from dominant educational institutions need to make "their own decisions about how knowledge is to be structured and used."[20]

Paradoxically, the conservative position on academic "standards" generally ignores the effects of the universities' bottom line crisis, and, hence, offers meager acknowledgement, not to mention resistance, to the severe budget cuts in higher education that have resulted in the elimination of entire academic departments, the raising of tuition, the firing of both nontenured and tenured faculty, and the downsizing of university services. The result has been a growing demoralization among faculty forced to teach larger classes and assume greater workloads, as well as a disillusioned working class student body of whites and minorities forced to pay higher tuition and bear the burden of reduced financial aid. In addition, such cuts open up the university to funding by private foundations and corporations who will support "only those programs deemed economically correct."[21] It is precisely the refusal to deal with such issues and their effects upon teaching and learning that betrays conservatives' obsession with the lowering of standards.

ACADEMIC FREEDOM AND THE ISSUE OF POLITICS

The dispute over standards is only one of the major considerations that defines the issues in the political correctness debate. Even more controversial than the issue of academic standards is the widespread perception that the public schools and universities are being increasingly politicized and that one casualty of this process is academic freedom.

According to anti-politically correct conservatives, the politicization of the discourse of schooling and higher education is evident on a number of fronts. First, it can be seen in the efforts of radical intellectuals to use the public space of the university to address issues of race, class, and gender. By challenging the university as a font of neutral scholarship, it is alleged that radical educators have compromised the integrity and moral purpose of the educational process. Rather than being linked to the search for truth and pure knowledge, the university, in this perspective, becomes merely a breeding ground for social transformation or what John Taylor calls "the new fundamentalism."[22] One response to the perils of political correctness that exemplifies this position can be seen in Boston University President John Silber's report of April 15, 1993 to the board of trustees. Silber proclaims:

> this University has remained unapologetically dedicated to the
> search for truth and highly resistant to political correctness. . . . We

have resisted the fad toward critical legal studies. . . . In the English Department and the departments of literature, we have not allowed the structuralists or the deconstructionists to take over. We have refused to take on dance therapy. . . . We have resisted revisionist history. . . . In the Philosophy Department we have resisted the Frankfurt School of Critical Theory. . . . We have resisted the official dogmas of radical feminism. We have done the same thing with regard to gay and lesbian liberation, and animal liberation. . . . We have resisted the fad of Afro-centrism. We have not fallen into the clutch of multi-culturalists.[23]

The defensive quality of Silber's engagement with political correctness suggests a dangerous ideological orthodoxy at work in his pursuit of the truth. Ironically, Silber's statement suggests that the threat to academic freedom comes less from left-wing professors than it does from administrative demagogues who are willing to police and censor knowledge that does not silence itself before the legitimating imperatives of the traditional academic canon.

Many conservatives believe that radical academics have no grounds for distinguishing between the literary and the nonliterary since they vacate the grounds of universal truth by arguing that knowledge is mediated historically, linguistically, and socially. Nor can they distinguish works that embody high aesthetic qualities and noble ideals from those everyday cultural texts that pass the political litmus test regarding race, class, and gender. William Kerrigan echoes this sentiment in arguing that those critics who claim that the dominant curriculum is racist or exclusionary can be dismissed as simply "liberal educators who have become pathologically sensitive to complaints of ethnocentrism." Ironically, he reinforces such a charge by declaring that "Black and Hispanic students must be taught in the language of the British and American intelligentsia, since integration will never succeed on any other level."[24]

Finally, one of the most visible rallying cries against political correctness comes from conservatives who link the expression of progressive ideas about gender, race, and power to forms of censorship. Citing excessive strains of anti-civil libertarianism among specific anti-racist and anti-sexist groups, some conservatives argue that both the discourse as well as the practices of such groups stifles traditional convictions and silences mainstream faculty and students. The result is an alleged marriage between intimidation and intellectual conformity. Camille Paglia, the author of *Sexual Personae*, goes so far as to claim that politically correct faculty and students in the university bear strong resemblance to "Moonies" and "the Hitler Youth."[25] Robert Rozenzweig, President of the Association of American Colleges, argues that the language of social criticism, whether it be anti-racist, anti-sexist, or anti-homophobic, closes down debate by simply "bludgeoning the opposition into submission."[26] These charges betray more than an exaggerated fear. They also suggest an act of bad faith on the part of conservatives who raise the specter of fascism against progressive faculty and students and at the same time remain indifferent to the alarming increase in hate crimes on American campuses against women, gays, and people of color. Within this critique, conservatives mobilize populist fears of violence while keeping the social order off the agenda for either criticism or change.

Moreover, evidence of the assault on free speech can also be found, according to anti-politically correct educators, in the emergence of hate-speech codes at American universities. Some conservatives claim that these laws are a threat to free speech. In this scenario, students who engage in hostile racial slander, for example, should be immune from disciplinary action under first amendment rights. Racism in this case is seen as less corrosive to democracy than the protection of the right of its advocates to translate their prejudices into speech acts.

Even more pernicious are the arguments made by conservatives regarding academic freedom and its relationship to particular teaching practices. Many liberals and conservatives argue that any form of pedagogy that takes as its goal the progressive transformation of either the classroom or society at large by definition engages in a form of pedagogical terrorism. Teachers who take a position of advocacy, who link knowledge to democratic commitment, or incorporate social issues into their classrooms are criticized for indoctrinating their students. Teachers who model leadership and civic courage in this view simply silence students who are allegedly refused the right to express opinions at odds with those of the teacher. However, it is precisely teachers with progressive visions who recognize the necessity of struggle and debate in the classroom as against those who advocate the transmission of orthodox world views. Conversely, conservatives reject the notion that teaching is a political and cultural practice that encourages critical debate and radical disagreement. In its place they advocate the promotion of pedagogical practices free of controversy and the clash of opinions.

In the final section, I will analyze the potentiality for redefining the purpose of education, the roles and interaction between teachers and students, and pedagogy itself as part of a wider effort to expand, deepen, and reconstruct the possibility for democratic public life.

POLITICS AND EDUCATION

We will begin by examining an assumption at odds with the anti-politically correct conservatives, one that has a long tradition in the United States. The assumption being emphasized claims that the meaning and purpose of schooling is imminently political. This suggests that schools cannot be understood outside of the meditations of history, power, and struggle. Schools are both sense-making and power-bearing institutions that are actively involved in the "struggle to control and contribute to the social circulation and uses of meanings, knowledges, pleasures, and values."[27]

Central to any notion of education is the relationship between authority and teaching on the one hand and knowledge and power on the other. Authority is both a condition and effect of teaching. Teaching itself is premised on making choices about the production and use of knowledge as well as helping students understand the linkages that mutually inform the relationship between schooling and the larger society. School as a site and teaching as a practice must always be seen as deeply moral and political. Schools like all social sites produce and organize knowledge through processes of inclusion and exclusion. Such processes do not exist outside of history nor are they untouched by the operations of power. Neither the curriculum nor the canon can be understood as expressions of the disinterested search for truth and knowledge. Such knowledges more often than not express an ongoing process of negotiation and struggle among different groups over the relationship between knowledge and power on the one hand and the construction of individual and social identity on the other.

What counts as legitimate knowledge, culture, history, and speech can only be understood by interrogating the conditions of exclusion and inclusion in the production, distribution, circulation, and use of power and authority in the classroom. The conservative view of knowledge as neutral and pedagogy as a transparent vehicle of truth overlooks important political issues regarding how canons are historically produced, whose interests they serve, and how they are sustained within specific forms of institutional power. Toni Morrison, the Nobel Prize winning novelist, illuminates the political nature of the relationship between knowledge and power by arguing that:

> Canon building is Empire building. Canon defense is national defense. Canon debate, whatever the terrain, nature and range (of criticism, of history, of the history of knowledge, of the definition of language, the universality of aesthetic principles, the sociology of art, the humanistic imagination), is the clash of cultures. And all of the interests are vested.[28]

Morrison suggests that both knowledge and its dissemination are filtered through the normative lens of history and tradition. Since histories are constructed and struggled over rather than merely received and passed on to future generations, it is imperative that teachers articulate a moral vision and social ethics that provide a referent for justifying how, what, and why they teach. After all, if education presupposes a vision of the future and always produces selective narratives and stories, it is crucial for teachers to both clarify and make themselves accountable for how their pedagogical practices contribute to the social consciousness, hopes, and dreams of their students.

For the anti-politically correct conservatives, tradition dictates what is taught in schools. But tradition in these terms is tied to the obligations of reverence rather than to what might be called the imperatives of respect. Reverence suggests treating tradition as an object, an artifact that is unproblematically transmitted and received by teachers and students alike. Conversely, respect situates tradition not as a fixed object of austere contemplation but as a cultural text that needs to be historically situated, open to debate, and central to helping students understand its limits and strengths as part of a wider attempt for them to narrate themselves as critical and engaging citizens.

Some conservatives would argue that such an approach to tradition vacates the terrain of values; on the contrary, it makes the very category of value problematic and in doing so enhances its potential for critical exchange. A critical attentiveness to the values that inform teacher work, the ways in which knowledge is constructed, and the structuring of teacher-student relationships is a precondition for making explicit and, when necessary, changing those values that inform common sense assumptions serving to structure oppressive conditions for students. Symbolic and material violence, whether expressed in the form of racially inspired tracking, sexist curricula, institutional inequality, authoritarian teaching, or academic insensitivity to the demands of Afro-Americans, women, the poor, and others cannot be challenged and transformed unless teachers become aware of how the values that sustain such practices are reproduced in the histories, institutional practices, and narratives that shape education and pedagogical practice. The issue for teachers is not to abandon judgments in the name of a false neutrality that suggests they simply be missionaries of an unproblematic truth, but to try to understand how the values that inform their work are conditioned, produced, and used to both inform their own sense of agency and its relationship to the wider issues of radical democracy.

I want to argue that the anti-political correctness argument against politics, along with its claim to disinterested teaching and scholarship, are really a prescription for deskilling teachers and masking how the dynamics of power work in the culture, pedagogy, and the institutional organization of schools. The conservative ploy of labeling critical educators as "the new fundamentalists" or "cultural barbarians" may provide a rhetorical strategy for making headlines in the popular press, but it offers no language for understanding how power has worked historically to silence, disable, and marginalize certain groups in society through the process of schooling. Removed from the context of history, theory, politics, and power, the discourse of anti-political correctness offers limited insights into a view of educational leadership that would provide a moral focus on suffering. It offers no language for discriminating between the pedagogical and ethical imperative of challenging racism, discrimination, and social injustice and the unacceptable behavior of teachers who in their excessive zeal commit pedagogical violence by preventing students from engaging in critical and open dialogue. Moreover, the claim that social criticism promotes censorship confuses acts of state censorship with the inability of many conservatives to actually engage in critical inquiries into how power works in public schools and higher education. Anti-civil libertarian behavior is unacceptable, whether its source is a public school teacher, college professor, or an anti-abortionist activist. But social criticism is not a liability in a vibrant democracy; in fact, it is both a political and pedagogical necessity if such a democracy is to become part of a dynamic tradition rather than a historical relic.

I don't want to suggest that teachers should tolerate expressions of anti-civil libertarian behavior that close down debate and silence others, but it is no secret that America has a long legacy of witch-hunts, show trials, and an appalling absence of public debate about crucial political issues. My point is that institutional authorities, the United States government, and industry have never passionately defended the right to dissent from established and consensual policies. Therefore, the call for free speech cannot be dismissed as a convenient trope of conservative discourse parading under the banner of the anti-political correctness campaign. What teachers need to address is the contradiction between the call for the defense of free speech and the simultaneous refusal to address the central and most urgent social problems of our time. The real crisis in schools may not be about censorship, freedom of speech, or the other alleged evils of political correctness, but whether students are learning how to think critically, engage larger social issues, take risks, and develop a sense of social responsibility and civic courage.

Finally, I want to argue in opposition to anti-politically correct advocates that teachers cannot abstract the issue of standards and excellence from a concern with equity and social justice. These should be mutually informing categories because the discourse of standards represents part of the truth about ourselves as a nation in that it has often been evoked in order to legitimate elitism, racism, and privileges for the few, as well as shutting down the possibilities for public schools and the academy to educate students for critical citizenship and the promises of a democratic society. Equally important, when standards are removed from their ethical and political referents, they mystify how educational practices shape what is legitimated or excluded as knowledge and truth. Teachers need to assert their vocation as a political enterprise, without necessitating that they need to politicize their students.

This is not an argument for indoctrination. On the contrary, it is a discourse that challenges the very nature of indoctrination by raising questions such as whose authority is secured through the form and content of specific canons? What does it mean to organize the curricula in ways that decenter its authority and power relations? What social relations have to come into play to give university teachers and students control over the conditions for producing knowledge? If educators are to take the precepts of radical democracy seriously in their pedagogy, they need to address what it means to decenter the curriculum. Students should be actively involved with issues of governance, "including setting learning goals, selecting courses, and having their own, autonomous organizations, including a free press."[29] Not only does the distribution of power among teachers, students, and administrators provide the conditions for students to become agents in their learning process, it also provides the basis for taking seriously the imperatives of citizenship for a radical democracy. Through student centered investigations of social problems, such as toxic waste dumping, homelessness, poverty, the high incidence of certain diseases, and other issues that bear upon their experiences, neighborhoods, and the larger society, students can develop community based curricula and initiate projects that link civic action to academic learning and ethical responsibility. Not only does such agency emerge through a pedagogy of lived experience and struggle rather than as the empty, formalistic mastery of an academic subject, but it also develops within a larger social and historical vision through which the student can both understand and challenge the imperatives of schooling.

The distinction I am making here refutes the liberal and conservative criticism claiming that since critical pedagogy attempts to both

politicize teaching and teach politics, it represents a species of indoctrination. Asserting that all teaching is profoundly political and that
critical educators should operate out of a project of social transformation should not mean that as educators we refuse to exercise an
auto-critique of our own authority, or to make such authority an
object of student analysis. Nor does the assertion that as educators we
should use authority in the interest of social transformation suggest
that we underestimate the pain and resistance involved in learning
(especially regarding the fear of theory) in making students accountable for their positions, and in their resistance to specific socio-political
discourses.[30] There is no excuse for an oppressive pedagogy, but at the
same time, it is politically and ethically irresponsible to suggest as
Gerald Graff has been doing for the last decade that radical pedagogy
represents a species of tunnel vision because it "is for those who have
already decided to be radicals, and . . . the others will pretty much stay
out of it, as presumably they will want to anyway."[31] Graff is being simplistic. He wrongly suggests that any pedagogy informed by a political
project is by nature oppressive. In opposition to Graff's reified
approach to pedagogy, I want to argue that as teachers we need to
make a distinction between what Peter Euben calls political and politicizing education. Political education, which is central to critical
pedagogy, advocates teaching

> students how to think in ways that cultivate the capacity for
> judgment essential for the exercise of power and responsibility
> by a democratic citizenry. . . . A political, as distinct from a politi-
> cizing, education would encourage students to become better
> citizens to challenge those with political and cultural power as
> well as to honor the critical traditions within the dominant cul-
> ture that make such a critique possible and intelligible.[32]

A political education means decentering power in the classroom and
other pedagogical sites so that those institutional and cultural inequalities that marginalize some groups, repress particular types of
knowledge, and suppress critical dialogue can be addressed. On the
other hand, a politicizing education is a form of pedagogical indoctrination in which the issues of what is taught, by whom, and under
what conditions are determined by a doctrinaire political agenda that
refuses to examine its own values, beliefs, and ideological construction.
While refusing to recognize the social and historical character of its
own claims to history, knowledge, and values, a politicizing education
silences in the name of a specious universalism and denounces all
transformative practices through an appeal to timeless notions of truth
and beauty. Ironically, the latter virtue seems much more endemic to
right-wing educational agendas, given their emphasis on pedagogy as
an unproblematic vehicle for conveying truth and knowledge as something to be handed down rather than critically engaged.

In short, the battle against political correctness is less a corrective to
bad educational and pedagogical practices than a prescription for remov-
ing debate, cultural differences, and diverse theoretical orientations from

the sphere of schooling. Moreover, it casts teachers within a discourse that strips them of the possibility to become public intellectuals actively engaged in the process of linking their own teaching and the institutional role of schooling to the struggle for radical democracy and social justice. Commitment is not the disease of an oppressive partisanship, it is the basis for making teachers aware of what it means to be the active subjects of history rather than the guardians of an unproblematic and nostalgic view of the past. What is at stake in the current debate about political correctness and education is not the recognition of the alleged tyranny of a handful of progressive educators but the fear that radical democracy inspires in the orthodox guardians of traditional culture. But there is more at stake in these debates than the fears conservatives have about the imperatives of democracy—there is also the frustration and hope that cultural, political, and economic democracy demands. Catharine Stimpson is right in suggesting that "being a cultural democratic can be exhausting and irritating," but she also recognizes that such hope and anguish can strengthen and expand our moral, cognitive, and cultural capacities as educators while simultaneously encouraging us to act in order to expand democratic public life as the deepest expression of individual and collective freedom.[33]

NOTES

1. The principles that inform such a democracy have been explicated in Stanley Aronowitz, "The Situation of the Left in the United States," *Socialist Review* 23, no. 3 (1994): 5–80; Chantal Mouffe, *The Return of the Political* (London: Verso, 1993).

2. For an extensive detailed analysis of the right wing theorists, foundations, and issues in the anti-politically correct movement, see Messer-Davidow (1993).

3. Schlesinger, Jr., *The Disuniting of America* (Knoxville, TN: Whittle Press, 1992).

4. Worth, "Postmodern Pedagogy in the Multicultural Classroom: For Inappropriate Teachers and Imperfect Spectators," *Cultural Critique* 25 (Fall 1993): 5.

5. It is worth noting how the genealogy of the term politically correct has been completely ignored by both the popular press and right wing critics. In its more fashionable usage in the 1960s, the use of the term "politically correct" had an ironic if not abusive connotation aimed at the ideological rigidity and excessiveness of certain radical groups and individuals.

6. Fraser, "Tyranny of the Media Correct: The Assault on the New McCarthyism," *Extra* 4(4) (1991): 6.

7. Patrick Buchanan, "Losing the War for America's Culture?" in *Culture Wars*, ed. R. Bolton (New York: The New Press, 1992), 33.

8. Charles Krauthammer, "U.S. Socialism's Dying Gasps," *The Cincinnati Enquirer*, Wednesday, 26 December 1990, B2.

9. Dinesh D'Souza, *Illiberal Education: The Politics of Race and Sex on Campus* (New York: Free Press, 1991), 182.

10. James Wilson, quoted in S. Diamond, "Notes on Political Correctness," *Z Magazine* (July/August 1993): 32.

11. Ehrenreich, "What Campus Radicals? The P.C. Undergrad Is a Useful Specter," in *Are You Politically Correct: Debating America's Cultural Standards*, ed. F. Beckwith and M. Bauman (New York: Prometheus Books, 1993), 33.

12. Balch, "A Symposium on Freedom and Ideology: the Debate about Political Correctness," *The Civic Arts Review* 5(1) (1992): 5.

13. Allan Bloom, *The Closing of the American Mind* (New York: Simon & Schuster, 1987).

14. Stanley Aronowitz and H. A. Giroux, *Education Still Under Siege* (Westport: Bergin and Garvey, 1993).

15. T. Short, "Diversity and Breaking the Disciplines: Two New Assaults on the Curriculum," in *Are You Politically Correct*, 92.

16. H. L. Gates, Jr., "The Master's Pieces: On Canon Formation and the African-American Tradition," *The South Atlantic Quarterly* 89(1) (1990): 89–111.

17. Jeffrey Hart, quoted in S. Diamond, "Notes on Political Correctness."

18. Christopher Newfield, "What Was Political Correctness? Race, the Right and Managerial Democracy in the Humanities," *Critical Inquiry* 19 (Winter 1995): 332.

19. D'Souza, *Illiberal Education*.

20. Newfield, "What Was Political Correctness?," 333.

21. Diamond, "Notes on Political Correctness," 33.

22. John Taylor, "Are You Politically Correct," in *Are You Politically Correct*, 17.

23. John Silber, quoted in Raskin, "The Great PC Cover-Up," *California Lawyer* (February 1994): 69.

24. William Kerrigan, "The Falls of Academe," in *Wild Orchids and Trotsky: Messages from American Universities*, ed. M. Edmunson (New York: Penguin Books, 1993), 167.

25. Camille Paglia, quoted in Taylor, "Are You Political Correct?," 19.

26. Robert Rosenzweig, "Symposium on Freedom and Ideology: The Debate About Political Correctness," *The Civic Arts Review* 5, no. 1 (1992): 8.

27. Fiske, *Power Plays, Power Works* (London: Verso, 1994), 13.

28. Toni Morrison, "Unspeakable Things Unspoken: The Afro-American Presence in American Literature," *Michigan Quarterly Review* 28(1) (1987): 1–34.

29. Stanley Aronowitz, "A Different Perspective on Equality," *Review of Education, Pedagogy, and Cultural Studies*, 16, no. 2 (1994): 148.

30. See the insightful discussion of this issue in Judith Frank (1995).

31. Gerald Graff, "Academic Writing and the Uses of Bad Publicity," in *Eloquent Obsessions*, ed. Marianna Torgovnick (Durham: Duke University Press, 1994), 215.

32. Peter Euben, "The Debate Over the Canon," *The Civic Arts Review* 7(1) (1994): 14–15.

33. Catharine Stimpson, "Can Things Ever Be Perfectly Correct?," *College Literature* 21(3) (1994): 197.

PEDAGOGY AND RADICAL DEMOCRACY IN THE AGE OF "POLITICAL CORRECTNESS"

3

RADICAL DEMOCRACY AND POLITICAL POSSIBILITY

16

EQUALITY, DIFFERENCE, AND RADICAL DEMOCRACY

THE UNITED STATES FEMINIST DEBATES REVISITED

NANCY FRASER

"DEMOCRACY" IS TODAY AN INTENSELY CONTESTED word, meaning different things to different people, even as everyone claims to be for it. Should we take it to mean free-market capitalism plus multi-party elections, as many ex-Cold Warriors now insist? Or should we understand democracy in the stronger sense of self-rule? And if so, does that mean that every distinct nationality should have its own sovereign state in an "ethnically cleansed" territory? Or, does it mean a process of communication across differences, where citizens participate together in discussion and decision-making to collectively determine the conditions of their lives? And in that case, finally, what is required to ensure that all can participate as peers? Does democracy require social equality? The recognition of difference? The absence of systemic dominance and subordination?

"Radical democracy" is distinguished from rival conceptions by a distinctive set of answers to these questions. To be a radical democrat today is to appreciate—and to seek to eliminate—two very different kinds of impediments to democratic participation. One such impediment is social inequality; the other is the misrecognition of difference. Radical democracy, on this interpretation, is the view that democracy today requires both social equality and multicultural recognition.

This, however, is only the outline of an answer. To flesh it out is to become immediately embroiled in difficult questions about the relation between equality and difference. These questions are variously debated today with respect to gender, sexuality, nationality, ethnicity, and "race." What are the differences that make a difference for democracy? Which differences merit public recognition and/or political representation? Which differences, in contrast, should be considered irrelevant to political life and treated instead as private matters? Which kinds of differences, finally, should a democratic society seek to promote? And which, on the contrary, should it aim to abolish?

Radical democrats, like everyone else, cannot avoid confronting these questions. But to answer them is not a simple matter. Current United States discussions are haunted by two unfortunate temptations, which we must now figure out how to avoid. One is the tendency to adopt an undiscriminating version of multiculturalism that celebrates all identities and differences as worthy of recognition. The other is the mirror-opposite tendency to adopt an undiscriminating form of anti-essentialism that treats all identities and differences as repressive fictions. In fact, both of these tendencies share a common root: a failure to connect the cultural politics of identity and difference to the social politics of justice and equality. Both tendencies impede efforts to develop a credible vision of radical democracy.

This, at any rate, is the thesis I shall argue in this essay. I shall approach it somewhat indirectly, however. I shall reconstruct the history of recent United States feminist debates about difference in order to show how and where our present difficulties arise. Where possible, I shall also suggest ways of getting around them.

This approach requires a clarification. Despite the explicit focus on feminist debates, primary interest here is not feminism *per se*. Rather, I aim to use a reconstruction of feminist debates to illustrate a more general cultural-political trajectory. Analogous lines of argument can be developed from other starting points, such as the debates concerning "race." They, too, would reveal a progressive tendency to divorce the cultural politics of identity and difference from the social politics of justice and equality—to the detriment of efforts to develop a credible vision of radical democracy.

"GENDER DIFFERENCE": EQUALITY OR DIFFERENCE?

United States feminist debates about difference divide roughly into three phases. In the first phase, which lasted from the late 1960s through about the mid-1980s, the main focus was "gender difference." In the second phase, which ran roughly from the mid-1980s to the early 1990s, the main focus shifted to "differences among women." A third phase, which is currently underway, is focused above all on "multiple intersecting differences." Of course, to plot the trajectory of debate in this way is necessarily to simplify and abstract. But it also makes possible the sort of bird's-eye view that can reveal an otherwise hidden inner logic.

In the first phase, the principal antagonists were "equality feminists" and "difference feminists." And the main questions that divided them were, first, the nature and causes of gender injustice, and second, its appropriate remedy; hence, the meaning of gender equity.

Equality feminists saw gender difference as an instrument and artifact of male dominance. What passes for such difference in a sexist society, they claimed, are either misogynist lies told to rationalize women's subordination (for example, we are said to be irrational and sentimental, *therefore* unfit for intellectual work but well-suited to domesticity) or the socially constructed results of inequality (we have actually *become* anxious about math or fearful of success *because* we have been differently treated). In either case, to stress gender difference is to harm women. It is to reinforce our confinement to an inferior domestic role, hence to marginalize or exclude us from all those activities that promote true human self-realization, such as politics, employment, art, the life of the mind, and the exercise of authority. It is also to deprive us of our fair share of essential social goods, such as income, jobs, property, health, education, autonomy, respect, sexual pleasure, bodily integrity, and physical safety.

From the equality perspective, then, gender difference appeared to be inextricable from sexism. The political task was thus clear: the goal of feminism was to throw off the shackles of "difference" and establish equality, bringing women and men under a common measure. To be sure, liberal-feminists, radical-feminists, and socialist-feminists might dispute how best to achieve this goal. But they nevertheless shared a common vision of gender equity, which involved minimizing gender difference.

This equality perspective dominated the United States women's movement for nearly a decade from the late 1960s. In the late 1970s, however, it was sharply challenged by the rise of a new, "difference" feminism, which has also been called "cultural feminism." Difference feminists rejected the equality view as androcentric and assimilationist. From their perspective, getting women included in traditionally male pursuits was an insufficiently radical goal, as it uncritically adopted the biased masculinist view that only men's activities were truly human, thereby depreciating women's. Far from challenging sexism, then, equality feminism actually reproduced it—by devaluing femininity. What was needed instead was another sort of feminism, one that opposed the undervaluation of women's worth by recognizing gender difference and revaluing femininity.

Difference feminists accordingly proposed a new, positive, interpretation of gender difference. Women really did differ from men, they claimed, but such difference did not mean inferiority. Some insisted, on the contrary, that nurturant, peace-loving women were morally superior to competitive, militaristic men. Others preferred to drop all talk of inferiority and superiority, to recognize two different "voices" of equivalent value, and to demand a respectful hearing for women's voices. In either case, they agreed that gender difference was real and deep, the most fundamental human difference. All women shared a common "gender identity" *as women*. All suffered a common harm when that identity was denigrated. All therefore were sisters under the skin. Feminists need only articulate the positive content of femininity in order to mobilize this latent solidarity. The way to do justice to women, in sum, was to recognize, not minimize, gender difference.

Here, then, were the stakes in the first difference debate within United States feminism. The movement stood poised between two conflicting views of gender difference, two alternative accounts of gender injustice, and two opposing visions of gender equity. The proponents of equality saw gender difference as the handmaiden of male domination. For them, the central injustices of sexism were women's marginalization and the maldistribution of social goods. The key meaning of gender equity was equal participation and redistribution. Difference feminists, in contrast, saw gender difference as the cornerstone of women's identity. For them, accordingly, androcentrism was sexism's chief harm. And the centerpiece of gender equity was the revaluation of femininity.

This debate raged for several years on both cultural and political planes. But it was never definitively settled. Part of the difficulty was that each of the two sides had convincing criticisms of the other. The proponents of difference successfully showed that the egalitarians presupposed "the male as norm," a standard that disadvantaged women. The egalitarians argued just as cogently, however, that the difference side relied on stereotypical notions of femininity, which reinforced existing gender hierarchies. Neither side, therefore, had a fully defensible position. Yet each had an important insight. The egalitarian insight was that no adequate account of sexism could overlook women's social marginalization and unequal share of resources; hence, no persuasive vision of gender equity could omit the goals of equal participation and fair distribution. The difference insight was that no adequate account of sexism could overlook the problem of androcentrism in the construction of cultural standards of value; hence, no persuasive vision of gender equity could omit the need to overcome such androcentrism. What, then, was the moral to be drawn? Henceforth, feminists would have to find a way to accommodate both of these insights. We would need to develop a new perspective that opposed social inequality and cultural androcentrism simultaneously.

"DIFFERENCES AMONG WOMEN"

As it turned out, United States feminists did not resolve the equality/difference impasse by developing such a new perspective. Rather, by the mid- to late 1980s, the entire framework of the debate had been altered so radically that the problem could no longer be posed in those terms. In the interim, leading feminist currents had come to reject the view that gender difference could be fruitfully discussed in isolation from other axes of difference, especially "race," ethnicity, sexuality, and class. And so the equality/difference debate was displaced. The focus on "gender difference" gave way to a focus on "differences among women," inaugurating a new phase of feminist debate.

This shift in focus was largely the work of lesbians and feminists of color. For many years they had protested forms of feminism that failed to illuminate their lives and address their problems. African-American women, for example, had invoked their history of slavery and resistance, waged work and community activism, to contest assumptions of universal female dependence on men and confinement to domesticity. Meanwhile, Latina, Jewish, Native-American, and Asian-American feminists had protested the implicit reference to white Anglo women in many mainstream feminist texts. Lesbians, finally, unmasked assumptions of normative heterosexuality in the classic feminist accounts of mothering, sexuality, gender identity, and reproduction.

Mainstream American feminism, all these voices insisted, was *not* a feminism for all women. It privileged the standpoint of the white heterosexual middle class women who had so far dominated the movement. It falsely extrapolated from their experiences and conditions of life in ways that were inappropriate, even harmful, to other women. Thus, the very movement that claimed to liberate women ended up reproducing within its own ranks the racism and the heterosexism, the class hierarchies and the ethnic biases, that were endemic in American society.

For many years, such voices had been largely confined to the margins of United States feminism. By the mid- to late 1980s, however, they had moved, in the prophetic words of bell hooks, "from [the] margins to [the] center" of discussion. Many erstwhile doubters were now willing to concede the point: the movement had been so exclusively preoccupied with gender difference that it had neglected the differences among women.

"Difference feminism" was the most obvious culprit. Its purportedly universal accounts of feminine gender identity and women's different voice could now be seen for what they actually were: culturally specific stereotypical idealizations of middle class, heterosexual, white-European femininity, idealizations that had as much to do with hierarchies of class, "race," ethnicity, and sexuality as with hierarchies of gender. And yet, equality feminism was culpable, too. Assuming that all women were subordinated to all men in the same way and to the same degree, it had falsely universalized the specific situation of white, middle class, heterosexual women and concealed their implication in hierarchies of class, "race," ethnicity, and sexuality. Thus, neither side of the old equality/difference debate could withstand the critique. Although one side had stressed male/female similarity and the other side male/female difference, the end result was effectively the same: both had obscured important differences among women. In both cases, consequently, the attempt to build sisterhood backfired. False universalizations of *some* women's situations and *some* women's identity-ideals had not promoted feminist solidarity. They led, on the contrary, to anger and schism, to hurt and mistrust.

But the difficulty went deeper still. In repressing differences among women, the mainstream movement had also repressed axes of subordination other than gender—once again, class, "race," ethnicity, nationality, and sexuality.[1] It therefore repressed what Deborah King has called "multiple jeopardy," the multiple forms of subordination faced by lesbians, women of color, and/or poor and working-class women. Consequently, the mainstream movement failed to grasp the multiple affiliations of such women, their loyalty to more than one social movement. For example, many women of color and/or lesbians remain committed to fighting *alongside* men of color and/or gays in anti-racist and/or gay-liberation movements, while simultaneously fighting *against* the sexism of their male comrades. But a feminism focused only on gender difference failed fully to grasp this situation. By suppressing axes of subordination other than gender, it also suppressed differences *among men*. And that created a double-bind for women who are subject to multiple jeopardy: it effectively pressured them to choose between loyalty to their gender and loyalty to their "race," class, and/or sexuality. The either/or imperative denied their reality of multiple jeopardy, multiple affiliation, and multiple identity.

The exclusive focus on "gender difference" proved increasingly counterproductive as "identity politics" proliferated in the 1980s. Now the political scene was crowded with "new social movements," each politicizing a "different" difference. Gays and lesbians were mobilized around sexual difference in order to fight against heterosexism; movements of African-Americans, Native-Americans, and other peoples of color had politicized "racial" difference in order to contest racial subordination; and a wide range of ethnically- and religiously-identified groups were struggling for recognition of cultural differences within an increasingly multi-ethnic nation.[2] Thus, feminists found themselves sharing political space with all these movements. But not in the sense of a parallel, side-by-side coexistence. Rather, all the various movements cut across one another. And each was going through an analogous process of discovering the "other" differences within itself.

In this context, the need for a re-orientation was clear. Only if feminists were willing to abandon an exclusive focus on gender difference could we cease interpreting other difference claims as threats to the unity of women. Only if we were willing to grapple with axes of subordination other than gender could we theorize our relation to the other political struggles surrounding us. Only by abandoning the view of ourselves as a self-contained social movement, finally, could we fully grasp the true situation: that gender struggles were occurring on the broader terrain of civil society, where multiple axes of difference were being contested simultaneously and where multiple social movements were intersecting.

By the early 1990s, therefore, the decisive United States feminist debate was poised to shift from "differences among women" to "multiple intersecting differences." The result was to be an enormous gain. What had appeared at first to be a turning inward—instead of focusing on our relation to men, we would focus on the relations among ourselves—seemed instead to invite a turning outward: instead of focusing on gender alone, we would focus on its relation to other cross-cutting axes of difference and subordination. In this way, the whole range of politicized differences would become grist for the feminist mill. Not only gender, but also "race," ethnicity, nationality, sexuality, and class would now require feminist theorization.[3] And all struggles against subordination would now need to be linked up with feminism.

"MULTIPLE INTERSECTING DIFFERENCES": ANTI-ESSENTIALISM OR MULTICULTURALISM?

This brings us to the third phase of United States feminist debate, which is currently underway. Its focus is how to develop a viable theoretical and political outlook oriented to "multiple intersecting differences." This is also the context for the recent revival of interest in "radical democracy." Today, radical democracy is being proposed as a rubric for mediating various struggles over "multiple intersecting differences," hence for linking various social movements. As such, it is appealing on at least two planes. On the one hand, it appears to correct the balkanizing tendencies of identity politics and to promote broader political alliances. On the other hand, and at the same time, it seems to offer a "post-socialist" vision of the good society and to contest hegemonic conservative understandings of democracy.

Yet the meaning of "radical democracy" remains underdeveloped. So far, it is unclear how precisely this project can connect a cultural politics of identity and difference to a social politics of justice and equality. Unless it manages to connect them, however, it will not succeed in forging democratic mediations among "multiple intersecting differences."

The difficulties become clear when we examine the current debates that form the context for discussions of radical democracy. These debates focus chiefly on group identity and cultural difference, and they divide into two related streams. One of the streams goes by the name of "anti-essentialism"; it cultivates a skeptical attitude toward identity and difference, which it reconceptualizes as discursive constructions. A second stream goes by the name of "multiculturalism"; it cultivates a positive view of group differences and group identities, which its seeks to revalue and promote. Both streams of discussion are insightful in many respects. Yet neither is entirely satisfactory.

The problem is that both discussions rely on one-sided views of identity and difference. The anti-essentialist view is skeptical and negative; it sees all identities as inherently repressive and all differences as inherently exclusionary. The multiculturalist view, in contrast, is celebratory and positive; it sees all identities as deserving of recognition and all differences as meriting affirmation. Neither approach is sufficiently differentiated. Neither provides a basis for distinguishing democratic from anti-democratic identity claims, just from unjust differences. Neither, as a result, can sustain a viable politics or a credible vision of radical democracy.

Let me sketch the main contours of each approach, focusing on its understanding of difference. I will show that the weaknesses—in both cases—can be traced to a common source; namely, a failure to appreciate that cultural differences can only be freely elaborated and democratically mediated on the basis of social equality.

I begin with anti-essentialism—as it is debated within feminist circles. Proponents of anti-essentialism propose to avoid the errors of difference feminism by radically reconceiving identity and difference. They begin from the assumption that the differences among women go "all the way down"; hence, there is no way of being a woman that is not already "raced," sexed, and classed. Therefore, gender has no invariant essence or core. They also reject approaches that divide women (and men) into ever smaller subgroups, each with its own distinct identity and its own claim for recognition. In contrast to such approaches, anti-essentialists appreciate that neither differences nor identities are simply given as a matter of fact in virtue of a group's "objective" character or social position. Rather, they are discursively constructed. Differences and identities are performatively created through cultural processes of being claimed and elaborated. They do not pre-exist such processes. They could always in principle be otherwise. Thus, existing differences and identities can be performatively undone or altered by being dis-claimed or differently elaborated.

What follows politically from this view? Clearly, anti-essentialism rejects any politics—feminist or otherwise—that essentializes identity and difference. But some of its exponents go further still. Stressing that all collective identities are "fictional" because constructed, they regard all with a skeptical eye. From this perspective, politicized identity terms such as "women" must always necessarily be exclusionary; they can only be constructed through the repression of difference. Any collective identification, therefore, will be subject to critique from the standpoint of what it excludes. Feminist identity is no exception. Thus, the black-feminist critique of white bias in feminism is not only a protest against racism; it also protests a logical necessity. Any attempt to claim a black feminist identity, therefore, could only repeat the exclusionary gesture.

I shall henceforth call this "the deconstructive version of anti-essentialism." In this version, the only "innocent" political practice is negative and deconstructive. It involves unmasking the repressive and exclusionary operation that enables every construction of identity. Thus, it is not the job of feminism, on this view, to construct a feminine identity or a collective feminist subject; it is rather our task to deconstruct every construction of "women." Rather than take for granted the existence of gender difference we should expose the processes by which gender binarism and, therefore, "women" are constructed. The political aim of feminism, then, is to destabilize gender difference and the gender identities that accompany it. The preferred means include dissidence and parody. But beyond this, we should ally with other social movements with analogous deconstructive aims; for example, with critical "race" theorists committed to deconstructing black/white difference and with queer theorists working to deconstruct the homo/hetero difference, but not, in contrast, with Afrocentrists seeking to consolidate black identity, nor with proponents of gay and lesbian identity politics.

What should we make of this discussion? In my view, the outcome is mixed. On the one hand, anti-essentialism makes a major advance by conceptualizing identities and differences as discursively constructed instead of as objectively given. But the politics of the deconstructive version are simplistic. By this I do not mean only the obvious difficulty that sexism cannot be dismantled by an exclusively negative, deconstructive practice. I mean also that further difficulties arise when deconstructive anti-essentialists try the theoretical equivalent of pulling a rabbit out of a hat, when they try, that is, to deduce a substantive politics of difference from an ontological conception of identity.

The problem can be put like this: Deconstructive anti-essentialists appraise identity claims on ontological grounds alone. They do not ask, in contrast, how a given identity or difference is related to social structures of domination and to social relations of inequality. They succumb, as a result, to a night in which all cows are grey: all identities are equally fictional, equally repressive, and equally exclusionary. This is tantamount to surrendering any possibility of distinguishing emancipatory and oppressive identity claims, benign and pernicious differences. Thus, deconstructive anti-essentialists evade the crucial political questions of the day: Which identity claims are rooted in the defense of social relations of inequality and domination? And which are rooted in a challenge to such relations? Which identity claims carry the potential to expand actually existing democracy? And which, in contrast, work against democratization? Which differences, finally, should a democratic society seek to foster, and which, on the contrary, should it aim to abolish?

Yet anti-essentialism has no monopoly on these problems. They are shared by the other major stream of United States discussion, the stream focused on "multiculturalism." Multiculturalism has become the rallying cry for a potential alliance of new social movements, all of whom seem to be struggling for the recognition of difference. This alliance potentially unites feminists, gays and lesbians, members of racialized groups and of disadvantaged ethnic groups in opposition to a common enemy: namely, a culturally imperialist form of public life that treats the straight, white-Anglo, middle-class male as the human norm, in relation to which everyone else appears deviant. The goal of the struggle is to create *multicultural* public forms, which recognize a plurality of different, equally valuable ways of being human. In such a society, today's dominant understanding of difference as deviance would give way to a positive appreciation of human diversity. All citizens would enjoy the same formal legal rights in virtue of their common humanity. But they would *also* be recognized for what differentiates them from one another, their cultural particularity.

This, at least, is the most common American understanding of multiculturalism. It has dominated intense debates over education in the mainstream public sphere. Conservatives have attacked proponents of Women's Studies, African-American Studies, Gay and Lesbian Studies, and Ethnic Studies, charging that we have inappropriately politicized the curriculum by replacing Great Works selected for their enduring universal value with inferior texts chosen on ideological, affirmative-action grounds. Thus, the argument turns on the interpretation of "difference." Whereas defenders of traditional education persist in viewing difference negatively, as deviance from a single universal norm, multiculturalists view difference positively, as cultural variation and diversity; and they demand its representation in educational curricula, as well as elsewhere in public life.

Radical democrats are understandably committed to defending some version of multiculturalism against the conservative attacks. But we should nevertheless reject the version just sketched, which I will henceforth call "the pluralist version." The pluralist version of multi-culturalism is premised on a one-sidedly, positive understanding of difference. It celebrates difference uncritically while failing to interrogate its relation to inequality. Like the American pluralist tradition from which it descends, it proceeds—contrary to fact—as if United States society contained no class divisions or other deep-seated structural injustices, as if its political-economy were basically just, as if its various constituent groups were socially equal. Thus, it treats difference as pertaining exclusively to culture.[4] The result is to divorce questions of difference from material inequality, power differentials among groups, and systemic relations of dominance and subordination.

All this should ring warning bells for feminists who would be radical democrats. We should recognize this view as a cousin of the old "difference feminism." The latter's core elements are recycled here in a more general form and extended to differences other than gender. Where difference feminism made cultural androcentrism the central injustice and revaluation of femininity the chief remedy, pluralist multiculturalism substitutes the more general injustice of cultural imperialism and the more general remedy of revaluing all disrespected identities. But the structure of the thinking is the same. And so are the structural weaknesses.

Like difference feminism, pluralist multiculturalism tends to substantialize identities, treating them as given positivities instead of as constructed relations. It tends, consequently, to balkanize culture, setting groups apart from one another, ignoring the ways they cut across one another, and inhibiting cross-group interaction and identification. Losing sight of the fact that differences intersect, it regresses to a simple additive model of difference.

Like difference feminism, moreover, pluralist multiculturalism valorizes existing group identities. It assumes that such identities are fine as they are, only some need additional respect. But some existing group identities may be importantly tied to existing social relations of domination; and they might not survive the transformation of those relations. Moreover, some group identities—or strands thereof—are incompatible with others. For example, one cannot consistently affirm a white supremacist identity and an anti-racist identity simultaneously; affirming some identities—or some strands of some identities—requires transforming others. Thus, there is no avoiding political judgments about better and worse identities and differences; these, however, pluralist multiculturalism cannot make.

Pluralist multiculturalism, finally, is the mirror image of deconstructive anti-essentialism. Whereas that approach delegitimated all identities and differences, this one indiscriminately celebrates them all. Thus, its politics are equally one-sided. It, too, evades the crucial political questions of the day: Which identity claims are rooted in the defense of social relations of inequality and domination? And which are rooted in a challenge to such relations? Which identity claims carry the potential to expand actually existing democracy? And which, in contrast, work against democratization? Which differences, finally, should a democratic society seek to foster, and which, on the contrary, should it aim to abolish?

CONCLUDING THESES:
TOWARD A CREDIBLE VISION OF RADICAL DEMOCRACY

It is no accident that both deconstructive anti-essentialism and pluralist multiculturalism fail in the same way. For the weaknesses of both share a common root: both fail to connect a cultural politics of identity and difference to a social politics of justice and equality. Neither appreciates the crux of the connection: *cultural differences can only be freely elaborated and democratically mediated on the basis of social equality.*

In this sense, both approaches are victims of an unmastered history. With the wisdom of hindsight, we can now see that both are haunted by echoes of the old equality/difference debate. The failure to resolve that debate left both current discussions with a truncated problematic. Both anti-essentialism and multiculturalism have sought to correct the deficiencies of difference feminism, but they remain on the latter's own terms. Both approaches restrict themselves to the plane of culture, which they treat in abstraction from social relations and social structures, including political economy. And so both try to elaborate a cultural politics of difference in abstraction from a social politics of equality. Put differently, both approaches repress the insights of equality feminism concerning the need for equal participation and fair distribution. As a result both are left without the resources needed to make crucial political distinctions. Thus, neither can sustain a viable politics in a period of multiple, intersecting difference claims. And neither can model a credible vision of radical democracy.

What, finally, can we learn from this story? How can we use its lessons to develop a credible vision of radical democracy? And where should we go from here?

Let me conclude by proposing three theses.

First, there is no going back to the old equality/difference debate in the sense of an exclusive focus on any single axis difference. The shift from "gender difference" to "differences among women" to "multiple intersecting differences" remains an unsurpassable gain. But this does not mean that we should simply forget the old debate. Rather, we now need to construct a new equality/difference debate, one oriented to multiple intersecting differences. We need, in other words, to reconnect the problematic of cultural difference with the problematic of social equality.

Second, there is no going back to essentialized understandings of identity and difference. The anti-essentialist view of identities and differences as relationally constructed represents another unsurpassable gain. But this does not mean that we should pursue an exclusively deconstructive politics. Rather, we should develop an alternative version of anti-essentialism, one that permits us to link a cultural politics of identity and difference with a social politics of justice and equality.

Third, there is no going back to the monocultural view that there is only one valuable way of being human. The multicultural view of a multiplicity of cultural forms is yet another unsurpassable gain. But this does not mean that we should subscribe to the pluralist version of multiculturalism. Rather, we should develop an alternative version that permits us to make normative judgments about the value of different differences by interrogating their relation to inequality.

In sum, we must find a way to combine the struggle for an anti-essentialist multiculturalism with the struggle for social equality. Only then will we be able to develop a credible model of radical democracy and a politics that is adequate to our time.

NOTES

1. An important exception were the socialist-feminist currents of the late 1960s and 1970s. They had always insisted on relating gender divisions to class divisions and, to a lesser degree, to racial divisions. But with the decline of the New Left their influence waned.

2. The relative absence of nationalist struggles—the exceptions being some Native-American and Puerto-Rican currents—distinguish United States identity politics from that in many other areas of the world.

3. The reverse is also true: gender must now be theorized from the perspective of these other differences.

4. In so doing, pluralist multiculturalism construes difference on the standard United States model of ethnicity, in which an immigrant group preserves some identification with its "old country" cultural heritage, while integrating into United States society; since the ethnic group is thought not to occupy any distinctive structural position in the political economy, its difference is wholly cultural. Pluralist multiculturalism generalizes this ethnicity model to gender, sexuality, and "race," which the model does not in fact fit.

17

A DIALOGUE ON DEMOCRACY

GAYATRI CHAKRAVORTY SPIVAK AND DAVID PLOTKE

R ECENT HISTORY HAS SHOWN THAT THE CONCEPT OF democracy can no longer be considered in purely national terms. In a post-cold war era lacking in super-power conflicts, conventional definitions of citizenship and identity have been thrown into question by ruptures in the global political landscape, changing post-industrial economic relations, and shifting population demographics. This growing transnationalism is only exacerbated by increasing globalization of capitalist "democracy" through such instruments as the North American Free Trade Agreement (NAFTA), the General Agreement on Tariffs and Trade (GATT), and the prominence of such institutions as the World Bank and the newly established World Trade Organization.

How will these new economic and political structures effect relationships between rich and poor nations in the world? What impact will the altered relationships have on workers? How might these changes influence the workings of democracy, both nationally and transnationally? In the interest of addressing these questions in an interdisciplinary context, Gayatri Chakravorty Spivak and David Plotke have created a dialogue for this book. Spivak is best known for her work as a literary critic. She is the Avalon Foundation Professor in the Humanities in the department of English and comparative literature at Columbia University and the author of such books as *In Other Worlds* (Routledge, 1987), *The Post-Colonial Critic: Interviews, Strategies, Dialogues* (Routledge, 1990), and *Outside in the Teaching Machine* (Routledge, 1993). Plotke is associate professor of political science at the Graduate Faculty of the New School for Social Research in New York City. He is the author of *Building a Democratic Political Order: Reshaping American Liberalism in the 1930s and 1940s* (Cambridge University, 1995). From 1976 to 1981 he was the editor of *Socialist Review*.

In the conversation that follows, Spivak and Plotke place current debates about radical democracy in a global context by discussing new institutional forms that are developing across national boundaries. Such organizations are becoming increasingly important in addressing such worldwide issues as population, economic development, and the environment. Yet in their varying origins and purposes, these new multinational institutions often reproduce many of the same political problems as the states from which they emerge. This conversation was recorded in New York City in October 1994 and subsequently revised for publication.

GLOBAL PERSPECTIVES

DAVID PLOTKE: One impetus for this conversation is the proposal that "the left" should define itself as favoring radical democracy. This view has been advocated in journals such as *Socialist Review*, *Rethinking Marxism*, and *New Left Review*, and in many articles and books.[1]

GAYATRI CHAKRAVORTY SPIVAK: The recent debates around radical democracy have been very useful in explaining the shortfalls of certain groups on the left in the United States: the Democratic Socialists of America, the New American Movement, and the Democratic Socialist Organizing Committee. The narrative of old-left-to-New-Left, waves of feminism, and New Social Movements is provincial—even in terms of the United States alone—in the post-Soviet world. Discussions of radical democracy occasionally mention economic restructuring, post-Fordism, and so on—but they do not think them through. Because of an absence of global vision, there is no awareness of existing models of economic resistance to "the United States" (a metonym for the forces of the North) in the South. When Stanley Aronowitz starts talking about economic restructuring, he must immediately shift to the labor movement in the United States, and how capital flight has decimated the industrial landscape in the United States, etc.[2] Or he speaks of national liberation movements in the old second world. You cannot think of a leftist solution—radical democratic or otherwise—if you do not consider the configuration of globality today.

DP: What do you mean by "provincial." What would the discussions address if they weren't provincial?

GCS: What they are not seeing is the specific place of the United States. It's been fashionable for some time for the United States left to say that it is no longer a world power, it's no longer a real economic power. But if you examine the United State's role in economic restructuring in terms of the Group of Seven, the World Bank, the International Monetary Fund, and the General Agreement on Tariffs and Trade (GATT), you would recognize the real dilemma. In fact, I would call it something bigger. Forgive my use of the somewhat trendy word, "aporia." A dilemma is just a task of thinking, whereas an aporia is a practical fact. An aporia is a situation where one choice cancels out another, but a choice must be made. You can't exist in an aporia. Discussions that focus on the United States fail to recognize that the best solution for real domestic problems in the United States may have no effect or a bad effect on the global situation. This is not to ignore the problems in the United States but to acknowledge that by virtue of its historical identity the United States is in a bind in terms of the left's international role. Much of the current discussion doesn't recognize the aporia between a vision of the left in the United States and a vision of the left in a global context.

DP: I don't think many participants in discussions of radical democracy have a clear image of the contemporary relationship between the United States and other parts of the world. The cold war categories that helped orient people from left to right are gone. One clear sign of that confusion was the difficulty even in discussing the North American Free Trade Agreement (NAFTA). Conventional left positions were inadequate to deal with NAFTA both in narrowly economic terms and more broadly as a political and social conception of relations between the United States and Mexico. I think that people on the left in the United States—and Mexico—often believed that the best policy for many countries, especially small and poor ones, was to be outside the world market, to remain outside the capitalist realm, and to exercise autonomy within that external space. Such autonomy no longer appears attractive or feasible, and its demise as a guiding aim leaves "the left" unequipped to analyze measures in favor of greater economic integration and political cooperation. No clear policy has emerged in place of the prior critique of participation in the international economy.

GCS: That's why I'm saying that there are places where the United States left can learn a bit more about this. These are problems that the organized left faces around the globe. I recall a conversation with a prominent member of the communist party of Bangladesh, who had come to consult with an alternative development collective worker just before the interim elections. The worker in the collective told him it was pointless to focus on the state of the communist party in Bangladesh. Instead, the left should rethink its role and begin negotiating with the major transnational agencies exerting economic influence in the region. He was suggesting that the left should think globally rather than in terms of the Bangladeshi left or the Indian left or the United States left. In this sense, radical democracy as confined to a particular national left is not going to make much of a difference.

DP: You (or I) refer to "the left," but I'm not sure what political content that term has today. The African National Congress is certainly "the left" in terms of its history and practical orientation, but it is not about resisting capitalism. It wants to create democracy, to shape markets, and sharply increase equality, but it's not anti-capitalist. The prevalent framework of the period after World War II has lost its pertinence. Two central pillars of left thinking—not just socialist but broadly left-of-center—were the national autonomy of subordinate countries and resistance to domestic capitalist development. I don't think national autonomy can now be conceived as a thorough separation from international capitalism and cooperation with similarly separated nations. Nor can general anti-capitalism in an earlier sense provide a basic political framework. The emphasis on "radical democracy" rather than "socialism" sometimes amounts to a tacit recognition of these conceptual and practical changes, but without really theorizing them. Still, a tacit recognition is better than none at all.

GCS: This is why I mentioned the suggestion that the nationalist communist parties should negotiate with the transnational agencies. I was referring to the way "development" often provides an alibi for exploitation. Everyone is familiar with the Bruce Rich statement that all of the money invested in so-called "aid" flows back finally to the ten richest capitalist countries. Let's consider both national autonomy and resistance to capitalist development—not resistance to small "c" capitalist, small "d" development. We're talking about resistance to capital "D" development, which is an exploitative front that does little or nothing for indigenous capital, about export-based investment, or about the world-bank's subcontracted so-called aid and development projects. Throughout Asia and Southeast Asia, economic resistance to such forms of exploitative development is well articulated. Moreover, it is organized into forms of collectivity that are global in structure like the Third World Network, for example, which meets all over Asia—also, I think, in Latin America—and is actively connected by e-mail.

In these transnational collectives people are tied together globally, and as a consequence they no longer act like nationalists talking about national autonomy. They are bound by the recognition that global economic restructuring is slowly breaking down the boundaries between fragile national economies and international economies. In that context the state has little relevance. Because of this the so-called "local" initiatives against ecological disaster brought on in the name of sustainable development are constituting themselves as a transnational network. This does not resemble the Euro/United States ecological movement in many important respects. On this front, local initiatives are immediately global. This is evident in the way that the World Bank protects itself against them by way of dubbing the collaborative Non-Governmental Organizations (NGOs) as the "international civil society."

This type of hard-core economic resistance sometimes uses a new model of nationalism. They have nothing to gain from mere "national liberation," for it is post hoc recolonization that they are facing. They use the word "nation" as Foucault uses the word "power" to name a complex strategic situation in a particular conjuncture. Amaryllis Torres in the Philippines uses the word "nation" to mean this kind of local initiative joining together to confront the shortfalls of global restructuring and capital development. At this point we are no longer talking about old models of nationalism. After all, the folks comprising these resistance movements were never identified with the state anyway. They are not a part of the nationalist culturalist front. This is precisely why they can use some kind of recognition from the so-called "left" or the so-called "United States-Third World" or the "European Third World." Those folks privilege the Anglo United States, the white United States, because it's only in such a relationship that they are constituted as "third world" at all.

Their resistance does not resemble European or United States new social movements. It is hard-core economic resistance, not sociocultural resistance. They could use some support, not leadership, from the left in the Group of Seven countries—even if it only leads to making the United States an enlightened donor country. That's practical, and it is not against capitalist development. There are enlightened donor nations like Canada, Holland, and some of the Scandinavian countries. Believe me, that would be much less provincial than this notion of radical democracy versus United States third world.

DP: Regarding this notion of small "d" development, it promises a big step forward. While it recalls development theory of the 1950s and early 1960s with the idea of a uniform path toward modernity, talking about small "d" development means one can have focused and concrete arguments about what kind of development one wants and doesn't want. During the cold war there was a typical association between notions of national liberation and socialist development. These were counterposed to capitalist or liberal development. The question now is precisely what forms of development are preferable and possible. How should we talk about the ensemble of desired changes?

GCS: My first answer is I do not care about the name we use. I am going to be a bit naive here because at times I think we should be prepared to be naive. You see, unlike many advocates of radical democracy, I am not so ready to throw Marx away. I do agree that it can not be the dominant model, but I do not think that happened because Marxism was particularly bad. I think it happened because Marxism was not suited for the adventures undertaken in its name. We should keep in mind that through the three volumes of *Capital* at least, Marx is not talking about the non-generation of capital, but the non-utilization of capital for capitalism.[3] It is like the difference between starving and dieting. You can agree to the production of capital, but restrict it (by common consent) so that it cannot be appropriated by one group of people, but remains a dynamic for social redistribution. If that kind of Marxist analysis is digested, it becomes the active core of these movements rather than a mere model for bureaucratic state capitalism that claims a particular name. Such is the case in the "new social movements" of the South; they are "globe-girdling" rather than international movements. They operate with the real goal of redistributing generated capital, reallocating the uses of capital. Alternative development becomes alternatives to "Development." This can't be something that you can solve once and for all by establishing a radical democratic model or a participatory democratic model or any single model. This wrench between the self and the other, between rights and responsibilities, appropriation and redistribution, taking and giving—this is extremely fundamental; it's not something that just came into being with capitalism. The push between competition and giving up is not something you can just solve by choosing one model of governance.

I was talking with one of the leaders of the subaltern collective last night. He was saying that what one has to keep in mind is that the subaltern project is not just an unfinished project, it is unfinishable. And in my view, in the current version of globality the struggle between international capital and local self-management *is* the arena of struggle between "capitalism and socialism." The tug-of-war between the two is not something you're going to solve with a program of radical democracy. It is an unfinishable project. This is what I see every day when I look at grassroots economic resistance within the southern hemisphere, the mode of operation of the network of non-elite NGOs in the South. That's why the leadership complex of the left in the United States has no particular role, as far as the left goes internationally. Rather than wanting to lead, the United States left should become aware of the aporia between domestic economic justice and international economic justice and be prepared to give support.

DP: In your description of these global economic justice movements, I'm struck by the lack of connection between their activities and historic socialist projects, except in the sense that they all regard social productivity as in some sense open to social control. Beyond that major point, socialism ceases to make a compelling claim. Instead you have a range of political positions concerning what "social control" might actually mean.

GCS: We have to think of such alternatives now. There has to be a transformation in leftist thinking that reaches beyond a European mode of making oneself recognizable as a system of government. If the world is truly post-national, then the role of the party has to be rethought, and old labels need to be rewritten. Again I find this whole notion of leadership a little absurd. For example, when someone like Aronowitz says that the popular left sees itself as the inheritor of the Third Estate after the French revolution, that is a problem. You just put your finger on it. I keep repeating that the positions of Aronowitz and Immanuel Wallerstein about new social movements—as "cultural" or interested in state power—does not apply in the Southern theater.[4] A different model is already at work there, and it is not a European model.

DP: The widespread attraction to "new social movements" can divert attention from national politics and state forms. One constructs an image of movements in advanced countries as movements apart from and outside of conventional politics, almost to spare oneself from worrying about the latter. Such talk about new social movements may have allowed people to evade thinking through the collapse of prior left ideologies in the advanced countries. In Western Europe the talk about new social movements in the 1980s was a useful way to distinguish some of these movements from the social democratic parties. It allowed people to be in favor of something, to support an actual movement amidst the general ideological unravelling that was occurring.

In the "southern" settings to which you're referring, the distinction between cultural and political movements is very hard to sustain. But the same is true if you look carefully at recent movements in advanced countries. The participants in movements of gay people care a lot about the character of their national political regime, and the large movements that existed for awhile—such as those regarding race and gender—have likewise had many dimensions. They have been concerned about how political and economic life is organized and how culture is shaped.

GCS: Unlike many new social movements in the United States and Europe, the non-elite Southern NGOs—not the World Bank's "international civil society"—have a very different attitude toward the state. Of course they are all located in relationship to various governments, but their political programs are not contained by their governments. Instead organizations like the Third World Network and the Asian Women's Human Rights Council concentrate on issues like GATT. You have no idea of the degree of expertise on GATT that exists among near-illiterate rural workers in these collectives; it is amazing how thoroughly they recognize the implications of what is going on. And what they are doing is not identity politics at all. The identitarians and the culturalists would belong to the sphere of the international civil society as it is being represented by the world bank.

That is partly why I am saying that the old models will not work. When these local—against global—resistance movements relate to the state, they stand behind the state to the extent that it is being disseminated by these transnational forces. At the same time, they are also against the state because it is collaborating with the agents of economic restructuring. In this sense, their relationship to the state is robustly contradictory; it cannot be compared to the "post-nationalist," "post-statist" talk that we get in the Euro-United States house of advanced theory. And I have already said that notions of culturalism and identity politics are not applicable to this kind of work. It subsists in the arena of cultural difference, but cultural identity is not their specific program. Instead their focus is hard-core economic resistance.

DP: People in what you're terming "southern nations" play imaginary roles in certain kinds of left theorizing—as cultural rebels, as people who have not been absorbed or modernized. You're familiar with those vocabularies. But in your argument those people aren't interested in playing such roles.

GCS: I know these people because I move around in their circles. Their relationship to the state is not what we would expect, and their relationship to the left is not uncomplicated. In the opening pages of his book *Imagined Communities*, Benedict Anderson argues that one can hardly distinguish between Marxist and non-Marxist parts of the third world.[5] That judgement is true if you attend only to party labels. In that sphere people are not necessarily working within the tug-of-war between a capitalist use of capital and a redistributive use of capital. The efforts of the economic resistance groups I am speaking of are very different. Their relationship to the left ranges from rejection and contempt when it's too Marxist (as with our friend Aijaz Ahmad; perhaps you've read his book, *In Theory: Classes, Nations, Literatures*[6]) to comradeship. So there is a whole spectrum of relationships between the globe-girdling networks and their local lefts. But the networks themselves cannot be identified as "the left" in the South. There are new models that the so-called United States left should become aware of. These networks need support because the United States is one of the major powers in the transnational financialization of the globe. It would indeed be a worthy goal for the United States left to play, to put itself to school, to see how nationalist and how provincial the constant invocation of American domestic economic justice is without this larger global view.

I'm not saying that the struggle for economic justice is wrong. I must emphasize this. I could not in terms of what's happening in France, in Belgium, or in California with undocumented immigrants. But it is specific to the United States domestic situation, and it is not commensurate with the United States role in the international capitalization and financialization of the globe. It may appear aporetic to the world of the South.

The narrow vision of the United States (and other northern nations) became very apparent at the 1994 International Conference on Population and Development in Cairo. I attended the conference as a member of the Asian Women's Human Rights Council, one of numerous non-elite NGOs seeking to discuss the connections *between* population and development issues. Regrettably, most of our attempts to raise these matters were silenced at the main conference sessions, although there were elaborate preparatory meetings in the previous months when Southern NGOs had been "allowed" to air their views. Due in large part to the controversy generated by the Pope, the northern-dominated women's caucus could only discuss population in terms of abortion rights. When at last they moved to the consideration of development, they ignored the connection between population control and development—coercive population control forced upon women in poor countries in the name of so-called capital "D" development.

To achieve what it perceived as a broader consensus, the northern women's caucus was willing to overlook the dumping of pharmaceuticals, the regulation of contraceptive information, and the use of ill-informed local doctors in the population control process. The northern caucus promoted this separation of population and development issues in the name of leadership. Perhaps more to the point, the caucus never really bothered to support the more holistic model of the southern NGOs, where economic resistance and women's struggle come together. Their feminist discussion remained confined to domestic justice in the arena of individual rights.

ᴅᴘ: I don't know enough about what happened in Cairo to question the specifics of your account. But if the choices that you attribute to the "northern" women's caucus were as you describe them, I am not

sure that these people deserve criticism for being narrow. It may be simply a matter of political disagreement about whether and how one improves women's position by linking rights claims with an overall program of economic and social reform. The question that has troubled relations between various incarnations of feminism and the left over the last century is made even more complex by contemporary uncertainty about what the content of such a program might be.

SUBJECTIVITY AND AGENCY

GCS: Speaking of subjectivity, when we think about agency from a global perspective, we can't simply speak of true hope or false hope, true or false understanding. "Consciousness" in "false consciousness" is not to be understood in the rich and robust sense of consciousness in Freud. In the area of agency and the empowerment of those women in the South who are "victims" of exploitation in the name of economic developments, it's important to understand that these southern victims are the agents of the preservation of the Northern lifestyle. The sense of "agency" that is useful here has rather little to do with theories of the subject.

For this reason, empowering these southern groups means giving them infrastructure support so that they can actually question the ones who victimize them. That is agency. In this context the distinction between true and false, the idea that intention is free, that one can be responsible—these ideas hold. Certainly, these ideas are limited and, likewise, the field of agency, however powerful, is also limited. So in regards to the subject, talking of Freudian metapsychology is counterintuitive and not relevant to the field of agency. One cannot simply turn Freud into pop psychology or raise and apply issues of Lacanian law to this notion of agency.

This returns us to the unfinishable tug-of-war between capitalism and the socialist uses of capital. This arena, because it relates to the self and other (taking and giving), relates to ethics. It is a pedagogical project. That is why I am so interested in rural literacy. It is a different project from putting ideas of subjectivity in the field of agency and saying that the idea of false consciousness is not philosophically correct. Of course it's not philosophically correct. It's the same as chronological time is not philosophically correct. In the domain of complex theories, chronological time is irrelevant. On the other hand, you have to have a chronological timepiece in order to run your life. That is the difference between agency and subjectivity. I do not think one can introduce notions of subjectivity to "enrich" the arena of agency. You acknowledge in the subject the limits of the agent. I wanted to say that so as not to shortchange my theoretical convictions.

DP: I partly disagree. When you encounter people in the circumstances you describe, you want to help them become autonomous and self-sufficient. To do so you use a liberal and democratic vocabulary, both as a tool and a partial indication of aims. This vocabulary is rich and relevant enough to be useful. Yet it presumes at least the possibility of constructing relatively coherent subjects. Does it make sense then to suggest that these concepts have only a crude usefulness, as an instrument that measures without explaining or analyzing? You clearly don't want to go to landless agricultural workers in Bangladesh and tell them that the unity of the subject is a myth.

GCS: I wouldn't say it to *anyone*. I would say that the seeming unity of the acting subject—the agent—is produced within a vast field. And as for, say, the Bangladeshi subaltern, she already knows it in a way—because we are dealing here with what is contemptuously named "ethno-philosophies," where the sovereignty of the individual has always been questioned. It's only if you imagine that this specific bit of sense is always dressed up in deconstructive language that there is a problem. We are dealing with utterly battered, compromised, and gender distorted responsibility-based ethics, but they do retain a useful and usable idea of the limits of agency. Such an idea cannot be entertained by concepts of infinite rights or rights-based ethics. These freedoms and rights I see as absolute means rather than ends. It's something I have learned in the last ten years. I was not suggesting at all that you need sophisticated theories here and agency theories there. I'm saying that even here the idea that one can use theories of subjectivity in the field of agency is confused.

Subjects and agents are not two different things, they are two different focuses. Everybody (not just subalterns or just the cultural dominant) can be seen as subject and/or agent. The idea of agency is a small and symptomatic part of a fuller theory of the subject's inaccessibility to itself. Let us use a crude example. Suppose a particle physicist sitting here said everything is full of holes. That theory is not wrong, but if you therefore decide that your body is nothing but holes, you would be confusing two things. That is all I am saying. Agency is a situated part of what we loosely call being. We have many names, but each name is talking about something else. We say subject, self, agent, individual, all kinds of things—person. But these are not synonymous. You cannot love someone in terms of their physiological and lymphatic systems. It is a misplaced and rather dangerous category of mistake. Actually it is not that dangerous. Because when we "bring" subject-theory into agency, what subjectivity turns into is a version of agency where the true or false stuff is supposed to be no longer amenable—except it always is when you are getting on with your practical life. Theories of subjectivity or subject production theories (not really subjectivities) are not amenable to manipulation in the field of agency. Psychoanalysis in clinical practice may try in transference to form a basis for agency, but the connection is tenuous.

DP: I agree that a distinction between subjectivity and agency is analytically important. And reducing agency to subjectivity is misleading. But you still seem more concerned to circumscribe the field of agency than to consider what goes on within it. Once subjects are constituted as agents, they really do exist, even if they are never wholly coherent or unified.

A Freudian account of psychodynamics doesn't explain how markets work. Nor does a sociocultural account of the production of liberal political subjects provide an account of political conflicts and alliances. In politics, there are agents. It is true they are always constrained, and deeply shaped in ways that are not evident in descriptions of their capacities as agents. But they do consider alternatives and make choices. It seems at least as important to seek to understand their judgement and their aims as to explicate the limits of their agency. For that reason I'm not sure, at least regarding politics, that it makes sense to consider an account of agency as inadequate or superficial with respect to something deeper and more substantial behind it.

GCS: Although I think we are disagreeing here, I respect that. My understanding is that the complexities of subject production give us a sense of the limits of agency. This does not make agency inadequate or "the subject" impotent. To that extent no political system is going to assure the final solution to that tug-of-war. When I was talking about the tug-of-war between competition and giving, between rights and responsibility, between justice and development, I took it as deep as I could—to the self and the other. One simply cannot dismiss this relationship as something produced by the capitalist system. The practical project is unfinishable. In its context we need subject production theories.

No discussion with Gayatri Spivak would be complete without a quotation from Derrida, so I will give you one: "It is just that there should be law, but law is not justice." The law part of it is the field of agency, and we absolutely must engage it; but the field of justice is the field where the complexities of subject production begin to play and go beyond the idea of mere subjectivity. We can try for empowerment in the field of agency. Rational expectations theories are a mockery of so-called subject theories. Their limits are lodged in the complexity of subject production. One of the problems of analytic philosophy is that there the mental theater is taken to be a given. Subject production theories can show us the limits of such an assumption. But if we were to stop to make those analyses at every point, assuming we could, we would become paralyzed. Even when compromised, the agent is stronger than the subject.

MEANINGS OF RADICAL DEMOCRACY

DP: A number of contributors to this book are asking whether we should think of ourselves (whoever "we" are) as socialists or radical democrats. That question seems to be some years out of date, in both its alternatives.

With "socialism," there are at least three main parts of the socialist tradition, broadly understood, that are in general terms unacceptable. One is its statist orientation. A second is its reluctance to acknowledge the special status of liberal and democratic rights. A third is its narrowly economic focus with regard to modes of domination. I realize that I am simply naming problems rather than making arguments. Nor do I claim that these problems make it impossible to create a defensible notion of socialism. But claiming a socialist or social democratic identity without having something serious to say about them is politically empty. Thus I am often not sure what it means for someone to say he or she is a socialist in the United States, whether that claim conveys any interesting political content. On the other hand, I would not take any pleasure in saying that I am not a socialist or that I am anti-socialist. This view, from someone who for years strongly identified with the socialist tradition, is another way of saying the socialism question does not seem useful as a marker for political identification.

I also want to ask what the adjective "radical" means in radical democracy. It is not the worst adjective one could come up with. If it simply means that one is really democratic or adamantly democratic, that is fine. But I suspect what is going on is less positive. As people whose prior referents were socialist or Marxist are giving up those markers and uneasily moving toward some version of a democratic framework, they prefer a term that distinguishes them as not fully on that terrain. Thus radical democrats do not want to say that they are socialists anymore, at least not in the ways they once intended. At the same time, they do not want to say that they are just plain democrats, much less liberal democrats.

"Radical" in this context may create the misperception that a position has been built and argued when such a term only outlines a stance. To avoid such confusion I think people might be better off just calling themselves democrats and then arguing what democracy should mean, as regarding representation, participation, and other matters. Claiming to be a radical democrat or a social democrat might then seem more like a conclusion and less like a defensive response to political theoretical uncertainty. And after the cold war there is ample room for creativity and experimentation in giving new meaning to democratic commitments.

GCS: I am not interested in what people call themselves. Like you, I would not like to call myself an anti-socialist. But I am more concerned that capitalism is being recoded as free choice, and that as a consequence the possibilities for democracy are being progressively lessened. Whether American ex-socialists call themselves "other" or "self" is not a pressing problem to me, although I respect it may be for some with certain specific histories.

There are two problems with this particular view of radicalness. One is the idea of pluralist universalism. If one took the issue of globalism that I have been discussing seriously, it would be more of a real task for the United States left than talking about universalism, number one. Some years ago I discussed Bruce Ackerman's book on the constitutional notion of "we the people."[7] What struck me about Ackerman's analysis was his assertion that within the normal operation of the United States "we the people" played no role. He said that it only came into play during moments of crisis—when a popular mandate was created, when transformative opinions were stated by the Supreme Court, and so on. That taught me something. Although my politics could not differ more from Ackerman's, my question is how anyone can transform that normal, day-to-day sense of civic alienation into a participatory democracy that will call itself radical. How can one force people into participation? For me the question can only be answered by way of an unfinishable pedagogic project, not by the fiat of a political system.

Another related question is if one considers globality in an informed way, if one looks at post-Fordism, one sees that the greatest burden of the so-called decentralized factory is being borne by women—and not only in the extraordinary global phenomenon of home-working of various kinds. Women also are absorbing the costs of management, work-place safety, recruitment, you name it—all kinds of costs. Now when the workforce is global, how on earth are the values going to operate that would lead to participation in the functioning of democracy. The challenges facing democracy in the United States center on effecting changes in the electoral process itself (getting rid of Political Action Committees [PACs], convincing people to participate, for example), addressing the role of the United States in the financialization of the globe, and working on how these changes might be made given the nature of the workforce. So I have practical questions.

DP: The radical democratic notion of permanent, lively participation is exactly the kind of confusion that the term encourages. Such a vision of participation is perhaps defensible and even inspiring as a horizon. Yet even as a horizon its infeasibility as a real objective can lead to passivity or even cynicism. When it becomes clear that there is no possibility of permanent ongoing participation by everyone, it is tempting to be "realistic" and consider whatever we actually have to be acceptable and unavoidable. If radical democracy means full, unlimited participation, or a simple critique of representation as such, it is more confusing than productive.

GCS: When you talk about it you also imagine participation.

DP: I do imagine and prefer expanded participation, but as a political project with limits due to time constraints and varied preferences among citizens. If you do not have an image of permanent participation by everyone, how do you change the character of participation to expand and improve it? That question is blocked from view if "radical democracy" is affirmed as an alternative to "normal" democracy and as a synonym for unlimited participatory democracy. If "radical democracy" is an invitation to post-socialist reflection on representation, participation, the extent of agreement required for a democratic polity, and other matters, then it is a great idea burdened with a bad name.

Here I think your notion of plural universalism is promising, at least underlining issues that do not get much attention in unitary images of radical democracy. The image of a fully participatory democracy is also an image of a community in which this participation makes sense—a virtually homogeneous polity, a republican polity. But in the United States, and presumably all advanced market countries, there is no such community, nor would we want to try to create one.

GCS: You know the name that constantly hangs in one's mind when this kind of participation is talked about? Jean-Jacques Rousseau. It is an extremely culturally specific concept. Every cultural inscription—given the world with its history of imperialism of various kinds, great movements, and so on—drags out some notion of participation in its past. But why do we want to create everyone in our own image? Why does the left in the United States cling to such a nostalgic image—Rousseau, town meetings, Thoreau, the sixties?

DP: Because to give up that image of homogeneous republican communication at the site of true democracy is very disruptive. Giving up this image undermines conventional left critiques of liberalism and limits the appeal of simplicity as a political value. If democracy does not signify radical participatory democracy, it is hard to sustain sharp distinctions between democratic and liberal positions. Liberal elements of democracy—many of which are partly constraining—are most plausibly rejected if a polity is itself homogeneous and unified. Absent such a notion, one directly faces deep conflicts among democratic, pluralist, and liberal commitments in a country like the United States. Thus rejecting an image of a homogeneous republican community (in socialist or democratic terms) makes politics far more complex and difficult. It may be more attractive to affirm radical democracy where all political goods go together.

GCS: In terms of what I have seen over the last few years, I agree with you. I have no faith in this permanent solution. Certainly this working solution of the activist as leader comes out of a certain European tradition. And the participatory notions that have evolved from Rousseau's thinking are similarly tied to an obsession with the politically energized European person. If the Euro/United States babbling about universalism and pluralism can dislocate itself from its local cultural context far enough to realize that the idea of participation is historically specific, then I will sit down for a discussion. Otherwise I'm not convinced. [8]

NOTES

1. Stanley Aronowitz, et. al., "Radical Democracy: An SR Symposium," Special Issue of *Socialist Review* 93/3 (1994); Jay Stone, "The Phenomenological Roots of the Radical Democracy/ Marxism Debate," *Rethinking Marxism* 7, no. 1 (1994): 99–115; Peter Bachrach and Aryeh Botwinick, *Power and Empowerment: a Radical Theory of Democratic Participation* (Philadelphia: Temple University Press, 1992); Chantal Mouffe, ed., *Dimensions of Radical Democracy: Pluralism, Citizenship, Community* (London and New York: Verso, 1991); Douglas Brown, *Toward a Radical Democracy: The Political Economy of the Budapest School* (Boston: Unwin Hyman, 1989); Ernesto Laclau and Chantal Mouffe, "Post Marxism Without Apologies," *New Left Review* 166 (November–December 1985): 79–106; Ernesto Laclau and Chantal Mouffe, *Hegemony and Socialist Strategy: Towards a Radical Democratic Politics*, trans. Winston Moore and Paul Cammack (London and New York: Verso, 1985).

2. Stanley Aronowitz, "The Situation of the Left in the United States," *Socialist Review* 93/3 (1994): 5–80.

3. Karl Marx, *Capital* vols. 1–3 (New York: International Publishers, 1977).

4. See Etienne Balibar and Immanuel Wallerstein, *Race/Nation/Class* (London and New York: Verso, 1991).

5. Benedict Anderson, *Imagined Communities: Reflections on the Origin and Spread of Nationalism* (London and New York: Verso, 1983).

6. Aijaz Ahmad, *In Theory: Classes, Nations, Literatures* (London and New York: Verso, 1992).

7. Bruce Ackerman, *Private Property and the Constitution* (New Haven: Yale University Press, 1977). See also, Bruce Ackerman, *The Future of Liberal Revolution* (New Haven: Yale University Press, 1992).

18

THE ERA OF ABUNDANCE

Barbara Ehrenreich

ALL DECENT AND HUMANISTIC LEFT MOVEMENTS—
Marxist or post-Marxist—have been predicated on one
central fact. That was the fact (or hope) of abundance.
Marx's great insight, stated very simply, was that there really
was *enough for everyone*, or could be, if production were aimed
at satisfying the needs of the majority instead of the greed of
the few. Industrialization had potentially made material
scarcity, and hence many forms of human misery, a thing of the
past. Frustratingly though, the potential abundance inherent in
new technologies and organizations of production was artificially constrained by the priorities of the ruling class. Replace
the present owners with the workers, and everyone could live in
material comfort and security; that is, everyone could start to *live*
in the fullest human sense.

The New Left was no less predicated on the idea of artificial scarcity and potential abundance. Generally speaking, we believed we had achieved material abundance (in the first world anyway—a rather serious qualification!) but still faced forms of "surplus repression" inherited from the long human struggle against scarcity. Thus we described our New Left/countercultural vision as "post-scarcity" politics. The means of production still had to be wrested away from the capitalists, but in many ways the great challenge of meeting people's material needs had been met (or could readily be met with a more egalitarian system of distribution.) Within the United States, a diminishing fraction of the population was required to grow food and produce goods for everyone else. If we democratized ownership and divided up the more disagreeable forms of labor, there would be enough of everything to go around.

It was the premise of abundance that inspired and sustained the left movements for almost two centuries. The economic egalitarianism of socialism was made palatable to many middle-class people through the understanding that if everyone had the same amount of material goods, that would still be a pretty generous amount. Later, the ecstatic politics of "sex, drugs, and rock 'n' roll" was made possible by the belief that our ancient enemies—hunger and want—had been or could easily be vanquished. In a world of plenty, we would need neither external hierarchies nor psychic structures of repression to keep the species going.

Does this premise of plenty still hold? Did it ever? There was always something embarrassingly provincial about New Left "post-scarcity" politics, as revealed in our encounters with third world revolutionary movements, which were very much "pre-abundance" in spirit and mission. In my experience, American radicals wanted to discuss themes such as sexual liberation, while the third world comrades were more interested in agricultural production quotas. Our assumptions of basic material abundance had never fully included the third world (or the second one, for that matter.) Somehow, we had pictured ourselves driving cars and playing electric guitars while the rest of the world would be content with a more picturesque and energy-efficient way of life.

I am not sure that there is any way to objectively determine whether there is, or ever could be, enough to go around. Obviously, human needs are elastic. If "enough" means a car for every adult or family, an air-conditioned home and a pesticide-rich lawn, then the answer is clearly "no." If "good" medical care includes a right to kidney dialysis and by-pass surgery, then again, we may never all have enough. At the same time though, the human capacity for meeting needs is endlessly expansive and inventive. New forms of energy, combined with the powerful drive toward miniaturization (and hence less need for energy to accomplish many kinds of tasks), could make some of the more pessimistic estimates obsolete.

But what is clear is that few people in the world retain faith in the premise of potential abundance. In the United States, we lost this faith almost overnight, though few on the left noted the change. Recall that in the fifties and sixties, American intellectuals fretted about the morally corrosive effects of "too much" affluence. Then suddenly, the seventies heralded an "age of limits." There were too many people, according to the demographic doomsayers, and probably not enough food or fuel to support them. In the last two decades, this new Malthusianism has been reinforced again and again by numbing images of starvation and disaster: Biafra, Bangladesh, Somalia, Haiti. Societies that once exported hopes of socialism now export raft-loads of people. At the same time, persistent economic stagnation in the "first world" has the effect of undercutting the old faith that general abundance could be readily achieved, if only we had the will to do so.

The perception of scarcity fuels political reaction in many forms. In the "first world," people who might once have felt pious sympathy for the "starving children of India," or wherever, now work to keep the immigrant hordes at bay. How can we take in more hungry souls, people ask, when there is not enough for us? Domestically, patronizing attitudes toward the poor have been replaced by a churlish impatience—eagerly fanned, of course, by right-wing and often overtly racist ideologues. Globally, the embrace of market economics becomes a mad scramble to get what you can while the getting is good. "Socialism" seems to entail everyone being equally poor, but capitalism means that at least the lucky and enterprising few can be rich. Instead of the lifeboat analogy of the seventies, we imagine a well-appointed yacht, sailing along merrily while the world's disposable masses flounder and drown.

Now all this is of course a "perception," and we know that it has long been the aim of elites to convince the less fortunate that their condition is "natural." Clearly the left has to expose the manufacture of scarcity wherever we find it—for example, the United States budget deficit. As long as almost a third of the federal budget is devoted to ritual militarism, any talk of deficits has to be regarded as right-wing chicanery. The first business of any leftist or liberal in public office should be to expose the artificiality of much of the scarcity we are encouraged to perceive—and not, like the New Democratic Party (NDP) in Ontario or the Socialists in France, to become the enforcers of a new fiscal austerity.

But not every kind of scarcity is a product of right-wing propaganda. Again, it is difficult to estimate what is "enough" and whether we are anywhere close to it, but sober ecologists warn that, in general, there is less and less arable soil, ozone in the stratosphere, fish in the sea, rainforests to recycle our carbon dioxide, species of wildlife, and uncontaminated water.

The scarcity of essential resources has grown ominously since that pinnacle year of post-scarcity politics, 1968. In that year the human population of the earth was 3.7 billion; today it is 5.5 billion. A quarter-century ago, deforestation was still a distant threat to places like the Philippines and Brazil. Seafood was a thrifty alternative to meat. Global warming was not yet a credible threat. Mass microbial contamination of American drinking water was almost unthinkable. In this (pre-scarcity?) context, environmentalism was a middle-class, aesthetic concern, ranking far behind the more urgent agenda of third world national liberation.

Real scarcity conflicts with the aspirations of most of the human population for better goods and resources. People pressed together in tenements also want houses and chemical-rich lawns and cars to get to work in, and why not? The ecology movement, however, cannot responsibly promise "more," at least not in the medium-term, and certainly not more cellophane-wrapped, cardboard-backed, plastic or metal *objects of any kind*. In the context of a frenetic consumer culture, with its endless promotion of new things of eat, wear, and clutter a home with, an ecological consciousness can only mean the prospect of *less*.

Obviously, things are far worse than they need to be. Just as the left has to expose the false scarcity of right-wing propaganda, we should relentlessly expose the scarcities created by sheer waste and, of course, maldistribution. The rich nations are being buried in their own waste while the poor everywhere forage through garbage to survive. We do have a responsibility to persuade our fellow citizens to live in a more modest and sustainable fashion.

But it will not be enough to graft some granola-style, less-is-better ecologism on to our radical democratic, socialist-feminist, or whatever we want to call it, politics. If the left wants to recover, if it wants to have anything at all to say in this jaded and depleted world, it is going to have to reinvent a credible vision of abundance.

How do we accomplish that? We start with what there is *enough* of and work from there:

First, there are *enough* people on earth. Some would say "too many," but let us instead acknowledge our reproductive success as a species. If our job was to go forth and multiply, we have done it, perhaps all too well. The consequences of our reproductive success are potentially enormously liberating: No one can reasonably argue (although many, of course, still do) that women must be subordinated to the cause of reproduction or that sexual pleasure must be instrumental to conception. Sex can be a form of play, and women can, if they choose, be childless individuals, ends-in-themselves, without in any way jeopardizing the continuation of the human race.

If most of us are still desperate to have children, it is because we see few other alternatives to loneliness. But a consequence of our reproductive success is that, theoretically, no one need ever be lonely. According to a silly but still thought-provoking estimate, a college-educated person needs a city of about 100,000 in order to have at least three good friends. In a world of 5.5 billion people, each of us must have dozens, if not hundreds, of potential soul-mates. The isolation of the peasant family, the provincialism of the village where even minor differences in appearance or outlook might be intolerable, are conditions we have potentially put well behind us.

This assertion depends on something else there is enough of: We have enough ways, finally, of socializing. Centuries ago, contact with strangers often occurred only at festivals and other rare events. Today, we all "know" hundreds of people—celebrities and public figures, for example—whom we will never meet in the flesh. Fifty years ago, a radio was a sizeable piece of furniture, unavailable to any but the affluent; today television antennas sprout from shanty-towns and rural hovels. The industrial revolution irrevocably soiled the earth, but the information revolution rushes ahead on feet that are light and relatively clean. Potentially we can all be wired, interacting, on line. We may never all have hot running water or regular meals of meat, but there is no longer any reason for anyone on earth to be starved for information, education, entertainment, or social contact.

Finally, there is enough to do. Perhaps the most unique of our artificial scarcities is the scarcity of jobs, which vividly reflects the divergence between market-priorities and human needs. How can there be so few jobs when there is so much to *do*? If profit were not the principle guiding human endeavor, we could easily employ a couple of generations just cleaning up the current mess: salvaging the environment, curing disease, educating the ignorant, and housing the homeless. Once that is done, we might throw ourselves en masse into the great adventures of scientific inquiry, artistic expression, and space exploration.

Much of this was, of course, implicit in the "post-scarcity," counter-cultural politics of the sixties. Because of our relative privilege, sixties radicals did not ask for more *things*: We had already seen the best that our consumer culture could offer and knew how far it fell short of meeting our real desires. Instead, we envisioned a new social order in which long suppressed human needs—for conviviality, adventure, self-expression, love—could finally be met. This may have been a "post-scarcity" vision, but, in a world of looming scarcity, it is now more urgent and relevant than ever.

19

REPRESENTATION AND DEMOCRACY

AN INTERVIEW

BELL HOOKS AND DAVID TREND

FOR NEARLY TWO DECADES, WRITER AND EDUCATOR bell hooks has worked to broaden understandings of the relationships between identity and political activism. In challenging conventional categories of race, class, gender, and the often arbitrary distinctions among them, hooks has consistently produced critical analyses that resist easy answers or universalizing dogma. From her early interrogations of gender politics and feminist discourse to her more recent discussions of contemporary culture and media, hooks has produced a broad body of work on such diverse topics as postmodern theory, freedom of expression, and community organizing.

hooks's work is of particular relevance to ongoing debates in radical democracy in the way it seeks out common political goals among diverse movements. While recognizing the dual dangers of essentialism and relativism, hooks has addressed the difficult task of developing shared strategies to combat injustice. Writing of hooks,

Cornel West stated that "bell hooks' unique contribution to intellectual life, American letters, and Black thought is that of producing a challenging corpus of work which proposes a singular human struggle to be candid about one's self and contestatory toward the dehumanizing forces in our world. Her works sing a polyphonic 'song of a great composite democratic individual' yearning for a principled connectedness that promotes the distinctive self-development of each and every one of us."[1]

A poet and playwright since childhood, hooks wrote her first book of criticism, *Ain't I a Woman: Black Women and Feminism* (1981), while an undergraduate at Stanford University in the 1970s. In that work, hooks addressed a theme that would occupy much of her later writing: the solipsism of political movements; in particular the failure of certain feminist movements to recognize race. Her later books include *Feminist Theory From Margin to Center* (1984)and *Talking Back: Thinking Feminist, Thinking Black* (1989), among numerous other titles. The following interview was recorded following the release of two new volumes by hooks: *Outlaw Culture: Resisting Representations* (1994) and *Teaching to Transgress: Education as the Practice of Freedom* (1994). The conversation took place in San Francisco in October 1994 and was subsequently revised and edited for publication.

—David Trend

DAVID TREND: Much of your writing has addressed the failure of universalizing claims made by the women's movement or "the left" to speak to diverse groups. Do you see a resurgence in such assertions?

BELL HOOKS: I think that the recent rise in religious fundamentalism has produced a context for the resurgence of totalizing claims. It is both interesting and dangerous that we find this totalizing happening in radical or liberal spaces where we've seen major challenges to those claims. Feminism is a prime example of this. Who would have thought that after all of the interventions calling for a recognition of race, gender, and class that we would have people like Naomi Wolf, and to a certain extent Susan Faludi, coming back and positing a more monolithic sense of women's identity. This is very dangerous for the future of radical and revolutionary feminist movements.

DT: Why do you think this impulse is creeping into liberal and left circles?

BH: The critical interventions surrounding issues of diversity and difference created a moment of chaos. In *Teaching to Transgress* I argue that it is not as though you have a revolution of thought and all of a sudden you have stability and peace. Whenever you try to introduce new thought and shift people's paradigms you often have a period of confusion and chaos. The inability to resolve that tension and the desire to restore some unitary sensibility led many people on the left to panic. They began to wonder whether this introduction of diversity and difference wasn't undermining our capacities for solidarity and collective struggle rather than enhancing them. That was a point of panic.

Once you destabilize static and unitary notions of commonalty, you require people who have certain kinds of privilege truly to engage in solidarity and to divest of their privileges in certain ways. That is very threatening to many of us with a certain status within the existing structure. It requires a whole new paradigm saying that your position as a major professor at such-and-such may not represent such a revolutionary moment, but in fact a reformist moment that potentially might undermine the need to go further and to transform society. That is very hard for people to grasp.

We are a very naive public about the processes of social change, and that naiveté is not accidental. This culture doesn't encourage us to think about transformation as a process. Instead, we are addicted to notions of radical revolutionary moments that transform everything overnight. We have difficulty recognizing the notion of struggle in protracted terms, which requires both a critical vigilance and a willingness to alter strategies when they aren't working. Rather than changing strategies, we see people falling back on what they feel worked at a different moment in time.

I would say a parallel shift can be seen in certain homophobic and sexist strains of Afrocentric thinking. This represents another desire to return to a unitary vision of blackness, which people feel can give some steady ground. But because this thinking is in its grossest forms so fascistic, so much in opposition to the freedom of women and gay people, it actually undermines progressive politics though it presents itself as a new stage in the struggle—much the same way that someone like Naomi Wolf presents her ideas as a new stage in feminist struggle.

DT: Another way of approaching this is from the perspective of the margin. In critiquing universalizing or assimilating impulses, why is it important to consider the margin as a site of radical openness? How do marginal spaces remain sites of possibility?

BH: One issue is that marginal spaces are not always just already there; they're also spaces we create. You and I began our meeting today talking critically about the star system and how people who start off subverting the existing social structure can get incorporated within the elitism and privilege of stardom. I was suggesting that we also have the capacities to subvert that process by maintaining a kind of marginality in the way we live our lives and in our habits of being. But it takes a certain critical vigilance. For example, I still answer my phone and still try to negotiate my engagements—and I do not want to privilege that because it's sometimes overtaxing. Although I inhabit the space of stardom, I also inhabit the space of someone who does mundane tasks, who doesn't see herself as above mundane tasks. I think that type of balance is crucial in maintaining a communalist notion of struggle, which does not reproduce the image of the gifted leader who stands above things ordinary people do. Such elitism is at the core of certain forms of domination.

These marginal spaces of oppositionality can be created in multiple ways in our lives—even in our personal relationships. I have a great nostalgia for the challenges made during the 1960s and 1970s to monogamous marriage and to the coupled household. In many contexts these challenges have died out. A powerful movement emerged during that period in our culture for people to think about buying property together and creating different kinds of relationships. I think that was an important space of oppositional thinking—a challenge to the way we thought about private property, about space, a reaffirmation of the primacy of community.

We hear less and less about marginal spaces where people try to create different kinds of kinship bonds, different kinds of living space. Instead, we increasingly see assertions in the mass media that gay people really just want to have their nuclear family, too. We are witnessing a similar reification and reprivileging of the nuclear family by black male leaders and others insisting on the family as the only potential trope of redemption and salvation. For example, a great deal of time is spent talking about single mothers, and particularly the single black mother on welfare. Many people view this household as a negative framework or a bad family unit. But what I see with one of my sisters who is on welfare and who lives in a housing project—but who has a communal kinship structure—is that her child has infinitely more healthy relationships toward male authority figures than we did growing up in a nuclear family.

It is not the condition of being poor or being a single parent that produces dysfunction. It is the lack of a surrounding community support structure that is so detrimental. Once you have a young single mother who has bought into the notions of liberal individualism, who doesn't live in a communal context, who doesn't try to raise her child with the support of people of different ages or from different circumstances, you're going to end up with a situation that's incredibly problematic in terms of time, and care, and parenting skills. After all, where does a sixteen-year old learn parenting skills? But if you're in a communal context where there can be a sharing of resources—the kind of culture of poverty that anthropologist Carol Stack first discussed in *All of Our Kin: Strategies for Survival in the Black Community*—poverty is not necessarily the site of despair and nihilism and deprivation.[2] It is clearly the site of material deprivation, but with a communal ethos it can also be a marginal space where people can create alternative ways to live their lives which can be meaningful.

DT: Why don't we shift the conversation from a discussion of critique to one of social possibility. Your writing often addresses the need to problematize issues of solidarity and to recognize interconnectedness among structures of domination. This notion of simultaneous separation and linkage among diverse struggles is similar to what people like Cornel West and Stanley Aronowitz are proposing in relation to radical democracy. To ask a question that you yourself once posed, "How can we locate ourselves from standpoints that allow us to be inclusive of difference while appreciating similarities of experience?"[3]

BH: Many people mistake a critique of the universalizing ethos with a rejection of commonalty and common bonds. They collapse the two. I feel that it's not that we want to do away with the notion of commonalty, but that we want to find the basis of commonalty in something other than a notion of shared experience or common oppression. That is to say that you and I may find ourselves joined by our commitment to justice and freedom, and that can be as much a common bond as whether or not we share similar attitudes about class or what have you. I find I need to explain this issue when I am working with students and trying to encourage them to think about solidarity rooted in chosen points of bonding and contact. You know, we do not choose our ethnicity; we do not choose the neighborhoods we grow up in. So we need to learn to think in terms of those common points.

For instance, none of our radical movements really fundamentally address the issue of housing. I still believe that feminism could have been the most powerful social movement of the twentieth century had it addressed housing and the rights of women to control it. Imagine what it would mean for low-income women in projects to cooperatively buy the spaces where they live. What would it mean to create cooperative housing where day care would exist in the building, where there would be both communal and private space. You would think that given the economic luxury of this country we might be able to develop some examples of housing that are safe for women and children, where men can live in harmony with women, and where no one has to fear being raped or harassed.

Housing was an issue that could have bound many groups of people together. It certainly will in the future because the dilemma of housing becomes more intense daily. We know that women and children are the fastest growing populations of the homeless. A basic issue like housing cuts across class and race. Having taught in nations where cooperative housing exists, I've seen what can be achieved when housing is regarded as an inalienable right like health care. Yet, one of the dilemmas we have in our capitalist society is that so few people believe that housing should be a basic right. I think the failure to address this issue has meant a loss of "possibility" in a sense.

Those kinds of actions could have said to the world that feminism should be taken seriously—not on the surface of our lives, but in concrete ways. If we had feminist housing where people could live more freely in a spirit of justice and freedom, then when I go and talk about feminism with young black women in housing projects it wouldn't be something they laugh at and say is only for white women. If we had concrete ways of illustrating radical thought and how it can transform how we live, we would have more converts to left thinking.

I have finished a new book, *Killing Rage, Ending Racism,* that ends with a chapter about the way many folks have given up on Martin Luther King's vision of "a beloved community." I discuss how individuals like myself live lives where we experience an incredible diversity that includes loving relationships with white people who have divested of white supremacy. I want to think about why we are not theorizing from those concrete experiences to say, these are the conditions that create this world, this beloved community. How can we tell people, you don't have to despair about whether racism can end because you can actually interact with somebody in your life who has undergone a conversion experience and who has changed how they relate to the world.

When I encounter young black people who are convinced that white people are racist white supremacists who will not change, I think about what I have seen in my life. During my high school days within a racial apartheid community, I encountered white people actively engaged in a struggle to concretely divest themselves of privilege. For that reason my sense that white people can transform themselves is not rooted in some sentimental, utopian feeling, but in the concrete reality of having seen white people change. What does it mean that we are so divided that those young black people never see white people in resistance. All they see is white people who hold the xenophobic, racist thinking that reinforces their own fundamentalism, reinforces the sense that the races could not possibly bond, that there could not be any way to share blackness with white people without them appropriating it and exploiting it.

Although many progressives in this country occupy social spaces where diversity is the norm in our lives, where being with people who are different is the norm, the vast majority of Americans are still living in a system of racial apartheid. It is a system where they do not know somebody who is a feminist, a system where they do not have a clue what being a feminist means in concrete terms. I am interested in why we are not talking about those things. Why we are not discussing what makes it possible for some of us to inhabit a beloved community in the marginal spaces of existing structures without talking about how other people can have it.

Those of us who live in those oppositional spaces, who are not sharing the thinking of what has allowed those spaces to develop, are hoarding a resource for ourselves. If those of us who enjoy privilege continue failing to share the process of change, I think we become complicit with the reproduction of a kind of nihilism and despair. Part of what I love about my conversation with Mary Childers in *Conflicts in Feminism* is that we were saying, let's share in a basic way how we come together as a black woman and a white woman from working class backgrounds in a professional setting and learn how to support and bond with one another. Now, people are doing that everyday, but we're not writing about how we do it. That is a failure of critical intellectualism in this society.

It is not enough to just write our books and to write them in a way that leaves out the kinds of concrete ways that we might bond. For example, in my new job I had never had a bond with a black woman secretary in my office. Here I was the highest you could go on that totem pole of academe, and she and I did not talk. At one point I stopped and registered with her how I felt that racism was shaping the manner in which I was being treated. She expressed surprise that we both thought about such things in relation to our daily work. Where do we read stories about how those of us who occupy positions of privilege bond with those who enhance our work space? Those are the concrete unions of theory and practice that offer hope and possibility, but they have to be articulated and named. Making these kinds of connections will inspire people to engage the left and to join us in the struggle to end domination.

DT: In addition to the notion of shared political commitments, I want to ask you if there is an ethical dimension to consider.

BH: I want to be frank with you about this. I am troubled about the issue of ethics because my own sense of an ethical relationship to life is rooted in spirituality. I am troubled when I meet so many young people who do not really have a relationship to religion or spirituality. I have been trying to struggle dialectically with this question. In one of my essays I speak about an ongoing conversation I have with a professor at Lewis and Clark University from Afghanistan named Zaher Wahib, who is very anti-religious and who feels that ethics only grows out of struggle. I am uncertain about that. In my own life the ethical dimension of my being is continually reinforced through spirituality, because I feel that it's so much easier for ego to take over in the secular realm of politics. Things are constantly balanced for me by my ethical and moral struggles with spiritual issues of faith, forgiveness, and compassion. I do not yet see where we have created that kind of ethical sensibility in the secular realm of left politics.

Let us talk about an ethics of compassion in relation to the Simpson case, and how we might teach these ethics—share that knowledge from a left standpoint. The kind of compassion I think about in terms of engaged Buddhism would say to me that I want to feel for both O.J. Simpson and Nicole Simpson. I do not want to select one party and say that this person is good and this person is bad, that she is a victim and he is a potential victimizer (and certainly he *was* a victimizer in terms of domestic abuse). But instead we view the situation in terms of the kind of compassion that Thich Nhat Hanh talks about. That form of compassion says that if we do not embrace him as well, we do not embrace what is within him that could change. We cannot then have a conversion experience. I mean if I give up on you, then I am not creating any kind of strategies for your conversion.

We certainly saw this in knee-jerk feminist rejections of male capacities to change. There was a kind of giving up on men, a certain hopelessness about men changing. Once you put that hopelessness in place you destroy a social context where men can strive. I feel that one of the most devalued chapters in my writing has been the work I have tried to do around men as comrades in feminist theory. I said that we cannot demand that men change without affirming them in the process. We cannot ask them to change and then dismiss the changes, dismiss the small steps that someone may be taking away from their sexism, their misogyny. That dimension of compassion comes into my life when I believe that this person may not always be locked in the position that they are locked into today, and it is my compassion that allows for the possibility of their enlightenment, their conversion to a different standpoint. I think it is very much in the interest of sustaining a politics of domination not to see compassion as integral to the process of revolutionary change. Everywhere around the globe we have seen the kinds of revolution take place where you just have a switching of oppressor and oppressed, or a binary of good and bad, rather than thinking of models of transformation that hold out for the possibility that people can have conversion experiences, that people who did not believe in justice can come to see justice as a good. That is very important.

DT: This returns us perfectly to the topic of your new book *Teaching to Transgress*, which discusses the role of education in all of these processes. You were just speaking of a very Freirian concept of oppressed people teaching lessons to their oppressors and the capacities of both parties to change. What about the place of education in political movements?

BH: Clearly the subtitle of *Teaching to Transgress*—"Education as the Practice of Freedom"—is completely appropriated from Paulo Freire's work. I like appropriations that are a public naming of solidarity and continuity in a continuum of struggle. So that when I use a phrase like "the struggle continues," it is not just a sentimental phrase, but a phrase that speaks to how I learn from Freire, how I can apply that learning to my own life, how I can share that learning with someone else. Education as the practice of freedom is just such a revolutionary notion in our society because I think that education remains one of the few locations where we can inspire people to have conversion experiences away from their allegiances to the oppressive norms. If we take it as a given that all of us from the time we are born and begin watching television are inundated with the ideology of domination, we have got to think of education as one of the rare sites where we can unlearn some of that. Although I have not enjoyed my experience in the academy at all, I cling to it precisely because I believe that the classroom remains a place of possibility and transformation, one of the few places in our anti-intellectual, ever-growing-in-its-fascism culture where we can have hope.

That is why Dinesh D'Sousa and Allan Bloom became so concerned. I do not think they became concerned simply because we were raising issues of diversity and multiculturalism. They saw that people really were responding. I said in an interview earlier this morning that ten years ago if you came to a bell hooks talk you might have seen mostly white women. Now if you come to a bell hooks talk you see men of all colors, small children, and so on. That is the potential, the possibility, the enactment of the real that is about our hunger for change, that is really threatening to the new right.

The new right is so concerned about blocking our radical interventions in education because the classroom is really a powerful place. After a talk I gave last night, a blue-eyed woman came up to me and said that in her high school in a class on modern political thought she read something of mine and it stayed with her. She said that being able to come there to hear me talk was important to her because I am somebody that she can pattern herself after. In another situation, a young black woman from Yale Law School told me that she had been all ready to join up with a corporate firm. She had signed up with them and all of a sudden this stuff that she had learned in my classroom came back into her head, and she switched and went to work for the National Commission on AIDS. She embarked on a road to becoming involved in biomedical ethics issues on race and AIDS. That's the potential.

This is the threat the new right feels in the presence of critical intellectuals in the academy, who have the capacity by their habits of being and political commitments to inspire young people. That young people can make their break with structures of domination and decolonize their minds is the joy in our struggle. It is the one thing that has kept me in the academy because it is the one thing that concretely happens. That's a small revolution; however, it is very threatening to the new right that progressive teachers and educators have the power to engender such activism.

NOTES

1. Cornel West, "Introduction to bell hooks," from bell hooks and Cornel West, *Breaking Bread: Insurgent Black Intellectual Life* (Boston: South End Press, 1991), 62.
2. Carol Stack, *All of Our Kin: Strategies for Survival in the Black Community* (New York: Harper and Row, 1974).
3. Mary Childers and bell hooks, " A Conversation about Race and Class," in *Conflicts in Feminism,* ed. Marianne Hirsch and Evelyn Fox Keller (New York: Routledge, 1990), 67.

CONTRIBUTORS

STANLEY ARONOWITZ teaches sociology and cultural studies at the City University of New York. He is a convener of the Union of Democratic Intellectuals and the author of *The Politics of Identity: Class, Culture, and Social Movements* (Routledge, 1992) and (with William DiFazio) of *The Jobless Future* (University of Minnesota, 1994).

SEYLA BENHABIB is a professor of political theory in the government department at Harvard University. She is the author of *Critique, Norm and Utopia: A Study of the Foundations of Critical Theory* (Columbia University Press, 1986) and *Situating the Self: Gender, Community, and Postmodernism in Contemporary Ethics* (Polity and Routledge, 1992). She is the editor (with Wolfgang Bonss and John McCole) of *On Max Horkeimer* (MIT Press, 1994).

BOGDAN DENITCH is a professor of sociology at the Graduate School and University Center of the City University of New York. He is the author of *The Socialist Debate: Beyond Red and Green* (Pluto Press, 1990) and *Ethnic Nationalism: The Tragic Death of Yugoslavia* (Minnesota, 1994). Denitch is also an editor of *Dissent*.

AMARPAL K. DHALIWAL is a doctoral candidate in the ethnic studies department at the University of California at Berkeley, where she teaches courses in Asian American and women's studies. She is currently writing a dissertation on Western popular culture and postcoloniality by analyzing the international readership of Western romance novels.

BARBARA EHRENREICH is an essayist for *Time* magazine and a columnist for *The Guardian* in London. Ehrenreich's recent books include the novel *Kipper's Game* (Farrar, Strauss & Giroux, 1993) and a collection of essays entitled *The Snarling Citizen* (Farrar, Strauss & Giroux, 1995).

BARBARA EPSTEIN teaches in the history of consciousness program at the University of California at Santa Cruz. She is the author of *Political Protest and Cultural Revolution: Nonviolent Direct Action in the 1970s and 1980s* (University of California, 1991)

JEFFREY ESCOFFIER is a freelance editor and writer living in New York City. He is the author of *John Maynard Keynes* (Chelsea House, 1994). Escoffier was previously the executive editor of *Socialist Review* and the publisher of *Outlook: A National Lesbian and Gay Quarterly*.

J. PETER EUBEN is a professor of politics at the University of California at Santa Cruz. He is co-editor of *Athenian Political Thought and the Reconstruction of American Democracy* and the author of *The Tragedy and Political Theory: The Road Not Taken* (Princeton University, 1990) and the forthcoming *Political Education and Democratic Discourse.*

RICHARD FLACKS teaches sociology at the University of California at Santa Barbara. Flacks is the author of *Making History: The American Left and the American Mind* (Columbia University, 1988), the co-author (with Jack Whalen) of *Beyond the Barricades: The Sixties Generation Grows Up* (Temple University, 1989), and the co-editor of the forthcoming *Cultural Politics and Social Movements.*

NANCY FRASER is a professor of philosophy and a research fellow of the Center for Urban Affairs and Policy Research at Northwestern University. She is the author of *Unruly Practices: Power, Discourse, and Gender in Contemporary Social Theory* (University of Minnesota, 1989) and the co-author of *Feminist Contentions: A Philosophical Exchange* (Routledge, 1994).

HENRY A. GIROUX holds the Waterbury chair in secondary education at Pennsylvania State University. His recent books include *Living Dangerously: Multiculturalism and the Politics of Difference* (Peter Lang, 1993), *Disturbing Pleasures: Learning Popular Culture* (Routledge, 1994), and the anthology (co-edited with Peter McLaren) *Between Borders: Pedagogy and the Politics of Culture* (Routledge, 1994).

BELL HOOKS is the Distinguished Professor of English at City College in New York. Her recent publications include *Outlaw Culture: Resisting Representations* (Routledge, 1994) and *Teaching to Transgress: Education as the Practice of Freedom* (Routledge, 1994).

MANNING MARABLE is a professor of political science and history and director of the Institute for Research in African-American Studies and the African-American Studies Program at Columbia University. Marable's recent books include *The Crisis of Color and Democracy: Essays on Race, Class, and Power* (Common Courage, 1992), *Blackwater: Historical Studies in Race, Class Consciousness, and Revolution* (University of Colorado, 1993), and *Beyond Black and White* (Lawrence Hill Books, 1994).

CHANTAL MOUFFE teaches at the Collège International de Philosophie in Paris, where she directs the program on Citizenship and Modern Democracy. Her publications include *Hegemony and Socialist Strategy:*

CONTRIBUTORS

Towards a Radical Democratic Politics (with Ernesto Laclau, Verso, 1987), *Dimensions of Radical Democracy: Pluralism, Citizenship, Community* (Verso, 1991), and *The Return of the Political* (Verso, 1993).

MICHAEL OMI teaches ethnic studies and Asian-American studies at the University of California at Berkeley. He is the co-author (with Howard Winant) of *Racial Formation in the United States: From the 1960s to the 1990s* and has written extensively on United States racial politics.

DAVID PLOTKE is an associate professor of political science at the Graduate Faculty of the New School for Social Research in New York City. He is the author of *Building a Democratic Political Order: Reshaping American Liberalism in the 1930s and 1940s* (Cambridge University, 1995). From 1976 to 1981 he was the editor of *Socialist Review*.

GAYATRI CHAKRAVORTY SPIVAK is the Avalon Foundation Professor in the Humanities in the department of English and comparative literature at Columbia University. Her books include *The Post-Colonial Critic: Interviews, Strategies, Dialogues* (Routledge, 1990) and *Outside in the Teaching Machine* (Routledge, 1993).

DAVID TREND teaches at San Francisco State University and directs the Center for Social Research and Education. He is the executive editor of *Socialist Review* and the author of *Cultural Pedagogy: Art/Education/Politics* (Bergin and Garvey, 1992) and *The Crisis of Meaning in Education and Culture* (University of Minnesota, 1995).

ELLEN WILLIS writes a column of media commentary for the *Village Voice* and teaches journalism at New York University. She is the author of *Beginning to see the light: sex, hope, and rock-and-roll* (Wesleyan University, 1992) and *No More Nice Girls: Countercultural Essays* (Wesleyan University 1992).

HOWARD WINANT teaches sociology and Latin American studies at Temple University. He is the co-author (with Michael Omi) of *Racial Formation in the United States: From the 1960s to the 1990s* (Routledge, 1994) and the author of *Racial Conditions: Theories, Politics, Comparisons* (University of Minnesota, 1994).

ELI ZARETSKY teaches in the history department of the University of Missouri. He is the author of *Capitalism, the Family, and Personal Life* (Harper and Row, 1976) and the forthcoming *Psychoanalysis: From the Psychology of Author to the Politics of Identity*.